UNEARTHING CHINA'S PAST

UNEARTHING CHINA'S PAST

Jan Fontein & Tung Wu

Museum of Fine Arts, Boston

Distributed by New York Graphic Society, Greenwich, Connecticut

Copyright 1973 by
Museum of Fine Arts
Boston, Massachusetts

Library of Congress Catalogue
Card No. 73-79825

SBN 0-87846-076-4

Cover illustration:
90. Lotus-shaped bowl (detail)
William Rockhill Nelson Gallery of Art,
Kansas City, Missouri

Frontispiece:
Interior view of tomb number 30.14, excavated
in the northwestern suburbs of Lo-yang, Honan
Province, in May 1953. The tomb dates from
the end of the 1st century A.D.

Typeset in Sabon by
Dumar Typesetting, Dayton, Ohio

Printed by
The Meriden Gravure Co.
Meriden, Connecticut

Designed by
Carl F. Zahn

Contents

Preface

The exhibition "Unearthing China's Past" is the result of an initiative of the Department of Asiatic Art to respond to the increasing public interest in Chinese archaeology stimulated by the news of the spectacular recent discoveries in China. The exhibition and the accompanying catalogue are the work of Jan Fontein and Tung Wu of the Department of Asiatic Art, who have conceived and planned this project in detail. Preparations for the exhibition began long before I assumed the responsibilities of the directorship of the Museum of Fine Arts, but since they are reaching the final completion at this time, the pleasant duty has devolved upon me to acknowledge the museum's indebtedness to the institutions and persons who made this exhibition possible.

Our thanks are due, first of all, to the generous lenders to the exhibition on both sides of the Atlantic; they freely consented to our requests for the loan of their often unique and almost always irreplaceable treasures. For the success of an exhibition of this type, in which works of art from Western collections are juxtaposed with photographs of objects recently excavated in China, much depends upon the quality of the available reproductions. We gratefully acknowledge the invaluable assistance rendered to our curator by the Permanent Mission of the People's Republic of China to the United Nations. It was through the good offices of this mission that the museum was able to obtain a series of photographs of recently excavated objects supplied by our Chinese colleagues. The friendly cooperation of the Chinese Organizing Committee for the exhibition of archaeological discoveries held at the Musée du Petit Palais, Paris, this summer, made it possible to supplement the material obtained from China with photographs taken at that exhibition. Werner Forman and Yasuhiko Mayuyama allowed us to use photographs taken during trips to China.

An undertaking of this international scope is the product of the coordinated efforts of many persons of different skills and interests in and outside the museum. We are profoundly grateful to all who contributed to the final realization of the project by their work, their advice and suggestions. It could never have been achieved without contributions from sources other than the exhibition budget of the Museum of Fine Arts. The initial costs of travel and research were covered by a generous donation of Mr. and Mrs. Paul Bernat. Substantial financial assistance for the exhibition was provided by the Massachusetts Council on the Arts and Humanities from funds appropriated by the Massachusetts General Court.

MERRILL C. RUEPPEL
Director
Museum of Fine Arts, Boston

Acknowledgments

To locate and assemble the objects shown in this exhibition and to compile the accompanying catalogue are tasks that could only be completed with the help of many other persons. Most of them are not even known to us by name, for they are the often anonymous authors of the archaeological reports in the journals *Kaogu, Wen Wu,* and *Kaogu Xuebao* in which we found the inspiration for our research. We thank our Chinese colleagues for the many valuable suggestions and stimulating ideas that we have excavated from their reports. We can only hope that we have succeeded in our efforts not to distort their views by our own, second-hand interpretation of the facts.

From the very beginning we were encouraged by the enthusiastic response to our ideas and the active support for our plans of Mrs. John K. Fairbank. The collector Dr. Paul Singer is perhaps the only other person who had pursued similar ideas in a systematic manner in connection with the art objects in his collection. He not only permitted us to choose from the many pieces that fitted into our program but also freely allowed us to use some of his most interesting discoveries. Laurence Sickman of the William Rockhill Nelson Gallery of Art, Kansas City, generously provided us with fine works of art and fresh thoughts on the problems of Chinese archaeology. The entry on the Late Chou set of bells (cat. no. 14) could not have been written without the help of an unpublished translation by Professor Max Loehr of Harvard University of the original Chinese musicological report that he kindly placed at our disposal. Essential information on the geography of Sian (cat. no. 73) was provided by Professor Arthur F. Wright of Yale University. Helmut Brinker of the Rietberg Museum, Zurich, Howard C. Hollis, New York, and Mrs. Lois Katz, curator of the Sackler Collections, New York, assisted us in various ways with information. Only with the constant help of Dr. Eugene Wu of the Harvard-Yenching Library was it possible to assemble the vast amount of recent Chinese publications needed for research.

The catalogue was written by two authors of widely different training and background in the course of a continuous exchange of opinions and ideas that extended over a period of almost a year. Although many of his thoughts found their way into other entries of the catalogue, Tung Wu is mainly responsible for the entries on swords (cat. nos. 36-39) and the section on painting and calligraphy (cat. no. 112-122). Ms. Sheila Canby, assistant in the department, wrote the entries on Sassanian and Byzantine coins (cat. nos. 96-97). She shared the tedious task of typing the manuscript with Mrs. Posie S. Cowan. Money L. Hickman, Chimyo Horioka and Yasuhiro Iguchi, all staff members of the department, contributed each in his own way to this venture.

JAN FONTEIN
TUNG WU

Introduction

China's re-entry into the family of nations has opened the barriers that had prevented for so many years the exchange of ideas between the West and the new China. With exposure to the Chinese alternative life style, acrobats, acupuncture, and archaeology have suddenly come into the news. Archaeology especially seems to have captured the imagination of the museum-going public. In Paris and Tokyo crowds of curious spectators jostle in front of the glass cases in which lie in state the resurrected jade men, who have become, almost overnight, the most celebrated relics of ancient Chinese culture.

During the last twenty-five years Chinese archaeology was often considered to be little more than the esoteric hobby of a few museum curators and university professors, but now the revival of an older, deep-rooted interest has created the need for up-to-date information about what has happened in China in the field of archaeology during the years in which China and America lived so far apart. The first aim of the exhibition "Unearthing China's Past" is, therefore, to provide the public with some general information on archaeological activities in China since the founding of the People's Republic of China in 1949.

While the political and economic developments in China received considerable attention all over the world, Chinese archaeologists, maintaining a low profile in world publicity, have been quietly advancing their knowledge of China's ancient cultural heritage. The results of their labors are most spectacular, and the way in which they have advanced Chinese archaeology is in many ways as revolutionary as the changes brought about in Chinese society itself.

At the time these lines are written, no firm schedule has yet been made public for a showing in the United States of the Chinese archaeological exhibition from the People's Republic of China, which is currently traveling in Europe. "Unearthing China's Past" is therefore likely to have closed its doors long before the American public will have had a chance to see the magnificent treasures that are the tangible fruit of almost twenty-five years of scientific excavation in China. Yet "Unearthing China's Past" should not be seen primarily as a forerunner of this great event, or, if schedules should change and the two shows were to run simultaneously, as a kind of side show, which merely tries to ride the crest of the sudden wave of public interest that the jade men, as by magic, have caused to appear. For "Unearthing China's Past," which cannot and will not try to compete with the dazzling display of masterpieces from Peking, has an additional purpose, which is quite different from that of the Chinese traveling exhibition.

During the last few years there has been much public debate on the extensive damage inflicted upon monuments and archaeological sites by looting, on the illegal exportation of artefacts, and on the role that dealers, public institutions, and private collectors have played in this process. It is hoped that this exhibition will provide some new insights into these complex problems by showing what has happened in China during the last twenty-five years.

The Chinese example is in many ways enlightening. Except, perhaps, for the extra dimension that modern Western technology has unfortunately added to an already desperate situation by providing such new tools as helicopters and mine detectors, the present state of affairs in the countries of Central America resembles in many respects the conditions that prevailed in China during the first half of this century. However, whereas in Central America the by now familiar process continues with unabated if not accelerated pace, the founding of the People's Republic of China in 1949 put a sudden and complete stop to all activities directed toward the clandestine excavation and exportation of ancient cultural relics. Almost twenty-five years have elapsed since that change took place, and although we can judge the events only from afar and many details remain unclear because of a dearth of complete, first-hand information, there can be no doubt that the solutions that the Chinese have applied to their old problems have now taken full effect. As China is probably the only country in which fifty years of clandestine and uncontrolled excavations have been immediately followed by a period of twenty-five years of concerted efforts to make up for the past, it would seem useful to study the Chinese example and see what we can learn from it.

In "Unearthing China's Past" a first and modest effort is made to explain some of the recent gains in our knowledge of Chinese archaeology by visual means. Each object in the exhibition came to the Western world during the first fifty years of this century. Most of them came to their final destination through so many intermediaries that, even if the excavators had taken pains to preserve essential pieces of archaeological information, these would have been lost in the course of the peregrinations of these pieces from one dealer to another. As a rule, therefore, the objects arrived on the Western art market with little or no indication as to their original provenance, date, or function; the context in which they had been discovered remained almost invariably obscure.

Next to most of the actual objects in the exhibition the visitor will find a photograph of a similar piece that was excavated by Chinese archaeologists during the last twenty-four years. Although only a few of these juxtaposed pieces are identical, many are so closely related in shape or style of decoration that it would seem permissible to apply the knowledge that Chinese archaeologists gathered on the pieces they excavated *in situ* to the actual objects of unknown provenance, date, or function that are included in this exhibition.

By including only objects that are comparable to recently excavated specimens, the limitations of choice far exceeded those normally imposed on the selection of pieces for a temporary exhibition. Naturally, some of the pieces that would fit into the plans could not be borrowed or transported. Also, in the field of prehistoric archaeology, not well represented in most American and European collections to begin with, so much depends upon the texture and color of artefacts—neither of which can be deduced from most of the Chinese reproductions—that it was decided to omit this phase of Chinese cultural history from the exhibition. This is all the more regrettable as this is one of the fields in which Chinese archaeologists have achieved their greatest successes. The juxtaposition of objects and photographs with the new information on the recently excavated pieces sometimes raises more questions than it solves; in other cases the results are somewhat inconclusive because an essential piece of the puzzle is still missing. In spite of all these limitations and uncertainties, however, most of the material presented here constitutes a gain in factual knowledge, the refutation of an old hypothesis, or, at least, a clearer perspective on problems still awaiting a solution. In order to illustrate these gains in knowledge, it was often necessary to quote older opinions that now have been superseded by new discoveries. Especially to those of our colleagues who find themselves quoted and contradicted in this catalogue, we should like to give assurances that this was not done in order to enlarge upon their mistakes with the glee of those who have the benefit of hindsight. If anything has become clear to the authors of this catalogue it is that Chinese archaeology has now moved into a phase in which each mail delivery from China may bring word of new discoveries that contradict and correct the opinions based on excavations carried out only a few years ago. If, therefore, within a few years this catalogue should already have completed its lifespan of usefulness, this would be an apt illustration not only of the impermanence of human knowledge but also of the remarkable speed with which changes take place in a field that has been far too long characterized by stagnation.

"Unearthing China's Past" covers approximately three thousand years of cultural history, from the early Shang bronze culture to late Ming porcelains. The examples have been chosen from this wide span of time in order that the visitor may get at least some impression of different moods and styles in the changing picture of China's cultural history. As the visitor follows the roughly chronological sequence of the exhibition he may also perceive certain analogies in the circumstances under which some of the objects on display reached their final destination. Some individual juxtapositions demonstrate in dramatic fashion how much knowledge can be gained by scientific excavation and by a careful observation of the site. Other examples, conversely, give us an inkling of how much must have been irretrievably lost in former times, not only in terms of objects but also in terms of information, when objects were inexpertly and hurriedly dug up by grave robbers in the course of their surreptitious and nocturnal gravedigging.

For the benefit of the uninitiated visitor some basic questions require a preliminary explanation before we can deal with the history of Chinese archaeology itself. The first question concerns the beliefs that inspired the Chinese to construct, during the three millenia covered by this exhibition, such elaborate subterranean tombs that they furnished so lavishly with a great variety of the most costly mortuary furniture. Classical Chinese literature explains at length the Chinese concept of the duality of the human soul, the two components of which remain inextricably bound together during man's life on earth, only to separate at the moment of his death. The component that ascends to heaven was of no further human concern, but it was considered of the utmost importance that the spirit that accompanied the body into the grave be coerced and humored to remain in the tomb and not to stray from it, causing trouble and mischief. To achieve this purpose it was considered necessary to preserve the body and to prevent its decomposition and also to create in the tomb an atmosphere sympathetic to the spirit of the deceased. Unlike the Egyptians, who successfully achieved the first aim by their special embalming techniques, the Chinese relied exclusively on the alleged magic properties of jade. The second purpose was achieved by placing in the tomb objects that the spirit might like to use in his life after death.

In ancient times, during the rule of the Shang dynasty (fifteenth-eleventh century B.C.), a king or nobleman would be accompanied into his grave by the slain bodies of his servants, his charioteer, his horses, and his hunting dogs. These were believed to be resurrected after death, accompanying and serving the spirit of their deceased master in the nether world. Soon, however, sacrificial victims and actual tomb furniture were replaced by servants in effigy, puppets carved from wood or modeled in clay, and by "spirit goods," i.e., reproductions or models of houses, livestock, household utensils, and musical instruments. The transition from the barbaric custom of human sacrifice to a mortuary culture, which used substitutes in wood and clay for men, animals, and various possessions, occurred during the Chou period and seems to have been completed toward the end of that time.

By then large numbers of ritual bronze vessels and bells accompanied the grandees into their tombs. The noblemen were still inseparable from their horses and chariots, but no longer did their charioteers follow them into the grave. The introduction of wood or clay figurines and the use of ceramic substitutes for the costly ritual vessels in bronze gave a great impetus to China's mortuary culture, which, though it underwent continuous change, flourished uninterruptedly from Late Chou times to the middle of the eighth century of our era, when civil war and economic depression deprived the rich of the means of perpetuating the pious tradition of giving one's relatives the best possible funeral one could afford. Buddhism, with its belief in immediate rebirth and its Indian tradition of cremation, offered an alternative to the ancient, deeply rooted Chinese way of death. Yet it was only economic and political disaster, not the teachings of the Buddha, which made the Chinese abandon the precepts of filial piety concerning the disposal of the dead. Although the custom of lavish burials revived as soon as peace and prosperity returned, it never regained its old momentum. However, the tradition of placing mortuary gifts in solid, well-constructed tombs continued to be observed by all who could afford it until well into the seventeenth century, when the custom finally went into decline.

Thus, throughout most of China's long history the subterranean wealth of "spirit objects" continued to accumulate. By modern times cemeteries had expanded to the extent that a far from negligible percentage of arable land was taken up by tombs. Naturally, these subterranean treasures attracted thieves, for although the taboos concerning burial sites were in general strictly observed, there were always a few enterprising individuals who were not afraid to incur the wrath of the spirits of the dead in exchange for rare treasures. Chinese literary and historical works of all periods abound with stories of grave robbery.

By far the most momentous discovery from a historical point of view occurred when a band of thieves broke into the tomb of a ruler of the Late Eastern Chou (third century B.C.) kingdom of Wei in A.D. 281. In the tomb the robbers found the *Bamboo Annals,* a historical record of the state of Wei from high antiquity to 298 B.C. written on bamboo slips. The annals turned out to follow a chronology of ancient Chinese history that is at variance with the official chronological tables. This sensational discovery was studied and commented upon by scholars of Chinese history of all times. But already at this early date we get a foretaste of the waste and destruction that have accompanied bootleg excavations throughout history all over the world. The *History of the Chin Dynasty* gives a vivid description of the ransacking of the tomb and continues "But those who broke into the tomb used the bamboo slips as torches to provide them with light as they proceeded to loot the tomb of its treasures. Hence, by the time the authorities got hold of the bamboo slips many had already been burned or misplaced, with the result that the inscriptions had suffered damage, and that parts were missing or had become undecipherable."

Although grave robbing by men in search of gold and treasures occurred throughout China's entire history, totally new prospects for treasure hunters opened up when during the Sung period the Chinese developed a profound interest in archaeology. It is only in recent years that scholars in the West, who had always been inclined to enlarge upon the many mistakes that these Sung pioneers committed, have begun to appreciate the critical sense of history with which the Chinese applied themselves to the task of identifying and dating ancient objects, deciphering their inscriptions, and combining the information thus obtained with the wealth of written information in classical literature. As Richard Rudolph in his article "Preliminary Notes on Sung Archaeology" (*Journal of Asian Studies* 22 [February 1963], 169-177) has demonstrated, their evaluation of archaeological material was very similar to that of the great German historian Leopold von Ranke seven hundred years later.

Naturally, these early pioneers had their limitations. The ancient Chinese bronzes that such avid archaeologists and collectors as the Sung Emperor Hui-tsung (reigned 1101-1126) assembled were primarily appreciated for their inscriptions. Cultural relics of the remote and idealized past of wise rulers and great philosophers, the bronze inscriptions were considered to be a direct message from that past, unalterably cast into bronze and unaffected by the human errors of countless generations of scribes that had modified the message as it was handed down in the classics. The profound historical interest remained a characteristic of Chinese scholarship through the ages, and although it created a type of connoisseurship that to our taste is perhaps too much occupied with problems of epigraphy, its monumental achievements should not be overlooked.

Next to the scholarly approach of such Sung archaeologists as Chao Ming-ch'êng, the author of the famous *Chin-shih lu,* much literate dilettantism was involved in the observations that Chinese connoisseurs made about ancient Chinese bronze art. Later, during the Ch'ing period, the comparison of archaeological finds with textural information contained in the classics developed further, when new methods of textual exegesis were applied to epigraphic and archaeological material. Thus Chinese research on the ancient artefacts of their traditional culture passed from the stage of an elegant pastime for erudite amateurs to that of a highly developed, typically Chinese type of armchair archaeology. The range of interest, however, remain largely the same. Ancient bronzes, from Shang to Six Dynasties, jades, and inscribed stone sculpture were the principal types of objects that the archaeologists studied. As to the multitude of other "spirit objects" from the Chou, Han, and T'ang periods, these were left in peace in their tombs. From folklore stories it is evident that the Chinese were perfectly aware of their existence, but such *ming-ch'i* were still too much associated with the inauspicious event of death to be considered worthy of a scholar's attention. Only the archaeologist and connoisseur of calligraphy Yüeh K'o (1173-1240) seems to have reproduced a single *ming-ch'i* in one of his books. Actually, through the ages collectors who surrounded themselves with objects recovered from tombs were often viewed with misgivings by their family and colleagues. Pi Shao-tung of the Sung period, the first gentleman dealer whose biography can be reconstructed from Chinese sources, named his studio in a self-deprecatory manner "The Pavilion of Death," and the great collector Viceroy Tuan Fang (died 1911) received a similar sobriquet from a visiting friend who was struck by the morbid atmosphere in the courtyard of Tuan Fang's residence, where moss overgrown stelae and mortuary inscriptions were lined up along the walls.

How little foreigners knew from personal observation about China's ancient mortuary culture becomes evident when we read J. J. M. de Groot's *The Religious System of China,* which appeared in installments during the last decade of the nineteenth century. De Groot's study is based on a brilliant combination of personal observations of contemporary burial and mourning customs, mostly in Amoy, and historical information, culled from an astounding variety of ancient literary sources. The sometimes slightly diffuse and vague quality of his otherwise highly accurate translations suddenly makes us realize that De Groot translated all this material relating to *ming-ch'i,* tomb figurines and burial customs of ancient China, without ever having laid eyes upon a real tomb figure of the Han, Wei, or T'ang period. It is amazing to see how much of the information he assembled, and which, at that time, must often have looked fanciful and unreliable, has been confirmed by excavations almost eighty years later. Even the jade men make a brief appearance in his account, only to become Sleeping Beauties again in the yellowing pages of De Groot's undeservedly long-forgotten volumes.

All this changed with the coming of the twentieth century, which for China began inauspiciously with the bloody Boxer Rebellion and the international military intervention that accompanied it. From that time on more and more foreigners came to

China. The imperial government, on the brink of collapse, invited foreign companies to construct a network of railways that would connect the major cities of north and west China. After the educational reforms of 1905 several Japanese came to China to teach the "new" subjects. German, Swedish, Russian, and British expeditions, which had first concentrated most of their attention on the caravan routes of Turkestan, now decided to move into China. Some of these expeditions, such as the one led by the French sinologue Edouard Chavannes into northern China, and that of Victor Segalen, which concentrated on Szechwan, were legitimate expeditions, which took rubbings and photographs establishing in many cases a priceless record of what was still there at the dawn of the age of destruction. Other expeditions were in reality little more than shopping trips—and some of them were even worse than that.

The discovery, on May 26, 1900, of a walled-up library, more than a thousand years old, in one of the caves of the deserted Buddhist temple complex at Tun-huang, on China's northwest frontier, as well as its tragic outcome for the Chinese, are well known, and its details need not be recounted here. British, French, Japanese, and Russian expeditions led by such famous scholars as Sir Aurel Stein, Paul Pelliot, and S. F. Ol'denburg induced the ex-soldier-turned-priest who had found the priceless library to part with the manuscripts for ridiculously small sums of money. Only what was left after these visits ended up in the National Library in Peking.

Perhaps the most thoughtful and fairest comments on these events have been made by Arthur Waley: "The Chinese regard Stein and Pelliot as robbers. I think that the best way to understand their feelings is to imagine how we should feel if a Chinese archaeologist were to come to England, discover a *cache* of mediaeval manuscripts at a ruined monastery, bribe the custodian to part with them and carry them off to Peking" *(Ballads and Stories from Tun-huang,* London: Allen & Unwin, 1960, p. 237). Waley also points out that it was part of nineteenth century archaeological tradition to assume that the removal of art treasures from the Near and Middle East was not resented by the local populace because their conversion to Islam had divorced them from their ancient cultural heritage. To some extent, perhaps, this argument may have seemed valid to von Le Coq and Grünwedel when they cut up the wall paintings of Qyzyl and Turfan and transported them to Berlin—where most of them became victims of the senseless destruction of the Second World War.

In China, of course, this argument had no validity at all. Even Pelliot could not match the skills of his Chinese contemporaries Wang Kuo-wei and Lo Chên-yü in evaluating the Tun-huang manuscripts. Twenty years later Pelliot said in a conference that there was only one manuscript that he regretted having overlooked when he spent three weeks on his haunches in a badly lit cave, unrolling and rolling the manuscript scrolls as fast as he could to make his selection. In all probability he referred to the Manichaean scroll, which the Chinese found among the leftovers and which was published by Lo Chên-yü. More than anything else, perhaps, this revealing remark shows that he was a man without doubts or regrets even twenty years *post facto.*

The archaeologists who ventured into China during the early years of this century did not find a single, huge cache of priceless treasures, such as the sinologues had found at Tun-huang, but they found plenty. The first to appear on the scene, it would seem, was Berthold Laufer, who arrived in Sian in August 1903. His expeditions were buying trips for the Field Museum of Natural History in Chicago, and instead of undertaking actual fieldwork, he spent most of his time in Sian and Peking acquiring archaeological material from Chinese antique dealers. In this respect the best scholars, to whom Chinese literature on the subject was accessible, were strongly influenced by the Chinese approach to archaeology. And they had one distinct advantage over their learned Chinese colleagues: they lacked the inhibitions created by the Chinese taboos concerning *ming-ch'i*. Lo Chên-yü, the great Chinese scholar, gingerly acquired his first two tomb figurines in the winter of 1907, at a time when Laufer had already amassed a considerable amount of material.

The cause of the suddenly developing interest in early Chinese funerary objects is not difficult to establish. When the railroad construction gangs reached Sian and Lo-yang, they cut straight through the huge necropolis that surrounds the twin capital cities of the T'ang Empire. Thus, for the first time tomb figurines came to light again. But whereas the Chinese had always been inclined to disregard and discard them, the figurines caught the fancy of the foreign railroad engineers, who began to send pieces back to Europe. Soon a fashion came into being and a foreign market was established. Less than ten years later the distinguished Japanese archaeologist Hamada Kōsaku was the first to draw attention to the appearance on the market of forgeries of T'ang statuettes. From total oblivion to fashion and from there to large-scale imitation had taken only ten years.

From that time on the conditions regarding archaeology remained in many respects the same until the founding of the People's Republic of China in 1949. The revolution of 1912, which made China into a republic, brought neither the peace nor the prosperity and the political unity that its organizers had hoped for. In the political chaos of civil war, rivaling war lords, floods, and famine, conditions were created that could only favor the activities of grave robbers. During the last decade preceding World War II, Chinese archaeologists began the excavation of the buried ruins of the ancient Shang capital near An-yang, Honan Province. They brought to light important evidence of cultural life during the Shang period. In many ways, however, it was a hopeless struggle. As soon as a site became known, the grave robbers, armed with their "Lo-yang spades"—a primitive but most effective instrument for tomb prospecting known at least since Ming times—would converge upon it. Only occasionally, when strong local authorities intervened, a newly discovered hoard would end up in a Chinese museum. Most of the finds reached the markets of Peking and Shanghai, to be immediately dispersed over private and public collections in Japan, Europe, and America.

In the Western world this situation does not seem to have caused much concern.

Many museum curators and connoisseurs simply accepted with gratitude and enthusiasm the inexhaustible wealth of ancient Chinese art objects that continued to turn up in the shops of Berlin, Paris, and London. They had no idea of the circumstances under which these pieces had been found, for to them China was a faraway country, and not a living, everyday reality. Moreover, the slightly more enterprising among them did not find China a hospitable tourist country. It lacked the law and order, the picturesque charm, and the civilized comforts of Japan, and the reports of those who ventured beyond the hustle of Liu-li-ch'ang, the famed antique dealers' street in Peking, or the foreign settlements at Shanghai make frequent mention of "brigands," a term indiscriminately applied to robbers, mercenaries, and political dissidents. Commemorating one of Europe's most enterprising dealers who regularly went to China, Otto Kümmel, the founder of the Far Eastern section of the Berlin Museum, praised him and his colleagues for having been willing to accept "the burden, and not seldom even the dangers, of a protracted residence in the Orient." To a generation of scholars who were never able to visit China such words sound as if they came from another planet.

But the greatest contribution to the growth of the important collections of Chinese art in the Western world was made not by those who admired Chinese art and culture from a safe distance but by people with a different frame of mind. Many of them went to China in another professional capacity but became interested in Chinese art and archaeology during their work in that country. Most remarkable are the Swedes Johan Gunnar Andersson (1874-1960) and Orvar Karlbeck (1879-1967). Andersson, a geologist who became an archaeologist, was one of the few foreigners who made an agreement with the Chinese authorities concerning the prehistoric material he excavated and who scrupulously lived up to its conditions. His compatriot Orvar Karlbeck, a railroad engineer, became the self-styled "Treasure Seeker in China" and collected most of the Bronze Age material that is now in Swedish collections. He was the first to keep a careful record of the provenance of the pieces he acquired.

Acting in accordance with his dictum "Asia is One," Okakura Kakuzō, from 1906 to 1913 Curator at Boston, went to China in search of the origins of Japanese civilization. He was accompanied on his travels by Hayasaki Kōkichi, the son of his stepsister, a painter who was the first Japanese to penetrate into China's interior armed with a camera, and probably the only person who ever did so dressed in a Taoist costume. Together these two are responsible for expanding the activities of the Boston Museum from Japan into China.

The many colorful personalities and dedicated scholars who were instrumental in assembling the great collections of Chinese art in the Western world cannot all be mentioned here. Visitors to the exhibition will see some of them make a brief appearance in the pages of this catalogue with objects they brought back or opinions they expressed. When we read their books and letters, remarks such as those made by Pelliot and Kümmel are far from exceptional, and we begin to realize how much our thinking has changed in the relatively few years that separate us from them. Perhaps only those who have now become their successors as custodians of these collections, and who owe them a great debt of gratitude, will eventually be able to understand their feelings, and to place their actions in historical perspective. It would be easy now to point to their shortcomings, but it would hardly be fair if we tried to judge them, meting out praise and blame in the best of China's historical traditions.

We tend to stress their selfless dedication to our institutions, at the same time aware of their often deeply emotional ties with China. Yet we have to understand also that the Chinese view the events of the first half of this century with totally different eyes. Perhaps, however, the satisfaction of having made up for the past entirely on their own may help to heal the wounds and take away some of their justifiable bitterness.

With the founding of the People's Republic of China in 1949 a new era began. For archaeology we should perhaps put its official beginning at May 24, 1950, when the new government passed legislation protecting cultural relics and monuments, preventing the exportation of works of art and regulating archaeological activities. With great energy a beginning was made in the training of young field archaeologists, and cultural teams were organized all over the country to anticipate the demand for salvage archaeology that the increased pace of industrialization would undoubtedly create.

As the new regime began to extend its authority over the entire country, the exportation of art objects ceased. The art dealers were the first to see the writing on the wall. One of them wrote a letter to his world-wide clientele in which he announced his retirement: "I am seventy years old now, and since half a century I have been collecting and selling Chinese antique works of art. A very interesting profession which has business combined with pleasure: rarely a day has gone by without some excitement of securing or planning to secure certain objects. The definite confiscation by the new authorities in power at Shanghai of a large collection containing a great number of very important objects, has made me suddenly realize that dealing in Chinese antiques is at its end, and that I would be deprived of all my enjoyment."

It would be unfair, however, to leave the impression that the spectacular changes in Chinese archaeology should be attributed to the punishment meted out to violators of the new law and the confiscation of their wares. The results of almost twenty-five years of archaeological discovery in China certainly required much more than the mere establishment of law and order in China's cultural life, for they could never have been achieved without the willing cooperation and the active support of large masses of the Chinese population. It is in educating the Chinese people in a new attitude toward the preservation of the cultural relics of their own past and in enlisting their help to achieve this aim that the communist rulers of China have been remarkably successful.

For confirmation of this impression we do not merely have to take their word. Reading the archaeological literature published in China since 1950 in chronological order, one soon observes certain patterns in the events leading to the discovery of the archaeological objects and works of art that are published in these journals. It would, of course, have come as a surprise if all Chinese had changed their ways overnight.

During the first few years of the new regime, therefore, the archaeological literature, not surprisingly, mentions a number of cases in which illegal excavators were apprehended *flagrante delicto,* after which the objects were deposited in a museum. A few years later, after the intensive cultural propaganda began to have its effects, the archaeological literature provides several examples of honest but misguided initiative. Local inhabitants, without the benefit of any archaeological training, would proceed to excavate a chance find, in the process of which most of the valuable archaeological information would be effaced. The proud but ignorant excavators would then present their treasure trove to the authorities, leaving it to the archaeologists to try to reconstruct the details of their discovery (see cat. nos. 43-45).

As the crash courses for field archaeologists instituted during the first year of the new regime began to deliver their graduates, it became more common practice to call for expert assistance whenever a chance find was made. The archaeological teams of the provincial and municipal cultural committees played a most active part in this new development. The increased pace of industrialization and the extensive work on new roads, railways, and reservoirs necessitated a large amount of groundwork. Some of the most significant new discoveries have been made as a result of these activities. However, everywhere in the world, regardless of whether private profits or production norms are at stake, archaeological treasures often become the victims of draglines, sacrificed in order not to delay construction. Naturally, China has not been spared such losses, but from the published criticism of the few known cases of this type one gets the impression that in China such mishaps are exceptions rather than the rule.

Teaching the people the importance of protecting and preserving archaeological sites and ancient tombs because they are a repository of knowledge of ancient Chinese culture was an urgent task for yet another reason. As the tenets of communist doctrine gained more and more acceptance among the broad masses of the Chinese people, many of the ancient superstitions began to disappear. With them went the fear of tombs and the ancient taboos surrounding graves. As the tombs often provided excellent building materials for roads and other construction projects, the danger was far from imaginary that too literal an interpretation of the slogan "stress the present, neglect the past" might lead to irreparable damage to archaeological sites, this time not for their treasures, as had happened so often in the past, but for the sake of the material of which they had been constructed. From the very beginning the authorities were well aware of this danger, as is indicated by an editorial in the official newspaper *Kuang-ming jih-pao* of March 26, 1956.

Perhaps the final stage in creating an awareness among the people for the necessity of preserving the cultural relics of their country's past was reached during the work on the architectural remains of Tatu, the capital of the Mongol Empire, at Peking. Ku Yen-wen, reporting on this recent excavation says "The investigations and excavations at the Yuan capital Tatu, like other archaeological work, have been done with the support and assistance of the workers, peasants, and soldiers. The discovery of the barbican entrance to Ho Yi Men, in particular, should be attributed to the workers tearing down the Peking city walls. When this city gate was brought to light, they carefully protected the site and copied down the inscriptions written in ink when the gate was rebuilt in the fourteenth year of Hung-wu in the Ming dynasty (A.D. 1381). The inscriptions rapidly became illegible after being exposed to the air." Although some of the readers of such archaeological news may be inclined to take it with a grain of salt, the consistency with which such examples of an increased cultural awareness emerge from the vast number of archaeological reports cannot fail to impress anyone who is even only vaguely familiar with the problems of educating people to protect their own environment against pollution.

To sum up, in a few pages, the results achieved by all of this concerted activity is not easy and should perhaps be left to Chinese archaeologists who have first-hand knowledge of the finds. Here only a few salient aspects of new Chinese archaeology can be pointed out as they appear to an observer whose knowledge is based exclusively upon the large stream of archaeological publications that have come out of China during the last twenty-four years.

A distinguished expert in the field of Chinese art recently expressed his surprise at the fact that so much of our basic knowledge of the typology and styles of Chinese art, most of which seemed based on hearsay and speculation, has been confirmed by recent excavations. Although this observation may be quite correct, one must immediately add that much of our earlier knowledge was of a rather general nature, and not very precise. Even if objects were correctly attributed to the Han, Six Dynasties, or T'ang period, there were few, if any reliable methods of dating objects with greater precision within these periods, each of which spans several centuries. A determined search through all of the early publications may perhaps reveal the existence of a dozen datable tombs from these periods, and recent excavations even tend to discredit the reliability of several of these rare pre-war milestones. There is evidence to suspect that some of these "closed finds" may have been fabricated by dealers, who assembled material from approximately the same time and completed their "set" with the first available mortuary inscription that seemed to fit the bill. Those foreign scholars who enquired most persistently into the provenance, date, and archaeological context of their acquisitions collected some of the most valuable data. Inevitably they were also the first to become the victims of dealers who cloaked their ignorance in made-up stories.

The first and most useful gain in knowledge of ancient Chinese art is the result of the fact that the Chinese archaeologists have unearthed a very large number of exactly datable tombs. A list of dated tombs that has been compiled from recent archaeological literature consists of more than 450 entries. The usefulness of these data for Western archaeological or art historical research varies greatly. Some of the datable tombs are mentioned only in one- or two-line references in archaeological reports. These are often tombs that had previously been denuded of all of their furniture by grave robbers. Even though they may be of little interest to us, they can often be of great value to Chinese archaeologists because the structure of the tomb may contain details that can be helpful in establishing the date of other undated tombs (see cat. no. 40). The combination of data derived from the structure of the tomb and the typology of the objects placed in it has helped to refine the archaeologists' tools for dating both tombs and objects. Even if the number of exactly datable tombs in a cemetery is small, its systematic excavation makes it possible to establish typological sequences to which absolute dates can be assigned with a reasonable amount of certainty.

The usefulness of this vast amount of new and exciting archaeological information to the scholar in the West is also affected by the fact that so many of the finds have never been fully published. In all fairness it should be pointed out that our Chinese colleagues must have been under constant pressure to excavate and salvage chance finds and that this heavy pressure of work kept them from applying strict standards of archaeological description to all of their reports. To make matters worse, especially during the early years of new archaeological activities, the quality of reproductions in the journals was extremely poor. On the other hand, in the publications of carefully planned excavations a much higher standard of description was maintained from the very beginning. Especially after the Great Cultural Revolution the quality of reproductions increased dramatically, with the result that some of the most important finds made during these turbulent years are accessible in excellent reproductions. In spite of these shortcomings, archaeological reports from China have, from the very first day of their appearance, filled a great void and have deeply affected our knowledge of ancient Chinese art. For example, the large number of datable tombs now makes it possible to trace the development of mortuary ceramics and tomb figurines from the Han through the T'ang period and to date these pieces with a precision hitherto impossible. The exhibition includes numerous examples that illustrate these new possibilities of dating the works of art in our collections.

Apart from a vastly increased insight into the chronological development of Chinese art, perhaps the most important gain of recent years lies in our expanded knowledge of its immense regional variety. In the past, when the provenance of only relatively few pieces was known with certainty, even some of the most typical local characteristics largely escaped our observation. The dealers' provenance attached to a large number of pieces was of little help in solving this problem. Much of what has been said about this topic in connection with other ancient cultures applies to China as well, but the recent excavations have given us a new possibility of assessing retrospectively the reliability of some of this hearsay information. The stated provenance of some pieces included in this exhibition has been fully confirmed by recent excavations. Perhaps the best example is the set of Han mortuary ceramics from the William Rockhill Nelson Gallery of Art, Kansas City (cat. nos. 48, 49). The dealer's stated provenance for these pieces was Shan-hsien, Honan Province, an area that, in spite of its many tumuli, never was known for its subterranean treasures. The recent excavation of almost identical pieces in the neighboring Ling-pao County clearly confirms the information supplied by the dealer.

Especially when the provenance is stated by the dealer to be an area not previously known for its antiquities, chances are that it is correct, since the dealers, when pressed for information on the subject, usually fell back upon such old and reliable standby names as An-yang, Hui-hsien, or Chin-ts'un. Perhaps the most enlightening example of this sort of provenance is provided by the *hu* vase from the Seattle Museum (cat. no. 20). Dealers consistently attributed this type of ceramics to Lo-yang and Chin-ts'un, two well-known Late Eastern Chou sites. The overwhelming weight of archaeological evidence now points to the immediate vicinity of Peking as the area in which vases of this type were made and buried. One would almost suspect that the dealers considered the site a little too close to Peking to reveal its exact location to their clientele.

The attribution of pieces of unknown origin to well-known archaeological sites was in many cases merely used as a selling point. It made all Shang bronzes come from An-yang, all inlaid Chou bronzes from Chin-ts'un, and all pieces that were different and unusual from Ch'ang-sha, although the name of this last site never acquired the glamor of the other two. From an archaeological point of view China thus consisted largely of *terra incognita*, with only a few place names written in. Yet such a map may have responded closer to the archaeological reality of those days than we may now be inclined to believe. Grave robbing, the source of most of our material, was an enterprise that was carried out on a strictly commercial basis. Unless they were attracted to a remote site by rumors of new discoveries, the bootleg archaeologists usually confined their activities to those areas that seemed to offer the best chance of finding rich treasures. These areas were, of course, those that had been most densely populated in historic times. The result of these methods of operation is that the bulk of the material now assembled in public and private collections in the Western world comes from a relatively restricted area in northern China.

In Western collections that have been entirely or largely assembled by a single individual, the limited geographic range was evident from the way in which the collections had been acquired. The material assembled by Berthold Laufer for the Field Museum of Natural History, Chicago, has a typical Sian flavor; the Bishop White Collection in the Royal Ontario Museum is an assemblage of Chinese art from Honan. Much of the material collected by other museums, however, comes from the same area, without this being immediately evident from the museum's history. Only occasionally, when a traveler offered to a museum pieces from a remote area of China to which he had traveled, the strictly local style of certain objects was fully recognized. The tomb figurines from Szechwan in the British Museum and the Ethnographic Museum, Munich, are perhaps the only examples of this local school of mortuary sculpture in Western museums. Recent excavations have now revealed the geographic spread and stylistic evolution of this interesting local art form. The preponderantly "northern" flavor of most of our collections, however, has become evident only after the art forms and styles of other Chinese areas were begininng to become known.

Whereas the activities of illegal excavators were restricted to the areas most likely to yield profitable discoveries, the program of industrialization that the People's Republic initiated affects the entire country. The ancient treasures that are brought to light as a result of digging connected with the construction of factories, roads, railways, and reservoirs presents a much wider regional variety than those excavated in pre-war days. The greater insight into regional variations and styles, and into local types of tomb architecture and burial customs, which is the result of discoveries made in many remote parts of China, extends into all periods of Chinese cultural history.

Before World War II, our knowledge of Chinese Bronze Age sites was largely confined to An-yang, Chin-ts'un, Li-yü, and Hsin-ch'êng, and even these sites were far from perfectly known. In recent years dozens of other sites, several consisting of large tombs or even of large cemeteries, have yielded a wealth of new information on the evolution of Chinese bronze culture. The geographic spread of these finds is surprisingly large; bronze vessels have been found in southern Manchuria, in western Kansu, and all the way down into China's deep south. In the past the frequent occurrence of feudal state names in bronze inscriptions had helped to establish the provenance of vessels of unknown origin. Now that a large amount of new material of well-established provenance has been discovered, the first outlines of the extremely complex picture of the development of regional bronze styles are beginning to emerge.

The colorful spectrum of Han art, of which we previously knew only the metropolitan styles, reveals itself in the many spectacular Han finds that have been made in an area extending from southern Manchuria and North Korea to Yünnan and Canton in the south, and from Szechwan in the west to Shantung in the east. The extraordinarily large number of finds in the ancient kingdom of Ch'u, combined with those made in the territory of its southern neighbors in Canton, Kweichow, and Yünnan, clearly suggests that the traditional labeling as "Chång-sha" of anything with a southern flavor will have to be revised (see cat. nos. 52-57).

The dryness of China's northern border regions is conducive to the preservation of otherwise perishable objects. In Manchuria and the autonomous region of Inner Mongolia a considerable number of interesting discoveries have added to our knowledge of the cultural relationship between China and its northern neighbors. Of particular interest are the numerous graves of the Khitans of the Liao dynasty. Although some preliminary work has been done during the Japanese military occupation, a large number of newly discovered tombs, many of which are exactly datable, has now made it possible to reconstruct the material culture of the Khitans in considerable detail (see cat. nos. 97-103).

As the example of the Liao crown (cat. no. 97) shows, this period is one where the combination of detailed information preserved in written sources with the rich harvest of archaeological finds may enable us to gain a very complete and detailed impression of the lives of these northern herdsmen. The steady flow of new discoveries has also provided a large amount of new material for the comparative study of objects and passages in historical sources of other periods. Although bamboo slips have been discovered in several Eastern Chou tombs (see cat. no. 14), these writings usually constitute an inventory of the tomb furniture, which in itself is interesting enough, but in no way comparable in importance to the *Bamboo Annals* (see above), a find that has not yet been duplicated in modern history. Inscribed stones that give a biography of the deceased first made their appearance during the Six Dynasties period. They continued to be in fashion during the T'ang period and were used occasionally as long as tomb art flourished. Sometimes the deceased turns out to have been a person of sufficient importance to have his biography incorporated in the dynastic history, in which case the text of his tombstone provides an interesting source of information to establish the accuracy of the official history. The political historian will find the tombstones of controversial political figures the most interesting, as they provide us with new material in which the events are viewed from another perspective. Art historians will find important information, not recorded in any historical work, in the tombstone of the famous painter of horses Jên Jên-fa (1254-1327). A special category of archaeological finds, long favored by Chinese scholars, is formed by objects that illustrate or elucidate passages in ancient Chinese texts. The Taoist classic *Tao-tê-ching,* the *Ritual of the Chou,* and several other Han and pre-Han texts refer to chariot wheels with thirty spokes. Recent excavations confirmed this number, the correctness of which had previously been doubted. The recent find of lacquered shafts of halberds in a tomb from the Ch'u kingdom explained a passage in the *Ritual of the Chou* that had previously been unclear (see cat. no. 31). The most spectacular example of this type is, of course, the discovery of the jade suits, to which many Han sources refer (see cat. nos. 41-42) How many of such pieces were found in the past will always remain a mystery, and it was only because the technical difficulties of restoring the collapsed jade suits to their original shape was far beyond both the interest and the capability of the grave robbers that Western museums now have to content themselves with a handful of jade or glass plaques.

The fate of the jade men brings us to the question of how much was lost in the past. Reviewing the many recent reports on excavations and studying the contents of tombs in search of comparable pieces, the organizers of this exhibition soon began to realize the price that must have been paid in terms of objects and information for the rich harvest of finds that came to be dispersed over the Western world during the first half of this century. The number of objects of certain types that reached Western collections is clearly connected with their fragility. From the archaeological reports it is quite evident that glassware is far from exceptional in Chinese tombs. In Western museums hardly any examples of early Chinese glass survive; most of them must have been destroyed by inexpert excavation or in transit to Peking and Shanghai. The effort to assemble pieces resembling the mortuary gifts deposited in the tomb of the nine-year old girl Li Ching-hsün (cat. nos. 76-82) made us realize how many Sui tombs must have been despoiled of their inventory to contribute to this reconstruction.

Perhaps even more important than the loss in terms of fragile objects is that of information. Now that the average inventory of a T'ang tomb is well established, one could make an educated guess at the number of T'ang tombs that provided the material preserved in Western and Japanese collections. But about the contents of all these T'ang tombs and the way in which the mortuary gifts were displayed in them nothing was known. The sketch drawn by a Japanese art dealer in China and, therefore, presumably knowledgeable, is almost the only record we have. Recent excavations would seem to indicate that the drawing is either incomplete or incorrect.

In the exhibition several examples are given of objects of unknown use, the function of which can now be explained with the help of information gained by Chinese archaeologists *in situ* when they excavated similar pieces. The most dramatic example, perhaps, is the ceremonial axe of the Shang period (cat. no. 10). Equally interesting is the discovery of the function of the bronze mask, which had been a topic of protracted discussion among scholars in the past (cat. no. 13). In other cases the original placement of an architectural fragment (cat. no. 40) or the complete shape of a broken vessel could be reconstructed (cat. no. 63). All of these examples, which could easily have been multiplied, demonstrate the immediate relevance of the new archaeological finds in China, not only for the Chinese themselves but also for those interested in Chinese art all over the world.

The final section of the exhibition consists of a group of well-known masterpieces of Chinese painting and calligraphy, largely from the collection of the Boston Museum. An effort is made to demonstrate the new light that the recent excavations can shed on problems concerning the date, style, and origin of some Chinese paintings and works of calligraphy. These are usually dealt with in the purely art historical context of stylistic analysis. Here some possibilities of using archaeological data to study Chinese paintings are suggested.

Although this exhibition was organized with a view to providing the public with new information and new ideas, without reference to political events in China, a few words have to be added here about the Great Cultural Revolution of 1966 and the following years. This is only because this movement has given rise to widespread misconceptions as to the fate of ancient monuments, museums, and archaeological sites in China. The stream of archaeological publications that had flowed from China since 1950 suddenly stopped in the middle of 1966, when the Great Cultural Revolution started. Visitors to China found museum curators busy removing their masterpieces from exhibition and putting them into storage. However, even though one of the primary objectives of the Red Guards was to "smash the Four Olds," which included ancient culture, no damage was ever inflicted upon any of the major museums and sites. A photograph showing slogans painted over the statuary of a famous Buddhist sculpture site near Hangchow was one of the few images of the Cultural Revolution that reached the West, where it created the erroneous impression that the Chinese were deliberately destroying their ancient cultural heritage. Nothing could have been farther from the truth.

When the archaeological journals resumed publication five years after being discontinued, it became evident that archaeological field work had continued throughout the upheaval of the Great Cultural Revolution. In fact some of the most important discoveries of the last twenty-four years occurred during this period.

The resumption of archaeological publications, and, above all, the new contacts between China and the West, will undoubtedly continue to focus the attention of the world on the extraordinary achievements of the Chinese in the field of archaeology. Making up for the losses of the past, Chinese archaeologists are setting an example for others to follow. And if we consider Mao Tse-tung's exhortation to "Make the Past Serve the Present," perhaps we can all benefit from this fascinating, exciting, and unique revolution in the field of archaeology.

Boston, August 1973   JAN FONTEIN

Chinese Chronology

SHANG DYNASTY (traditional dates)	1766-1122 B.C.
CHOU DYNASTY	1122-255 B.C.
CH'IN DYNASTY	255-206 B.C.
FORMER OR WESTERN HAN DYNASTY	206 B.C.-9 A.D.
WANG MANG INTERREGNUM	9-23 A.D.
LATER OR EASTERN HAN DYNASTY	25-220 A.D.
THE THREE KINGDOMS	220-265 A.D.
WESTERN CHIN DYNASTY	265-313 A.D.
EASTERN CHIN DYNASTY	317-419 A.D.
WEI DYNASTY	385-557 A.D.
NORTHERN CH'I DYNASTY	550-577 A.D.
NORTHERN CHOU DYNASTY	557-580 A.D.
SUI DYNASTY	581-618 A.D.
T'ANG DYNASTY	618-906 A.D.
FIVE DYNASTIES	907-960 A.D.
NORTHERN SUNG DYNASTY	960-1127 A.D.
SOUTHERN SUNG DYNASTY	1127-1279 A.D.
YÜAN DYNASTY	1279-1368 A.D.
MING DYNASTY	1368-1644 A.D.
CH'ING DYNASTY	1644-1912 A.D.

Shang Bronzes

The site of the ancient Shang capital near An-yang, Honan Province, first began to attract the attention of Chinese archaeologists around the turn of this century, when the "dragon bones" of a local apothecary were identified as oracle bones, sometimes inscribed with an archaic type of Chinese writing. About thirty years after this momentous discovery Chinese archaeologists began to excavate the site. They unearthed the foundations of large buildings and large, royal tombs, some of which still contained their rich funerary treasures of bronze ritual vessels, marble sculpture, jades, and a great variety of ceramics. They also found large numbers of oracle bones inscribed with questions and answers.

It soon became evident that the bronze culture of the Late Shang period was of a technical perfection and an artistic maturity that could only have been achieved during a long period of evolution. Although some scholars assumed that the sophisticated decor of the Late Shang must have been developed in material of a perishable nature, this hypothesis never gained universal acceptance. Moreover, the Chinese historical tradition, the prestige of which was greatly enhanced by the frequent confirmation on several important points by oracle bone inscriptions, clearly states that the Great City of Shang was only the last of several capitals of the Shang dynasty.

A fortunate discovery, followed up by systematic excavation in China, and stylistic analysis, initially without the benefit of archaeological information, have now clarified some of the uncertainties concerning the origins of the Late Shang bronze culture. The chance find of a potsherd by a schoolmaster, dutifully reported to the authorities, directed the attention of archaeologists to the city of Chêng-chou, Honan Province. Buried under the present city of that name, and extending outside its present city limits, lie the remnants of a Shang city. The daring hypothesis, advanced by a Chinese scholar, that Chêng-chou should be identified with the ancient city of Ao, the capital of the Shang before

they moved to An-yang, has perhaps found more adherents than its narrow basis of fact would seem to warrant. However, from the bronzes found at Pai-chia-chuang, a suburb of Chêng-chou (see cat. nos. 2, 3, and 7), it is evident that these vessels represent a phase in the evolution of Chinese bronze culture that precedes that of the highly developed later Shang style.

Most vessels are of relatively small size, cast in thin metal and decorated with a very simple geometric or animal design. Similar characteristics can be observed in bronzes excavated at the village of Liu-li-ko near Hui-hsien, Honan Province. At this site, excavated in 1950, unmistakable stratigraphic evidence demonstrated that the bronzes are of an earlier date than the vessels of the Late Shang period. The discoveries at Liu-li-ko and Pai-chia-chuang lent new historical interest to a number of bronze vessels dispersed throughout Western collections that displayed the same characteristics. At least one of them had already been identified as one of the earliest examples of Chinese bronze art long before the new excavations provided the definite archaeological proof of this supposition (see cat. no. 2).

Another interesting discovery was that these Middle Shang vessels, once their true historical importance was realized, turned out to be found not only in the relatively small territory traditionally considered to be the realm of the Shang dynasty but far beyond its borders. The first find of this type occurred in 1958 at Huang-pei-hsien, near Wuhan, Hupei Province. This suggests that Middle Shang culture was spread over an area far larger than previously assumed, a fact that may have been of great importance for the evolution of local bronze cultures during the following Chou period.

Just at the time when these first excavations were undertaken, Max Loehr published an article in which he classified the bronze art of Shang into five successive style phases. Without the benefit of the archaeological information still to be published, he classified under his style I and II a number of bronzes

that obviously belong in the same category as the vessels found at Liu-li-ko and Pai-chia-chuang. There is no other example in the history of the study of Chinese art in which a bold and far-reaching hypothesis found such immediate confirmation in the results of archaeological excavations.

In the meantime Chinese archaeologists began to penetrate even deeper into the secrets of the origins of Chinese bronze culture. In a series of archaeological excavations carried out in and around the village of Erh-li-t'ou, east of Loyang, Honan Province, between 1959 and 1964 archaeologists uncovered evidence of a bronze culture that even antedates the Middle Shang culture of Chêng-chou and Liu-li-ko. The discovery of a huge terrace of rammed earth has given rise to the supposition that Erh-li-t'ou may have been the first capital of the Shang dynasty, but inasmuch as the hypothesis concerning the city of Ao is already uncertain, this last suggestion seems to belong to the realm of pure speculation. The bronzes found at Erh-li-t'ou are clearly the product of bronze casting technique in its infancy; they are of utter simplicity and consist of plain bells, arrowheads and fishhooks. A piece resembling one of the excavated bells represents the earliest phase of Chinese bronze casting in this exhibition.

The spectacular gains in knowledge in the field of prehistoric cultures, an area not covered in this exhibition, combined with this deep thrust into the dark area of the origins of Chinese bronze culture clarify the cultural developments in the second millenium B.C., during which Chinese bronze culture evolved toward its greatest perfection.

References: Max Loehr, "The Bronze Styles of the Anyang Period," *Archives of the Chinese Art Society of America,* 7 (1953), 42-53; Alexander C. Soper, "Early, Middle and Late Shang: A Note," *Artibus Asiae* 28 (1964), 5-38.

1
Bell with a single flange
Bronze
Early Shang period, ca. 16th century B.C. (?);
h. 9 cm.
Collection of Dr. Paul Singer

The small bell, cast in heavy metal, has a narrow flange on one side and a small loop at the top. The tapering body has been left plain, except for a trapezoid frame of raised lines on both sides.

Published: Chinese Institute in America, *Art Styles of Ancient Shang,* New York, 1967, no. 6.

Among the few small bronzes excavated at Erh-li-t'ou in northwest Honan is a bell (fig. 1) of the same type as the piece exhibited here. Perhaps it represents a slightly more primitive stage in the development of bronze casting, for although the two pieces are very similar in shape, the Erh-li-t'ou piece does not even have the simple design of raised lines. A considerably larger (h. 13 cm.) example, presumably from Loyang, is illustrated by Bishop W. C. White.

References: Alexander C. Soper, "Early, Middle and Late Shang: A Note," *Artibus Asiae* 28 (1966), 5-36; The Loyang Archaeological Team of the Archaeological Institute of Academic Sinica, "A brief report on excavations at Erh-li-t'ou in Yen-shih County, Honan Province" (text in Chinese), *Kaogu,* 1965, no. 5, pp. 215-224; William Charles White, *Tombs of Old Loyang,* Shanghai: Kelly and Walsh, 1934, pl. 177, fig. 515.

1

fig. 1

2
Tripod of the *chia* type
Thinly cast bronze
Middle Shang period, ca. 14th century B.C.;
h. 24.7 cm.
Royal Ontario Museum, Toronto.
960.234.12

This bronze vessel comes from the collection of Dr. James M. Menzies, a missionary of the Presbyterian Church of Canada near An-yang, Honan Province, who pioneered the study of oracle bone inscriptions in the west. According to Dr. Menzies this vessel was unearthed in 1913 or 1914 about twelve *li* (approximately 3 miles) north of the An-yang railway station, just to the west of the Peking-Hankow railway.

Menzies noted that the vessel was "a very early form of Shang dynasty *chia*." The voluminous, hollow legs are extensions of the bulbous lower part of the body. The decorative band consists of crosshatching and a zigzag design in thin, raised lines. The two posts consist of stubby, triangular, and flat-topped projections. Although the piece has been extensively restored by its former owner, its shape seems to have been faithfully preserved.

Published: Barbara Stephen, "Early Chinese Bronzes in the Royal Ontario Museum," *Oriental Art,* n.s. 8, no. 2 (summer 1962), 62-67.

In recent years excavations in China have yielded new information on the early stages of Chinese bronze art that tends to confirm the claims made by Dr. Menzies as to the age of this *chia*. A vessel quite similar in shape but lacking the two posts (which may have been broken) was found in the village of Yang-chia-wan, Huang-p'o County, Hupei Province. Although this is not visible on the small reproduction, the report described the piece as having a decorative band consisting merely of two raised horizontal lines. Because of its southern location, this find could perhaps have strengthened the argument of those who still believed these primitive bronzes to be "provincial" *ming-ch'i* (objects used as substitutes for mortuary purposes) but the *chia* was found together with a

chüeh of a well-established Middle Shang type.

From the large (h. 2.9 m., w. 1.17 m., d. 2.13 m.) Middle Shang tomb no. 3 at Pai-chia-chuang, a village to the northeast of Chêng-chou, Honan Province, in the heartland of Shang culture, comes a *chia* that closely resembles the Toronto vessel in shape (fig. 2). The principal difference is that the two posts are of a type, fitted out with caps, that would seem to constitute an advance from the triangular projections on the Toronto vessel. The tomb at Pai-chia-chuang, in which one person had been buried together with a single sacrificial victim, contained ten bronze vessels. Most of these are decorated with simple *t'ao-t'ieh* bands in low relief against a plain background, as was customary during the Middle Shang period.

Although the two parallel pieces mentioned above differ from the Toronto *chia* in their decoration, the use of crosshatched patterns in raised lines is occasionally seen on early bronzes found at Chêng-chou. A *li* tripod found at Yang-chuang has a decoration similar to that of the Toronto *chia*.

References: First Cultural Working Team, Honan Province, "Brief report on the excavation of Shang burials at Pai-chai-chuang, Chêng-chou City" (text in Chinese), *Wen Wu,* 1955, no. 10, pp. 24-42; Kuo Ping-lien, "Investigation of ancient remains at Yang-chia-wan, Huang-p'o County, Hupei Province" (text in Chinese), *Kaogu,* 1958, no. 1, pp. 56-58; *Ch'üan-kuo chi-pên chien-shê kung-ch'êng-chung ch'u-t'u wên-wu chan-lan t'u-lu* [Illustrated catalogue of cultural relics excavated at construction sites in the entire country], Peking, 1954, vol. 2, pl. 140.

fig. 2

2

3
Tripod of the *chia* type
Bronze, light grayish green patina
Shang period, ca. 13th century B.C.; h. 27 cm.
The Sackler Collections

fig. 3

The round vessel has a flat bottom and three pointed legs. Around the middle of the vessel runs a band of conventionalized zoomorphic design in bold relief with large bulging eyes. On the lower part of the vessel are flat, low bosses with four spirals curling in toward the center in the shape of a small circle. On the flaring lip stand two square, tall, capped posts.

This vessel, related to a piece in the British Museum, seems to combine characteristics typical of the Middle Shang period with some of a slightly later date. Among the bronzes from the large tomb no. 3 at Pai-chia-chuang, Chêng-chou (see cat. no. 2) is a *chia* of the same shape decorated with similar whirling bosses (fig. 3). The shape of the vessel conforms to Middle Shang standards, but the well-developed capped posts, the handle decorated with an animal mask, as well as the brief inscription under the handle are all usually associated with vessels of a slightly later date.

In comparing this *chia* with cat. nos. 2 and 4, however, it becomes evident that it represents a transitional phase between the most archaic type (cat. no. 2) and the fully developed late Shang type (cat. no. 4).

References: William Watson, *Ancient Chinese Bronzes,* Rutland, Vt.: Tuttle, 1962, pl. 3a; First Cultural Working Team, Honan Province, "Brief report on the excavation of Shang burials at Pai-chia-chuang, Chêng-chou City" (text in Chinese), *Wen Wu,* 1955, no. 10, pp. 24-42.

3

4
Tripod of the *chia* type
Bronze with lustrous black and green patina
Late Shang period, ca. 12th-11th century
B.C.; h. 42.2 cm.
Museum of Fine Arts, Boston, William
Sturgis Bigelow Collection. 34.65

The large vessel with slightly convex bottom stands on three pointed legs; it has a simple, undecorated handle on one side. The decoration, cast in flat relief, is divided by a plain band into two horizontal registers and by notched flanges and the handle into six vertical sections. The decoration consists of confronting dragons, which form *t'ao-t'ieh* (animal) masks with bulging eyes where they meet at the flanges. The background consists of spiral filling. On the outside of the flaring rim are rising blades, a simplified form of which appears on the caps of the two vertical posts, and an elongated version of which covers the legs.

The vessel, which resembles quite closely a *chia* in the Freer Gallery of Art, Washington, D.C., is a typical example of the highly developed art of the Chinese bronze casters of the late Shang period. A comparison with the two preceding *chia* illustrates the rapid development of bronze casting during this period.

The inscription, cast in the inside of the vessel, represents the word "father" flanked by two pictographs of an eye, the whole presumably standing for a name.

Published: Sueji Umehara, *Shina Kodō Seika*, vol. 1, Ōsaka: Yamanaka, 1933, pl. 67.

4

5
Tripod of the *chüeh* **type**
Bronze
Middle Shang period, ca. 14th century B.C.;
h. 14.6 cm.
Collection of Dr. Paul Singer

The archaic type of *chüeh* is characterized by thin casting of the body and slender legs, which are triangular in section and attached to a flat bottom. The decoration around the narrow waist consists merely of three raised lines. On both sides of the spout has been added a stumpy, triangular projection of the same type as that found on the Toronto *chia* (cat. no. 2).

Published: Paul Singer, "Pre-Dynastic and Dynastic Shang material," *Oriental Art*, n.s. 6, no. 2 (summer 1960), 42-48; Max Loehr, *Relics of Ancient China from the Collection of Dr. Paul Singer*, New York: Asia Society, 1965, no. 6.

As early as 1950 Chinese archaeologists began to excavate a cemetery at Liu-li-ko, a short distance to the east of Hui-hsien, Honan Province. It was there that they discovered clear evidence of a stratigraphical sequence in Shang culture. An old stratum was found to have been disturbed by later burials. These dated from the Late Shang period, as evidenced by their contents, which resembled the Late Shang artifacts found at An-yang.

One of the burials (no. 203) in the earlier stratum and older, northern section of the cemetery yielded a bronze of the same type as the Singer *chüeh*, but slightly larger in size (h. 15.2 cm., fig. 4). The older stratum at Liu-li-ko is thought to be roughly coeval with some of the finds at Chêng-chou (see cat. no. 2), where a more complex stratigraphical sequence has been observed, and with the earliest phase of bronze culture found at An-yang. These remains can all be attributed to the Middle Shang period.

The casting technique and the vessel shape connect the Singer *chüeh* with a number of other Middle Shang vessels of this type in Chinese and Western collections. Most have the typical Middle Shang decorative band of animal motifs and are provided with a single

5

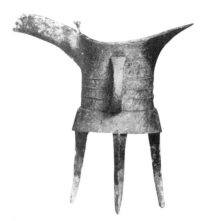

fig. 4

post or two posts of a slightly more advanced type, fitted out with a rounded cap. Although these features made it possible to assign pieces of this type to the Middle Shang period on stylistic grounds alone, the first clear stratigraphical support for this theory was found at the site where the *chüeh* of the same type and design as the Singer vessel was excavated.

Reference: The Archaeological Institute of Academia Sinica, *Hui-hsien fa-chüeh pao-kao* [Report on the excavations at Hui-hsien], Peking: Science Press, 1956, pp. 23-27, pl. 13.

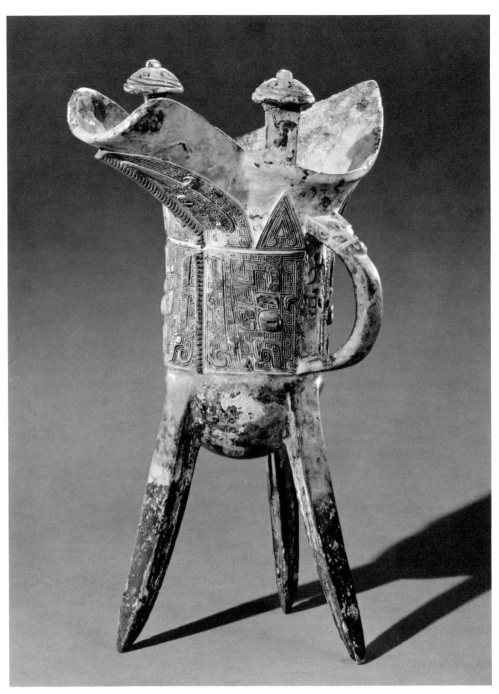

6

6
Tripod of the *chüeh* type
Bronze with light green patina
Late Shang period, ca. 11th century B.C.;
h. 20.5 cm.
Museum of Fine Arts, Boston, Seth K.
Sweetser Fund. 46.396

This vessel represents the Late Shang *chüeh* type that had evolved from the archaic type exhibited as no. 5. The capped posts of the *chüeh* reveal a development which parallels that of the same part of the *chia* vessel (see cat. no. 2). The bottom has turned from flat to round. A decorative band of *t'ao-t'ieh* on a *lei-wên* (meander pattern) ground encircles the piece. Flanges with deeply carved segmentation are placed vertically on three sides; together with the handle and the space for inscriptions underneath it the flanges divide the band into four sections. Under the handle is an inscription consisting of the graph *tzu* ("son") and a square surrounded by four footprints; the meaning of this graph has not yet been satisfactorily explained.

7
Beaker of the *ku* type
Bronze
Middle Shang period, ca. 14th-13th century
B.C.; h. 20 cm., diam. (at mouth) 13.1 cm.
Royal Ontario Museum, Toronto, gift of
Mrs. H. D. Warren

The beaker has the flaring mouth that is typical of all vessels of the *ku* type, but its slender waist lacks the bulging section. The foot has three large cross-shaped perforations. Above them is the upper frieze with a rectangular meander band bordered by circlets; around the foot is a band of diagonally slanted design arranged around rings containing flat eyes.

When Max Loehr first formulated his ideas on the bronze styles of the An-yang period, this vessel was one of those he singled out as a typical example of the Shang I style.

Published: Max Loehr, "The Bronze Styles of the Anyang Period," *Archives of the Chinese Art Society of America* 7 (1953), 42-53, fig. 2; idem, *Ritual Vessels of Bronze Age China,* New York: Asia Society, 1968, no. 2, pp. 20-21.

Although no exact counterpart of this *ku* has been excavated, the two *ku* recovered from tomb no. 3 at Pai-chia-chuang, Chêng-chou (mentioned in connection with the *chia* vessel; see cat. no. 2), come very close to the Toronto vessel in shape and style of decoration. On these the decorative band in the upper register is bordered by the same circlets, but between them is a simple animal decor typical of the Middle Shang period. The foot of one of the two *ku* has the same type of diagonal design with rings around flat eyes as is found on the Toronto piece. A recently excavated piece from tomb no. 2 at Ming-kung-lu, Chêng-chou, belongs to the same category (fig. 5).

Reference: First Cultural Working Team, Honan Province, "Brief report on the excavation of Shang burials at Pai-chia-chuang, Chêng-chou City" (text in Chinese), *Wen Wu,* 1955, no. 10, pp. 24-42.

7

fig. 5

8

9

8
Beaker of the *ku* type
Bronze with green and reddish brown patina
Late Shang period, ca. 11th century B.C.;
h. 29.6 cm.
**Museum of Fine Arts, Boston, Arthur Tracy
Cabot Fund. 46.780**

The flaring upper part is decorated with four
blades of a conventionalized cicada motif.
The waist and spreading foot, separated by
plain bands, are equally divided into sections
by four vertical flanges. The surface of the
waist and lower section is covered with
t'ao-t'ieh masks standing out against a background of *lei-wên* (meander pattern).

The slender shape and the finely cast decoration are typical of the *ku* of the Late
Shang period; numerous examples of this
type of ritual vessel have been found at An-
yang, the last capital of the Shang Empire.
Whereas in the earlier type of *ku* (cat. no. 7)
the cross-shaped perforations in the plain
band around the waist are large, the later
type has only thin crosses or none at all. It is
possible that these holes were a technical
necessity, essential to the casting process, and
that the need for them disappeared as the
casting technique reached a higher level of
perfection.

9
Spatula
Bronze covered with green patina
Shang period, 12th-11th century B.C.;
l. 33 cm.
Victoria and Albert Museum, London

This curious bronze object somewhat resembles a dagger, but the part corresponding
to a dagger's blade has the blunt shape of a
spatula and cannot have been used for cutting. The part corresponding to the hilt resembles the body of a snake; it is separated
from the tip of the spatula by two spirals
resembling a sword guard and ends in a
pommel in the shape of a snake's head, which
is hollow, with a movable tongue inside. The
tongue produces a rattling sound when the
piece is shaken. The eyes of the snake may
have originally been inlaid with malachite.

Several examples of this type of bronze,
ranging in length from 42 to 31 cm., some inlaid with malachite and some with a pierced
handle, are in Western collections (The
Sackler Collections, New York; the Royal
Ontario Museum, Toronto; and the collection of the late Girolamo Varaschini, Castel-
novo Vicentino, Italy). Of none of these
pieces can the provenance be firmly
established.

W. Perceval Yetts, describing the piece exhibited here for the Eumorfopoulos catalogue,
offered no explanation of its style and merely
called its date "doubtful." Alfred Salmony
was probably the first scholar to classify
these pieces as examples of so-called Ordos
or Sino-Siberian art, which flourished in the
northern Chinese border regions during the
late Chou and Han periods. He also suggested that these pieces could be shamans'
wands, wielded by these exorcists during
ceremonies. No information has come to
light that could lend support to this most
original and ingenious explanation.

At the Victoria and Albert Museum the
spatula is exhibited together with other
Ordos material, and Emma C. Bunker included it in the Asia House exhibition
" 'Animal Style' Art from East to West"

(New York, 1970), tentatively dating it in the Han period.

Published: W. Perceval Yetts, *The George Eumorfopoulos Collection of Chinese and Corean Bronzes,* vol. 1, London, 1929, no. A171, p. 69, pl. 74; Alfred Salmony, *Sino-Siberian Art in the Collection of C. T. Loo,* Paris, 1933, pl. 44, figs. 1, 2; Emma C. Bunker et al., *"Animal Style" Art from East to West,* New York: Asia Society, 1970, no. 132.

Although Emma Bunker believed that no example of this type of bronze had been found during controlled excavation, Chinese archaeologists had already discovered one such piece in 1957. The excavation is of considerable interest because, on the one hand, it seems to confirm the northern provenance first suggested by Salmony, while at the same time it suggests a date far different from that previously proposed.

In August 1957 a group of bronzes was discovered at the village of Hou-lan-chia-kou in Shih-lou County, Shansi Province. Shih-lou is located on the western edge of central Shansi, close to the Yellow River and less than one hundred and fifty miles from the Ordos region as the crow flies. The bronze hoard, consisting of twenty-four pieces, came to light as a result of erosion of the soil and was discovered by Youth Pioneers. A subsequent archaeological investigation of the site yielded only a few scattered fragments of human bones, and it was not possible to establish the original conditions in which the pieces had been found.

It is necessary to stress this uncertainty, as the find itself seems to be of a somewhat heterogeneous character. The presence in this hoard, so close to the Ordos region, of a spatula, or shaman's wand, of the type exhibited here, seems to lend greater credibility to the classification of such objects as "Ordos" bronzes than this admittedly inadequate art historical term deserves. The spatula, tentatively described as a knife, has a reticulated snake's body and a movable tongue; it measures 35 cm. in length. What is most remarkable, however, is that all other pieces found together with this mysterious

object are all vessels and weapons in a pure Shang style.

Any notion that the spatula was unrelated to the Shang find and had somehow come to be mixed up with it, was dispelled by the excavation of yet another spatula of the same type at I-tieh in the same county in May 1969 (fig. 6). This piece, smaller than most other objects of this type (l. 25 cm.), was again found in conjunction with Shang vessels and weapons. The People's Cultural Office of Shih-lou County, which published this last find, has drawn attention to the considerable number of Shang bronze finds made in this county before as well as after the founding of the People's Republic of China. The map published by the office shows the location of four pre-war finds, as well as five finds made in recent years. The Shang bronzes found in these different sites closely resemble one another in shape and decoration. Of the two spatulae the report says that they are identical. Another piece of a somewhat different type was found to the southeast of I-tieh, but no particulars are given, and no illustration has been published.

The fact that two pieces of this type have been found in two sites within the same Shansi county suggests that the spatula could be a typical local production. Although its function still remains a mystery, there can be little doubt that such pieces date from the later years of the Shang period.

References: Kuo Yung, "Brief report on the Shang bronze vessels discovered at Hou-lan-chia-kou, Shih-lou" (text in Chinese), *Wen Wu,* 1962, nos. 4-5, pp. 33-34; The Shih-lou County People's Cultural Office, "Shang bronzes discovered at I-tieh, Shih-lou County, Shansi Province" (text in Chinese), *Kaogu,* 1972, no. 4, pp. 29-30.

fig. 6

10

Ceremonial axe
Bronze, covered with green patina
Shang period, 12th-11th century B.C.;
h. 30.4 cm., w. (at edge) 35 cm.
Staatliche Museen Preussischer Kulturbesitz,
Museum für Ostasiatische Kunst, Berlin-
Dahlem

This broad axe of a type usually called *yüeh* is remarkable for the expressive human face covering the upper part of the blade on both sides. The grinning mouth, filled with regular rows of teeth, the nose, and the bulging eyes all stand out in bold relief. The ears have been accentuated by piercing their contours. The hair, arranged in two symmetrical rows of pointed strips, forms the upper edge of the blade. The two horizontal slits just above the hair served to attach the blade to a handle.

The axe was supposedly found at Hsin-ts'un, a well-known Shang and early Chou site in Hsün-hsien (Honan Province), but no definite proof of its provenance exists. The curvilinear motifs in thread relief below both ears clearly characterize it as a work of the Shang period. Although a number of broad axes have been preserved, all of those in Western collections are decorated with conventionalized animal masks, the so-called *t'ao-t'ieh*, and until recently this axe was, therefore, the only known example with a representation of a human face. In the catalogue of the collection of its former owner, the Hongkong collector Ch'ên Jên-t'ao (J. D. Chen), the face is identified as that of the ancient God of War Ch'ih-yu, even though it lacks the customary attributes associated with this deity. As to the original function of the axe the catalogue of the Berlin Museum observes "this axe, on account of its size and weight unsuitable as a weapon, may have been used in ceremonies or in a ritual execution."

Published: S. H. Minkenhof, "An early Chinese bronze mask," Vereeniging van Vrienden der Aziatische Kunst, *Bulletin*, n.s., no. 29 (April 1950), 17-21, fig. 8; Ch'ên Jên-t'ao, *Chin-kuei lun-ku ch'u-chi*, Hongkong, 1952, 27-29; Chêng

Tê-k'un, *Archaeology in China*, vol. 2, Cambridge, 1960, pl. 34d; Staatliche Museen Preussischer Kulturbesitz, Museum für Ostasiatische Kunst, *Ausgewählte Werke Ostasiatischer Kunst*, Berlin-Dahlem, 1970, no. 1.

The recent discovery of two bronze axes of a type similar to the Berlin piece has thrown some light on the problem of the original function of such pieces in Shang China (figs. 7-8). The new find was made in a tomb of the Shang period located in the village of Su-fu-t'un near Yi-tu (Shantung Province). The existence of an important Shang site at this village had been known since 1931, when farmers accidentally discovered a tomb and dug up several Shang bronzes. In 1936 a team of Chinese archaeologists, engaged in archaeological activities at An-yang, paid a brief visit to the village, and a report of their findings, written by Ch'i Yen-p'ei was published posthumously in 1947. It was not until 1965, however, that an archaeological excavation was carried out by the Shantung Provincial Museum. The excavation brought to light four Shang tombs. The largest of these, which is designated as tomb no. 1, is comparable in size and structure to the largest Late Shang tombs in the vicinity of An-yang (Honan Province), which are generally considered to be royal Shang tombs.

The rectangular, slightly sloping pit of tomb no. 1 has passages leading into it from four sides. It is 8.25 m. deep and measures 9.45 by 5.9 m. at the top. The burial pit has the shape of a square with recessed corners (fig. 9). Under the floor on which the wooden coffin stood are two additional pits known as *yao-k'êng*. The burial pit is surrounded by raised platforms of pounded earth.

Grave robbers had succeeded in penetrating into the tomb, taking with them or destroying the tomb furniture. That the two axes escaped this fate was probably due to their location. Instead of being placed in the immediate vicinity of the deceased, they were found in the upper layer of pounded earth, just at the point where the northern raised platform ends and the passage begins. This location suggests that the axes were not part

of the mortuary gifts, destined to accompany the deceased into the nether world, but that they served a ceremonial purpose connected with the burial rites, and that they were left in the tomb when the pit was filled with earth after the funerary rites had been completed.

Although there is no definite indication what kind of ritual the axes were used for, the suggestion in the Berlin catalogue that the ritual may have been an execution finds grim support in the large number of sacrificed human bodies found at this grave site. The first human sacrifice must have been made after the deepest point of the pit was dug, for it is in the *yao-k'êng* that the first sacrificial victim was found. At successive stages of the filling and sealing of the tomb human beings as well as dogs were sacrificed. The total number of sacrificial victims is forty-eight persons and six dogs. Most of them were found in three strata in the southern passage leading into the tomb. Judging from the size of their bones and the condition of their teeth, the victims all seem to have been youthful persons.

Human sacrifices are repeatedly mentioned in ancient Chinese historical sources. The *Shih-chi (Historical records)* by Ssu-ma Ch'ien (ca. 145-86 B.C.) claims "In the twentieth year of his reign (678 B.C.) Duke Wu (of Ch'in) died. He was buried at P'ing-yang in the district of Yung. For the first time human victims were made to follow a dead person into the grave. Those who were thus sacrificed numbered sixty-six persons." As early as 1843 Edouard Biot quoted this passage as proof for his theory that the immolation of human beings in China was a relatively late tradition, inherited by the Chinese from their northern, barbarian neighbors. Fifty years later J. J. M. de Groot more prudently explained the words "for the first time" as referring only to a "first" in the history of the duke's family. Archaeological proof that this tradition goes back to the very beginnings of Chinese civilization was provided by the excavations at An-yang, which started in 1929. The immolation of human beings at the founding of buildings as well as at burials of

10

fig. 7

fig. 8

the grandees of the Shang dynasty seems to have been common practice in those times; it is even mentioned in the oracle bone inscriptions. The excavation at Su-fu-t'un has demonstrated that this practice was not reserved for Shang kings, but that it had spread to other parts of Shang China as well.

How long this tradition persisted in China is not known. The historical work *Tso Chuan* records no less than four cases of human sacrifices during the sixth century B.C. The veracity of these records is vouched for by an example of human sacrifices found by archaeologists at Hou-ma-chên (Shansi Province). There four men had been sacrificed and buried in a trench surrounding a twin burial dating from the period of the Warring States (480-222 B.C.). The position of the skeleton suggests that a struggle took place before the victims were killed. The involuntary character of this type of sacrifice in Late Chou times has been recently confirmed by an excavation of a burial at Ch'ü-yao, Shensi Province, where victims were found with bronze bands around their necks to gag them. At Su-fu-t'un, on the other hand, there is no indication that the victims were resisting their fate, and all bodies seem to have been laid out successively in an orderly fashion.

That some sort of funerary ritual involving a pair of axes may have been practiced as late as the Han period, long after the tradition of sacrificing human beings had been completely abolished, is indicated by an excavation of Han tombs at Ho-fei (Anhui Province). The author of the excavation report, Ma Jên-ch'üan, makes the following observation: "The unearthing of four iron axes attracted special attention. Previously people had thought that the iron implements in tombs could have been left behind unintentionally when the tomb was sealed. Others said that these implements were weapons that the deceased had personally used during his lifetime. However, if we look at the iron axes found in tomb no. 22, we see that all four iron axes are of the same shape and manufacture, and that two of these were placed on either side of the tomb entrance on

top of the raised platform; this may have a definite meaning." Other sorts of ritual use of axes are suggested in Chinese classical literature. For example, the *Po-hu-t'ung* (Comprehensive discussions in the White Tiger Hall) in describing the system of examination and degradation of feudal lords during the Chou period mentions "those who are able to punish the culpable are granted ceremonial and battle-axes; those who are able to chastise the unprincipled are granted bows and arrows."

Although the two axes from Su-fu-t'un resemble the Berlin axe in many ways, there are a number of notable differences. The Su-fu-t'un axes have a less pronounced modeling than the Berlin piece, and the basic facial features are indicated by reticulation. Of special interest are the two inscriptions below the ears of the face of the smaller of the two axes from Su-fu-t'un (fig. 7). The two inscriptions are the same, one being the reverse of the other. The graph appears to be a pictogram representing a man pouring a libation. He is framed by the so-called *ya-hsing,* a square with recessed corners. Although the meaning of the *ya-hsing* is unclear, it is sometimes thought to perform a function in Shang script that is somewhat comparable to that of the royal cartouche in Egyptian hieroglyphics, i.e., to indicate clan names. Some Chinese experts read the pictogram inside the *ya-hsing* enclosure as *ch'ou;* it is possible that it represents the name of a clan. Another interpretation, found in the bronze catalogue *Mêng-p'o-shih hu-ku ts'ung-pien* (*chin,* 9), maintains that Shang weapons provided with the *ya-hsing* graph were not actually used but served merely a ceremonial purpose.

Whatever the exact meaning of the inscription may be, it occurs quite frequently on bronzes. According to Noel Barnard in *The Freer Chinese Bronzes* (p. 211), "More than a hundred examples of the *ya-hsing* graph with libation pourer inside have been recorded since the 18th century. The motif manifests a number of minor changes in detail which, when studied systematically and extensively, may offer clues as to the authenticity of many of these items. The graph has been most popular with forgers and the Freer *yu* (no. 51) is certainly not the sole example of forgery."

Although it is not possible to trace here each of the pieces bearing this inscription, two should be pointed out as possibly connected with the same find as the two axes. Among the bronzes that Ch'i Yen-p'ei saw at Su-fu-t'un during his brief visit in 1936 was a *chüeh* carrying the same inscription. A lack of reliable information about the original discovery of the Su-fu-t'un site makes it impossible to establish whether this bronze vessel came from the same tomb. That other pieces may have been removed from the site is suggested by a bronze spearhead published by Yü Hsing-wu in 1934, a few years after the discovery. It is inscribed with the same graph and is described as having also come from Ching-chou, Shantung.

References: Ch'i Yen-p'ei (posthumously published), "A report on the investigation of the bronze vessels excavated at Su-fu-t'un, Yi-tu, Shantung" (text in Chinese), *Chung-kuo k'ao-ku hsüeh-pao,* 1947, no. 2, pp. 167-178; "A tomb of the Late Shang period at Su-fu-t'un, Yi-tu" (text in Chinese), *Wen Wu,* 1972, no. 1, p. 81; Shantung Provincial Museum, "Tomb no. 1 at Su-fu-t'un, Yi-tu, Shantung, with sacrificed slaves" (text in Chinese), *Wen Wu,* 1972, no. 8, pp. 17-30; J. J. M. de Groot, *The Religious System of China,* vol. 2, Leiden: Brill, 1894, p. 274; for the tomb at Hou-ma-chên, Shansi, see *Wen Wu,* 1960, nos 8-9, pp. 15-18; Ma Jên-ch'üan, "Cleaning out Han tombs at Ho-fei, Anhwei" (text in Chinese), *Kaogu,* 1959, no. 3, pp. 154-155; Yü Hsing-wu, *Shuang-chien-i chi-chin t'u-lu,* ch. 2, p. 28a, explanation p. 9a, Peking: Lao-hsün-ko, 1934; John Alexander Pope et al., *The Freer Chinese Bronzes,* Washington, D.C.: Freer Gallery of Art, 1967, vol. 1, pp. 210-211, 293; Tjan Tjoe Som, *Po hu t'ung* [The comprehensive discussions in the White Tiger Hall], Leiden: Brill, 1952, p. 505.

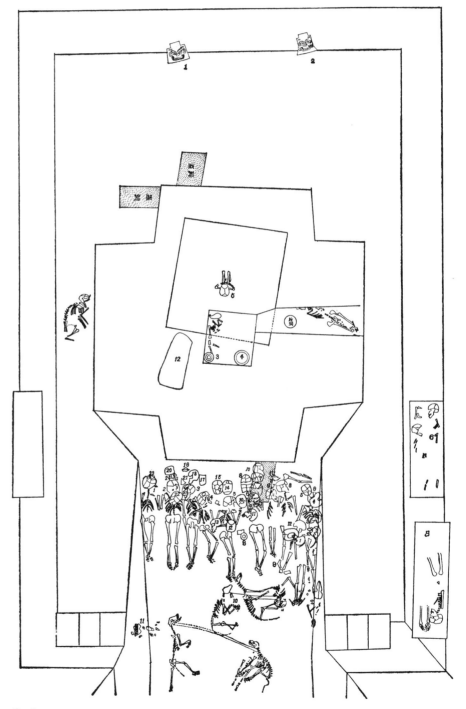

fig. 9

11-12

Two ceremonial vessels: *Chia* **and** *Yu*
Lead and antimony alloy
Early Western Chou period, 11th-10th century B.C.; *Chia:* **h. 24 cm.;** *Yu* **(without handle): h. 21 cm.**
Museum van Aziatische Kunst, Rijksmuseum, Amsterdam, gift of Dr. and Mrs. Anton F. Philips.

Although both vessel types belong to the standard repertoire of early Western Chou bronze art, this *chia* and *yu* are highly unusual pieces because they have been cast not in bronze but in an alloy of lead (95 percent) and antimony (5 percent). The two vessels belonged to a group of at least eleven pieces, all of which were excavated in China in 1936 or slightly earlier. William Charles White, who investigated their provenance, reported his findings as follows: "In December 1936 the Yamanaka Company of New York showed the writer a group of ten pewter vessels recently arrived from China, and furnished him with photographs of the vessels, that he might publish them when a suitable opportunity should occur. He was informed that their Chinese purchasers had obtained them in Cheng Chou, Honan, which means that in all probability their provenance was the Loyang area. Antiques from western Honan invariably came to Cheng Chou, a busy junction city for the Kin-han and Lung-hai railways, where the buyers for the trade in antiques did much of their marketing, and from there the objects would be taken north to Peking, east to Shanghai, and in more limited quantities out to Hankow. It was learned that a Hsien, or colander, was among the vessels but it was not clear where it had gone. One of the set, a Chüeh or libation cup, was obtained by the William Rockhill Nelson Gallery of Art, Kansas City. From the shapes it would appear that the vessels are from two sets, and there must have been many more items in the original sets than these few" (*Bronze Culture of Ancient China,* p. 176). A number of pieces of this set have been dispersed.

The *chüeh* of the Nelson Gallery is now in the Freer Gallery of Art, Washington, D.C. The two pieces in the Rijksmuseum were acquired from Yamanaka by Dr. Anton F. Philips. Professor Yang of Harvard University was the first to notice that these two vessels belonged to the Yamanaka set. When its stock was being liquidated by the Alien Property Custodian in 1943, the Yamanaka Company still owned seven vessels of the set. Several of these are now in the Hermitage Foundation Museum, Norfolk, Virginia.

Although a few lead vessels had been excavated at An-yang, so little was known about these early Chou pieces that their authenticity was often doubted. Both Yamanaka and White referred to these vessels as being made of pewter. As commonly used by antiquarians, however, the word "pewter" stands for an alloy consisting mainly of at least 80 percent tin with lead or copper as a secondary component. As a first step toward resolving the problems that these pieces posed, the Amsterdam museum had the alloy of its vessels analyzed, with the result mentioned above.

Published: Museum van Aziatische Kunst; *Catalogue,* Amsterdam, n.d., nos. 5, 7; William Charles White, *Bronze Culture of Ancient China,* Toronto: University of Toronto Press, 1956, pp. 175-176, pls. 97 -100; *Tōhō Gakuhō, Journal of Oriental Studies* (Kyoto), no. 23, March 1953, pl. 10; *Collection of Chinese and Other Far Eastern Art, assembled by Yamanaka & Company, Inc., now in process of liquidation under the supervision of the Alien Property Custodian of the United States of America,* New York, 1943, nos. 55, 56, 58-62; Lien-sheng Yang, Review of *Bronze Culture of Ancient China,* by W. C. White, *Harvard Journal of Asiatic Studies,* 20 (December 1957), 771-775.

The authenticity of the lead vessels from the Yamanaka set was confirmed by an excavation carried out by a team of archaeologists of the Bureau of Culture of Honan Province on June 9, 1953. The excavation even gave additional support to White's idea about their provenance, for the tomb (designated number 3:01) was found near the northeast gate of the Old City of Loyang. The excavators found eight lead vessels in the tomb: one *ting*, one *tsun*, one *yu*, two *chüeh*, one *ku*, one *chia*, and one *chih* (fig. 10). The *chia* is practically identical with the Rijksmuseum piece, except that the latter has a V-shaped band on the body of the vessel. One of the *chüeh* is very close to a vessel of the same type in the Yamanaka set (White, *Bronze Culture*, pl. 100).

Noel Barnard illustrated the Loyang set in his *Bronze Casting and Bronze Alloys in Ancient China* and made the following remarks: "their purpose may have been purely that of *ming-ch'i* 'funerary objects,' but because of the low melting point of lead and its general ease of casting, it may be surmised that such lead vessels might have been 'trial casts'. However, their placement in a tomb would, of course, indicate more definitely the possibility that the relatives of the deceased may have been obliged to effect such economies in place of the highly valued bronze" (caption, pl. 34).

That the casting of lead was practiced with some frequency in the Loyang area during the Shang and Chou periods is indicated by several other finds in the area. A Shang dagger-axe is among the earliest examples of lead implements found in Loyang (Kuo Pao-chün and Lin Shou-chin, "Report of excavations in the eastern suburbs of Lo-yang during the 1952 fall season" (text in Chinese), *K'ao-ku hsüeh-pao, 1955, pl. 4*). Of a considerably later date than the set of vessels is the lead figure of a kneeling man, found in tomb no. 2717 of the excavations at Chung-chou-lu, Loyang *(Lo-yang Chung-chou-lu,* Peking, 1959, pl. 70). This figure dates from the Eastern Chou period.

References: Second Cultural Working Team, Bureau of Culture, Honan Province, "A pair of Western Chou tombs at Loyang" (text in Chinese), *Kaogu,* 1956, no. 1, 27-28; Jan Fontein "Loden vaatwerk uit de Chou Periode," Vereeniging van Vrienden der Aziatische Kunst, *Bulletin,* 3d ser., no. 9 (December 1957), 144-148; Noel Barnard, *Bronze Casting and Bronze Alloys in Ancient China,* Monumenta Serica Monograph, 14, 1961, pl. 34.

fig. 10

11 and 12

13
Mask
Bronze covered with green patina
Western Chou period, ca. 9th century B.C.;
h. 26.5 cm., w. 27.5 cm.
The Art Institute of Chicago, Lucy Maud
Buckingham Collection

The mask in the shape of a demon's or animal's face was hammered out of a thin sheet of bronze. The eyebrows, nose, and eyes stand out in bold relief; other details have been incised or pierced. Small holes around the edge of the piece indicate that it may have originally been attached to cloth or leather.

Most masks of this type seem to have been hammered in a mold. This manufacturing process probably accounts for the existence of an almost identical example, brought from China during the late twenties by the dealer Jörg Trübner, who stated that it had been found near K'ai-fêng, Honan Province. The only difference between the two pieces is that the diamond shape between the eyebrows of the Chicago piece has been perforated, whereas in the Trübner mask this shape is merely indicated in thin lines. (The present whereabouts of the latter is unknown.)

In addition to these two pieces, there are several other, similar masks in Western collections. A mask formerly in the collection of Mrs. Dagny Carter has been provided with a "crown" consisting of seven triangles. A much more fragmentarily preserved mask is in the Wessén collection in Stockholm.

As all the masks just mentioned came from clandestine excavations, their original function remained unknown. Even the first controlled excavation, carried out by Kuo Pao-chün at Hsin-ts'un, Hsün-hsien (Honan Province) in 1932 and 1933, did not definitely settle the problem of the function and placement of these pieces in Chinese tombs. At Hsün-hsien about thirty masks, several of which were broken, came to light. According to Herrlee Glessner Creel, who visited the site in 1935, "what look like grotesque bronze masks, having some resemblance to human faces, were affixed to the south wall of the

13

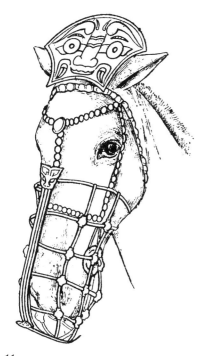

fig. 11

fig. 12

tomb, on either side of the approach. Chariots were also buried in the south." The photographic record of this early excavation is very incomplete, and no clear pictures are available that would allow us to compare the excavated examples with masks in Western collections. P. W. Meister, the first Western scholar to study these masks, pointed out that K'ai-fêng, the alleged provenance of the Trübner mask, is not far from Hsün-hsien, and that this mask may be one of the pieces previously excavated there by grave robbers. Like Kuo Pao-chün, Meister sees one type of mask found here as part of the paraphernalia of the shamans or exorcists, deposited at the tomb exit after the burial ceremonies had been completed.

Kelley and Ch'ên, who described the Chicago mask, conclude from the association of the masks with chariot burials that these pieces were attached to chariots, possibly to frighten the enemy. To what extent explanations of the same type of object can differ when there is a dearth of archaeological data, is demonstrated by the proposal of Bernhard Karlgren, who tentatively suggested that the masks of this type may have belonged to ceremonial puppets.

None of these masks carries elements of decoration that can be directly related to those on bronze vessels. Consequently, considerable uncertainty existed as to their date. Karlgren wrote "The dating of the few masks so far has been merely arbitrary guessing. The present mask (i.e., that of the Wessén collection) might be anything from Yin to Middle Chou." The tombs at Hsün-hsien can be dated in the early part of the Western Chou period, and Meister therefore proposed to date all of the masks in this period. An exhibition catalogue of the Metropolitan Museum, New York, describes the mask in the Carter collection as "Middle Chou"; Kelley and Ch'ên attribute the Chicago mask to the "Eastern Chou Dynasty or earlier."

Published: Charles Fabens Kelley and Ch'ên Mêng-chia, *Chinese Bronzes from the Buckingham Collection,* Chicago: The Art Institute of Chicago, 1946, pp. 74-75, 157-158; Otto Küm-

mel, *Jörg Trübner zum Gedächtnis,* Berlin: Klinkhardt & Biermann, 1930, pp. 48-49; P. W. Meister, "Chinesische Bronzemasken," *Ostasiatische Zeitschrift,* n.s. 14 (1938), 5-11; The Metropolitan Museum of Art, New York, *Chinese Bronzes,* New York, 1938, no. 153; Bernhard Karlgren, "Bronzes in the Wessén Collection," The Museum of Far Eastern Antiquities, Stockholm, *Bulletin,* no. 30, 1958, pp. 191-192, no. 23, pl. 32; Kuo Pao-chün, "Preliminary Report on the Excavations of the Ancient Cemetery at Hsin Ts'un, Hsün Hsien, Honan" (text in Chinese), *T'ien-yeh K'ao-ku Hsüeh-pao* (Shanghai) 1 (1936), 167-200; Herrlee Glessner Creel, *The Birth of China,* London: Jonathan Cape, 1936, p. 248.

The uncertainty as to the possible function and placement of these masks, prolonged by the lack of detailed information in the preliminary report on the excavation at Hsünhsien, definitely came to an end with the excavation, between 1955 and 1957, of a chariot burial at Chang-chia-p'o in Fêng-hsi County near Sian, Shensi Province. The best-preserved burial of the group of four turned out to be trench no. 2, which contained one chariot drawn by four and one drawn by two horses. A charioteer was buried together with the four-horse chariot.

The discovery at Chang-chia-p'o is of special interest for the study of the history of the Chinese chariot, for Chang-chia-p'o lies in the heartland of the Chou people, and this find makes it possible to observe the innovations in the structure of Shang chariots introduced by their Chou successors. In the present context only the bronze fittings of the horse's muzzle and, more specifically, the masks, can be mentioned. The horses of chariot no. 1 in trench no. 2, when examined by the excavators, revealed the following interesting feature: "On top of the horse's head was a large bronze ornament in the shape of an animal mask. The two lower ends of this ornament fitted between the horse's ears. Along the upper and lower edges of the masks are three pairs of small holes. It is possible that the masks were riveted to leather bands placed over the horse's head" (fig. 11a). (In translating this passage the word

fig. 11a

"mask" is read as plural, for although the published drawings omit the mask on one of the horse's heads, the best photograph taken *in situ* [published in *Archaeology in New China*, Peking: Wen Wu Press, 1962, pl. 37] clearly shows both horses had been provided with such a mask.)

The drawings published by the excavators give us a clear idea of the headstalls of the two horses (fig. 11). One of them had a muzzle consisting merely of leather straps, which were covered with double rows of cowrie shells. The headstall of the other horse was considerably more elaborate. It consisted of a bridle assembly, made of leather straps with bronze knobs, over which fitted a muzzle, made of straps connected by cruciform bronze fittings. Two grooved bronze strips topped by *t'ao-t'ieh* masks covered the nose and mouth of the horse. Although the position in which the mask was placed on top of the horse's head is clear, the exact means by which it was attached to the head remains unidentified. Perhaps a more perishable material such as cloth was used instead of leather, which would account for the fact that no trace of it was found.

One of the typical features that the four masks in Western collections have in common with the horse's mask from Chang-chia-p'o is the curved shape, somewhat resembling that of a Japanese folding fan (fig. 12). From this recent excavation it becomes evident that this shape was required in order to make the mask fit between the horse's ears. There can be little doubt, therefore, that these masks were not, as was so often believed, connected with shamans, exorcists, or ceremonial puppets, but that all of them served the same equestrian purpose as the mask excavated at Chang-chia-p'o.

As far as the archaeological data collected at Hsün-hsien are concerned, one wonders whether these cannot be reconciled with the incontrovertible evidence presented by the find at Chang-chia-p'o. That none of the chariots found at Hsün-hsien could be reconstructed seems to be the result of chaotic conditions in this site. Perhaps the masks found there should be associated with the horses rather than with the chariots. That some of the masks were found close to the south wall need not necessarily indicate that they were attached to the wall, for this seems to be the location where the horses were found as well. The excavation at Chang-chiao-p'o seems to strengthen the case of those who argued in favor of a Western Chou date for the masks. In this respect the finds at Hsün-hsien and at Chang-chia-p'o point to the same direction.

References: The Fêng-hsi Archaeological Team of the Institute of Archaeology, "Brief report on the excavations at Fêng-hsi, Ch'ang-an, Shensi, during the years 1955-1957" (text in Chinese), *Kaogu*, 1959, no. 10, pp. 528-530; J. D. Chên "Gold Animal Ornament for Horse's Head," *Archives of the Chinese Art Society of America* 15 (1961), 32-33; John F. Haskins, "The Pazyryk Chanfrons, the T'ao-t'ieh, and Late Chou China," *Archives of the Chinese Art Society of America* 16 (1962), 92-97.

14
A set of six bells
Bronze with green patina
Eastern Chou period, ca. 6th-5th century B.C.; h. 42.5, 38.7, 35.5, 31.1, 29.2, 25.4 cm.
The Sackler Collections

The six bells are identical in shape and gradually diminish in size, forming a graduated set or chime. The body of each bell is elliptical in section. Its flat top is surmounted by a long, tapering shaft (*yung*) to which a ring and a loop for suspension have been attached. On the body of the bell the different zones are marked off with rope patterns. A plain, central panel, trapezoid in shape, is flanked on both sides by three rows of three projecting knobs, alternating with bands of a conventionalized animal design. The curved lower section carries a symmetrical decoration of conventionalized interlacing dragons in typical Eastern Chou style.

Ancient Chinese bronze bells have no clapper and were struck on the outer surface to produce a tone. In addition to the type represented by this set of six bells, there are bells with loop handles and bells of which the handle has been modeled into an openwork design of confronting dragons or back-to-back animals. Of these pieces, often large in size and likewise made in sets of gradually diminishing sizes, the projecting knobs have been flattened into round bosses in the shape of coiling animals. The lower panel is often decorated with a large *t'ao-t'ieh* mask.

A not inconsiderable number of bells of the type exhibited here are found dispersed over collections all over the world, but a set of six of such bells is a great rarity in Western collections. The reason for the absence of larger sets should be sought, in all probability, in the way in which these pieces were found and exported to Western countries.

The case of one set of bells may be cited here as a typical example. During the late twenties a set of bells was excavated at Wei-hui, Honan Province, together with a pair of vases of the *hu* type carrying an inscription referring to an event that took place in 482 B.C. The two vases entered the Cull collection, London, and have recently been donated to the British Museum. The excavators of the bells, or, more likely, the Chinese dealer to whom they sold them, decided to dispose of them one at a time with long intervals in between in order to maintain the extraordinarily high prices that these pieces commanded at that time. Consequently, when the first piece appeared on the international art market, nobody realized that several similar pieces, different only in size, were to appear within the next few years. Two ended up in the Winthrop collection and are now in the Fogg Museum of Art, Harvard University; one went to the Stoclet collection, Brussels, and has now been reunited with the vases from the Cull collection in the British Museum. One bell is in the Museum of Asiatic Art, Amsterdam, and one disappeared from the Berlin Museum after World War II. Another set of bells, which appeared on the market a few years later, shared a similar fate. That the bells of the Sackler set stayed together is not due to a coincidence. These bells were once part of the collection of Emmanuel Gran, a long-time resident of Shanghai, who acquired many pieces in his collection at the Shanghai Railway Station, where farmers arrived to dispose of their wares in the city (see also cat. no. 51).

It is hardly surprising that under these circumstances even the most basic information concerning provenance, the number of pieces found, and their archaeological context was completely lost. When the Swiss musicologist Winfred Ellerhorst made the first effort to study the Wei-hui bells from a musicological point of view, it was not even known that such bells could be part of a set rather than individual pieces. W. Perceval Yetts, who made a study of the bronzes in the Cull collection, realized the possibility that these bells could have formed a graduated set, but he was unable to establish of how many bells it had originally consisted.

References: W. Perceval Yetts, *The Cull Chinese Bronzes,* London: University of London, 1939, pp. 52-53; H. F. E. Visser, *Asiatic Art in Private Collections in Holland and Belgium,* Amsterdam:

14

14

14

De Spiegel Publishing Co., 1948, pp. 38-39; Otto Kümmel, *Jörg Trübner zum Gedächtnis,* Berlin: Klinkhardt & Biermann, 1930, p. 58; Winfred Ellerhorst, "Glocken aus drei Jahrtausenden," *Atlantis* 1, no. 13, pp. 1-10.

During the last twenty years a considerable number of sets of bells have been excavated. The complete sets usually vary in number from seven to nine bells. The largest set of bells of the *yung* type exhibited here is one originally consisting of twelve; it was among the 456 bronze objects excavated near Shou-hsien, Anhwei Province, in 1955, from the tomb of a Marquis of Ts'ai, a small principality in the alluvial plain of the Huai River. In addition to twelve bells with shafts, of which only eight were found more or less intact, there was a set with straight, elongated loop handles consisting of nine pieces, and one set with elaborate zoomorphic handles, consisting of eight bells. The *yung* bells

(fig. 13) range in height from 79 to 48 cm., but the report of the excavation does not mention individual measurements of the pieces, and no comparison can therefore be made with the Sackler bells.

As to the date of the tomb there has been considerable discussion. Most major pieces in the find are inscribed with the name of a Marquis of Ts'ai, but the ancient type of graph used for his personal name has not been identified. He may be Marquis Chao, who was assassinated in 491 B.C., or his elder brother, who died in 519 B.C., or Chao's grandson, who ruled the principality from 471 to 457 B.C. The earliest possible date for the *yung* bells would be between 518 and 508 B.C.

Like most Chinese bronzes, practically all of the sets that have been excavated in recent years are corroded to a considerable extent. In this respect, however, the Ch'u tombs,

which so often have produced pieces in a remarkable state of preservation, yielded another surprise. In the antechamber of tomb no. 1 at Ch'ang-t'ai-kuan (see cat. no. 21) the excavators discovered a set of thirteen bells with rectangular loop handles (*pien-chung*). From the inventory of the tomb, written on bamboo slips in typical Ch'u fashion, it can be concluded that the thirteen bells represent the complete set that was deposited in the tomb. The bells are in a pristine state of preservation; they have no patina and are covered with only a thin film of oxide or carbonate, which does not even dull the gloss of the gold-colored bronze underneath.

The bells from Ch'ang-t'ai-kuan were originally suspended from a wooden frame, which, although decayed, could be reconstructed from the existing fragments. The bells had been suspended from a wooden beam, 242 cm. in length, supported by two

14

14

14

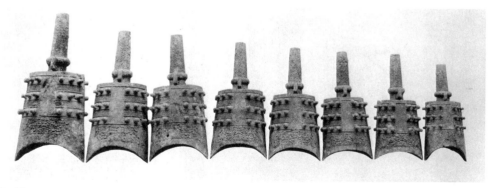

fig. 13

vertical posts, the upper ends of which were decorated with tigers' masks. The posts were tenoned into square bases decorated with cloud scroll patterns. The posts and blocks together raised the horizontal beam to a height of about 80 cm. Two wooden hammers with handles measuring 53 cm. in length were used to strike the bells; a musician sitting or kneeling on the ground could play the entire chime without moving from his place.

On the inner side of each bell are scraped grooves and other traces of scratching and scraping. These small modifications served to regulate the pitch. An analysis of the sound produced by these thirteen bells resulted in the first reliable information on the sound of ancient Chinese music ever obtained. The team of the Research Institute of Ethnomusicology, Peking, established the tone for each bell and carefully recorded the intervals, frequency, and pitch in terms of cents. Usually the difference in pitch exceeds 100 cents, or approximately one semitone interval; in most cases it is at least double that amount. Between bells no. 3 and 4 is a difference of a minor third, but by far the largest difference is between the twelfth and the last bell, which amounts to a value of 452 cents. Unless the series were originally larger (which is unlikely in view of the figure mentioned in the inventory), one could imagine the function of the last and by far the smallest bell to have been different from that of all the other bells of the chime.

From references to music contained in the texts of the ancient Chinese philosophers it would appear that Chinese music entered into a state of transition toward the end of the fifth century B.C. There was a shift toward string and reed instruments at the expense of the percussion instruments, which had dominated the solemn court music since Shang times. The critics of the new music characterized it as lewd and decadent. Marquis Wên of Wei (ruled 424-387 B.C.), expressing his preference for the new music of Chêng and Wei, confessed to a disciple of Confucius that he would fall asleep listening to the Old Music.

From literary sources one can glean some idea of these developments, but the discovery of this perfectly preserved set of bells and the analysis of their tonal system have produced, for the first time, tangible evidence to document the sound of ancient Chinese music.

References: Anhwei Cultural Committee and Anhwei Provincial Museum, eds., *Shou-hsien Ts'ai-hou-mu ch'u-t'u i-wu* [Ancient relics excavated from the tomb of the Marquis of Ts'ai at Shou-hsien], Peking: Science Press, 1956; A. Soper, "The tomb of the Marquis of Ts'ai," *Oriental Art*, n.s. 10, no. 3 (autumn 1964),152-157; Research Institute for Ethnomusicology, Central Music Academy, Peking, "Preliminary investigation into Warring States musical instruments from the State of Ch'u, excavated at Hsin-yang (text in Chinese), *Wen Wu*, 1958, no. 1, pp. 15-23; David Hawkes, *Ch'u Tz'u, The Songs of the South*, Oxford: Clarendon Press, 159, p. 6.

15
Belt hook in the shape of a rhinoceros
Bronze, inlaid with gold and silver
Late Eastern Chou period,
ca. 3rd century B.C.; l. 25.1 cm., h. 9.5 cm.
The Sackler Collections

The body of the buckle consists of a lifelike representation of a rhinoceros, covered with an inlaid ornament of spirals and teardrops, which follows and accentuates the natural shapes of the jaw, shoulder, haunch, and toes of the animal. From the snout extends an elongated tongue terminating in a curved bird's head, which acts as the hook of the buckle. At the back of the body is a protruding stud by which the buckle may once have been attached to a leather belt.

Published: Arthur de Carle Sowerby, *Nature in Chinese Art*, New York: John Day, 1940, p. 60; *Selections of Chinese Art*, exhibition catalogue by Mrs. Gilbert Katz, New York: China Institute in America, 1966, p. 19, no. 17.

Representations of the rhinoceros, which seems to have become extinct in China before the beginning of the Christian era, are relatively rare in Chinese art. The most celebrated representation is the ritual vessel in the shape of a rhinoceros from the Avery Brundage Collection (Center for Asian Art and Culture, San Francisco), excavated in Shantung Province before 1843 and dating from the Late Shang period. A recent discovery is a bronze vessel with an inlaid gold ornament, excavated at Tou-ma-ts'un, Hsing-p'ing County, Shensi Province. It dates from the Late Eastern Chou period.

The belt hook exhibited here is practically identical with a pair of pieces excavated in June 1956 from a group of boat-shaped coffin burials at Pao-lun-yüan, Chao-hua County, Szechwan Province. In other excavations belt hooks have occasionally been found near the head or feet of the body, indicating that buckles (*tai-kou*) may have been used on different parts of the garments. In the burials at Pao-lun-yüan, however, the buckles were invariably found close to the waist of the deceased. Their position indicates that the buckles must have been used either as belt hooks or as a means of suspending other objects from the belt. One of the two rhinoceros belt hooks was found right next to a sword and its sheath, but there is no clear indication that the buckle could have been used to suspend the sword from the belt.

The buckle in the Sackler collection has lost some of its inlay, but a comparison with a drawing of one of the excavated specimens (fig. 14) permits us to reconstruct the entire design. The examples from Pao-lun-yüan reveal the original shape of the large horn, of which the tip in the Sackler piece has broken. In the complete pieces the natural size of the horn is exaggerated; it is made to describe a gracious curve, almost touching the secondary horn on the forehead.

For lack of reliable archaeological data in the past, gold and silver inlay in bronzes was almost exclusively associated with the site best known for pieces decorated in this technique, the tombs near Chin-ts'un, Loyang (Honan Province). Although the possibility that these pieces had come from other parts of China should not be excluded, the recent excavations seem to indicate that in Late Chou times the technique of gold and silver inlay had spread over a large part of the area of Chinese bronze culture.

References: Fêng Han-chi, "Boat-shaped Coffin Graves in Szechwan Province" (text in Chinese), *Kaogu Xuebao*, 1958, no. 2, pp. 75-95; The Szechwan Provincial Museum, comp., *Report on the Excavation of Boat-shaped Coffin Graves in Szechwan Province* (text in Chinese), Peking: Wen Wu Press, 1960, p. 58; Chêng Tê-k'un, *Archaeology in China*, vol. 3, *Chou China*, Toronto: University of Toronto Press, 1963, pp. 254-255; Berthold Laufer, "History of the Rhinoceros," *Chinese Clay Figures*, pt. 1, *Prolegomena on the History of Defensive Armor*, Chicago: Field Museum of Natural History, 1914, pp. 73-173.

15

fig. 14

16

16

16

fig. 15

16
Head of a tiger
Bronze, inlaid with silver
Late Eastern Chou period,
ca. 3rd century B.C.; l. 5.5 cm.
Museum für Ostasiatische Kunst, Cologne

The tiger's head is entirely hollow; it ends in a round, socketed neck on one side and opened jaws, connected by a vertical bar in the middle, on the other. In the bottom is a leaf-shaped opening. With the exception of the hollow, open eyes and the bottom the entire surface of this expressively modeled piece is covered with a design of spirals and volutes inlaid in silver. The design emphasizes the natural forms of the face in a way quite similar to that seen on the rhinoceros buckle (cat. no. 15). In the bottom is an engraved and inlaid inscription reading "tso chêng." Its meaning is uncertain, but in a catalogue of the Cologne Museum the plausible suggestion has been made that these words may represent an official title. Less likely to be correct is the explanation of Eleanor Consten, who maintains that the words represent both the name and the title of the owner.

The original use of this charming object has not yet been successfully determined. The Cologne Museum has tentatively suggested that it may represent a bronze knob for a wooden lid. The compiler of the catalogue of the Venice exhibition (1954) and Eleanor Consten have suggested that it may have been the handle of a sword.

Published: Eleanor Consten, *Das Alte China*, Stuttgart: Kilpper Verlag, 1958, pl. 79; Edith Dittrich, *Ausstellung ausgewählter Kunstwerke in der Eigelsteintorburg*, Museum für Ostasiatische Kunst der Stadt Köln, Cologne, 1961, no. 47 (where all earlier literature is given).

The tiger's head of the Cologne Museum remained for many years one of those puzzling and unique objects that are considered among the finest treasures of Chinese art in Western museums. An excavation in 1953 of a tomb at Yang-tzu-shan near Ch'êng-tu, Szechwan Province, yielded for the first time a pair of objects resembling the Cologne tiger's head (fig. 15). However, although it may deprive the object of its previous uniqueness, the excavation does not solve the problem of the original use to which such pieces may have been put.

The grave at Yang-tzu-shan, to which the excavators of the Cultural Committee of Szechwan Province assigned the number 172, consisted of a large wooden chamber, which at the time of the discovery was already in an advanced state of decay. In accordance with a burial custom common in China during the Late Chou period, most of the mortuary gifts were placed at the head of the grave. Among the objects found in the northwest corner were two bronze heads of a tiger with gold and silver inlay. There are certain differences in style between these two masks and the Cologne piece, which would seem to argue against a common origin of the three. The rendering of the whiskers and eyebrows in thin lines resembles that of an animal's head inlaid with gold, excavated at Ku-wei-ts'un near Hui-hsien (see *Kaogu*, 1955, no. 3, color plate). The design of spirals and volutes is much simpler, less sophisticated. On the other hand, other objects in the Yang-tzu-shan tomb bear inlaid designs that resemble much more closely the decoration on the Cologne mask and are artistically the equal of this fine piece. The reproductions and summary description of the Yang-tzu-shan masks indicate that those pieces are solid, except for two holes through which a cord can be run to attach them.

No suggestion has been made as to the original function of these two animal masks. Although proof is lacking that their function was identical with that of the Cologne piece, it is of interest to note that the circumstances under which the two masks were excavated do not lend support to the previously advanced ideas concerning the original use of the Cologne mask. The remnants of swords and sword furniture were found in another corner of the grave, making it unlikely that the two masks could have been parts of such weapons. If the masks had served as knobs on some sort of lid, we could have expected

them to have been found at least some distance apart. Instead, they were found close together.

From the plans of the tomb and the summary report of its excavation we gather that the two masks were found in the immediate proximity of a number of fittings of a horse's harness and right next to a bronze bit. Perhaps these masks should therefore be placed in the category of harness fittings. This class consists of a great variety of objects, and although a considerable amount of information has been gained by scientific excavations conducted during the last twenty years, there are still many questions remaining to be solved. The leaf-shaped opening in the bottom of the Cologne mask could have served the functional purpose of attaching the mask— and, possibly leather straps running through it—to some sort of bronze button. However, no clear examples of such an arrangement have so far come to light. As these problems cannot be solved with the help of the information at present available, we must wait for further archaeological discoveries to shed new light on them.

References: The Cultural Committee of Szechwan Province, "Report of the excavation of tomb no. 172 at Yang-tzu-shan, Ch'êng-tu" (text in Chinese), *Kaogu Xuebao*, 1956, no. 4, pp. 1-20.

17
Covered vase
Bronze with yellowish green patina, patches of azurite
Late Eastern Chou period,
ca. 3rd century B.C.; h. 37.5 cm.
Collection of Dr. Paul Singer

The tall, slightly tapering vase stands on a spreading footring. The body is entirely plain, except for two *t'ao-t'ieh* animal masks in low relief to which rings are fastened. The slightly domed cover has three concentric circles of raised lines; four ring-shaped loops, standing in radial position, are attached to it.

The shape of this piece is rare in the repertoire of Chinese bronze art. Max Loehr, who twice published this vase, found few comparable vessels, except for a piece in Japan and two much smaller examples in the Singer collection. The eighteenth century bronze catalogue *Hsi-ch'ing ku-chien* (ch. 21, no. 55) illustrates a similar piece that has lost its cover. It is attributed to the Han period, whereas Max Loehr attributes the Singer vessel to the Late Eastern Chou period.

Published: Max Loehr, *Relics of Ancient China from the Collection of Dr. Paul Singer,* New York: Asia Society, 1965, no. 69a; Max Loehr, *Ritual Vessels of Bronze Age China,* New York: Asia Society, 1968, no. 66.

In the spring of 1970 a group of bronzes was discovered at the village of Tsang-chia-chuang, Chu-ch'êng County, Shantung Province. From the summary report that has been published the nature of the hoard is not clear, but from the type of bronzes included in this find it would seem that the bronzes came from a single, important burial. On the opposite bank of the Wu River, across from Tsang-chia-chuang, lies the village of Shih-fu-tzu, where the ruins of an ancient city wall have been located. These ruins are thought to belong to the ancient city of Ku-mu. The bronze find of Tsang-chia-chuang is considered to be one of the cultural relics of this ancient settlement.

The bronzes include a set of *po* bells and nine *chung* bells (see cat. no. 14), seventeen vessels of different shapes, a ladle, as well as

fig. 16

some fragmentary pieces. Among the vessels are two that are described as tumbler-shaped vessels. Judging from the single small reproduction that has been published (fig. 16), these appear to be very similar to the tumbler exhibited here. Not discernible from the illustration is whether the rings are attached to *t'ao-t'ieh* masks. On the cover are three instead of four ring-shaped loops in radial position. The height of one of the pieces is given as 32.9 cm., slightly smaller than the vessel from the Singer collection.

The shapes of the vessels and bells, as well as their decoration, suggest a date in the Late Eastern Chou period. As the excavators point out, the decoration of several pieces resembles that on objects found in the great Ch'u tombs of Chang-t'ai-kuan (see cat. no. 21) and the Han tombs at Man-ch'êng (see cat. nos. 42 and 45). On the basis of the small number of illustrations published to the present it is not possible to give a more precise dating, but it would seem probable that the bronzes date from the very end of the Eastern Chou period.

References: Ch'i Wên-t'ao, "Preliminary report on the bronze vessels of the Shang and Chou dynasties discovered in Shantung in recent years" (text in Chinese), *Wen Wu,* 1972, no. 5, pp. 14-15.

17

18

18
Vessel with a cover in the shape of a bird's head
Bronze with green patina
Late Eastern Chou period,
ca. 3rd century B.C.; h. 43.2 cm.
William Rockhill Nelson Gallery of Art,
Kansas City, Missouri

The vessel has a large, bulbous body and a tapering neck. The lid has the shape of a bird's head, the beak of which is hinged. The U-shaped handle is hinged to two S-shaped arms, which are attached to the neck of the vessel. The lid is secured to the arms by two rings.

The eighteenth century bronze catalogue *Hsi-ch'ing ku-chien* (ch. 21) contains woodblock illustrations of three similar pieces. One bird is identified as an eagle, another as an owl, whereas the lid of the third vessel is thought to have the shape of an animal. The body of each of the three pieces is plain, with only a single horizontal raised line around the middle. One piece has an animal mask with a ring on the side, while the other two have a ring attached to the back of the piece on the middle of the body. Jung Kêng illustrates a similar piece, the entire body of which is covered with horizontal grooves. The bird's lid has two ears, enhancing its resemblance to an owl. The only other major difference is that the arms are not S-shaped, but straight; they have been provided with an additional hinge in the middle. This piece carries an inscription that is probably not authentic; it may have been copied from that of an early Western Chou *tsun* beaker, illustrated in the *Hsi-ch'ing ku-chien* (ch. 9, no. 24). The vessel illustrated by Jung Kêng bears a striking resemblance to, and could even be identical with, a piece last known to be in the collection of Baron Paul Hatvany (see William Watson, *Ancient Chinese Bronzes*, pl. 64a).

As to the date of these vessels, there seems to exist considerable uncertainty. The Nelson Gallery piece was published by Mizuno Seiichi, who attributed the vessel to the Han period. Mizuno may have followed the *Hsi-*

ch'ing ku-chien, in which all three vessels of this type are assigned to the same period. The most recent publication is William Watson's *Ancient Chinese Bronzes,* where the vessel in the Hatvany collection is ascribed to the fifth-fourth century B.C.

Published: *Sekai Bijutsu Zenshū, 7, China,* no. 1, Tokyo: Heibonsha, 1952, pl. 9 (caption by Mizuno Seiichi); "Arts of the Han Dynasty," *Archives of the Chinese Art Society of America* 14 (1960), 32, no. 36; William Watson, *Ancient Chinese Bronzes,* Rutland, Vt.: Charles E. Tuttle, 1962, pl. 64a; Jung Kêng, *The Bronzes of Shang and Chou,* Peking: Yenching University, 1941, vol. 2, p. 378, fig. 713.

The find of bronzes at Tsang-chai-chuang near Chu-ch'êng, Shantung Province, which produced the tumblerlike covered vase (cat. no. 17), also produced a bronze (fig. 17) of the type of the vessel exhibited here. It differs from the Nelson Gallery vase in that its body is covered all over with horizontally grooved bands. In this respect it is much closer to the vessel in the Hatvany collection. The S-shaped arms are cast in one piece and resemble those of the Kansas City vessel. Judging from the archaeological context in which the vessel was found, there can be little doubt that the dating of these vessels to the Han period, as proposed by the editors of the *Hsi-ch'ing ku-chien* and by Mizuno Seiichi, should be revised to Late Eastern Chou.

Vessels with an allover decoration of horizontally grooved bands are comparatively rare. One of the earliest examples is a covered vessel of the *ling* type, excavated at I-shui, Shantung Province, in 1925. Although these few isolated examples do not provide sufficient evidence to support such an idea, the use of grooved bands without additional bands of other types of decoration could perhaps be a feature typical of the Shantung area.

References: Ch'i Wên-t'ao, "Preliminary report on the bronze vessels of the Shang and Chou dynasties discovered in Shantung in recent years" (text in Chinese), *Wen Wu,* 1972, no. 5, pp. 14-15.

fig. 17

19
Semicircular roof tile
Gray pottery
Late Eastern Chou period,
4th-3rd century B.C.; l. 41 cm., w. 21.5 cm.
William Rockhill Nelson Gallery of Art,
Kansas City, Missouri

The roof tile resembles a tube cut in half lengthwise. On one end its surface is roughened by hatching; on the opposite end the tile is covered with a semicircular ornamental plaque, the entire surface of which is taken up by an animal mask of the *t'ao-t'ieh* type, modeled in a style characteristic of the Late Eastern Chou period. Of most of the pieces of this type in Western collections only the ornamental mask has been preserved. A roof tile of this type was formerly in the Hellström collection, Mölndal, Sweden. The catalogue of the London exhibition of 1935-36 described it as a "brick" and dated it in the Han period; a similar piece from her own collection is described by Eleanor Consten as dating from the Late Chou period. About the provenance of these pieces nothing is known.

References: Royal Academy of Arts, London, *International Exhibition of Chinese Art,* 1935, no. 549; Eleanor Consten, *Das Alte China,* Stuttgart: Kilpper Verlag, 1958, pl. 42.

19

19A
Semicircular roof tile
Gray pottery
Late Eastern Chou period,
4th-3rd century B.C.; w. 22.5 cm.
William Rockhill Nelson Gallery of Art,
Kansas City, Missouri

The elongated, semicylindrical part of this
tile is largely broken. The ornamental end
is decorated with a design of two animals
facing one another, each with one claw raised
in a threatening gesture.

In recent years extensive investigations and
excavations at the site of the former Lower
Capital (Hsia-tu) of the Late Chou feudal
state of Yen have definitely established this
site as the provenance of the semicircular
roof tiles of the types exhibited here. The site
had been known for many years. As early as
1930 a preliminary investigation was carried
out by Chinese scholars headed by Ma Hêng
in the company of Japanese colleagues.

Extensive excavations carried out in 1957-
58, 1961-62, and 1964-65 have brought to
light a considerable amount of material of
archaeological and art historical interest. A
careful survey of the site made it possible to
retrace the remnants of the city ramparts of
the Lower Capital and the extensive system
of waterways and protective moats connect-
ing the systems of the Northern Yi River and
the Middle Yi River, between which the capital was laid out. The Lower Capital of Yen
consists of an Eastern and a Western City,
together measuring eight by six kilometers, a
surprisingly extensive area for a Late Chou
capital, considerably larger than any other
capital of the period that has been surveyed
so far.

Close to the mound investigated by Ma
Hêng and his associates, which now turns out
to have been situated just outside the perim-
eter of the city walls, archaeologists found
one of the most fascinating pieces recovered
during all of the excavations in the area, a
large gargoyle in the shape of a dragonlike
animal with gaping jaws. One of the finest
pieces in the current traveling exhibition of

Chinese archaeological treasures is a large
(h. 45.5 cm.) bronze t'ao-t'ieh mask with
ring, excavated from this site in 1966.

The so-called Wu-yang mound, situated in
the northern part of the Eastern City, probably was the site of the Royal Palace. A large
number of semicircular roof tiles were excavated here (figs. 18-19). Among the numerous bronze halberds excavated from the
site several are inscribed with the names of
Yen royalty, leaving no doubt as to the dynastic affiliation of the ruined city. Archaeological evidence, confirming historical
records, suggests that the Eastern City was
built before the middle of the Warring States
period (481-221 B.C.), whereas the Western
City may have been built later, when the city
expanded.

Roof tiles are among the most characteristic objects found in architectural remains of
the Late Chou period. Among the few sites
that have been surveyed are Han-tan, the
capital of Chao in Hopei Province, and Lin-
tzu, the capital of Ch'i in Shantung Province.
The semicircular ornamental roof tiles from
each of these capital cities have their own
style and local color. At the Lower Capital of
Yen t'ao-t'ieh masks are the most common
(fig. 18); they comprise more than ninety percent of all pieces found there. The decoration
is on the whole more lively and less simplified than that of pieces from the other two
sites. (For another typical relic of the ancient
state of Yen see cat. no. 20.)

References: Yang Tsung-ying, "Semicircular tiles
from the Lower Capital of Yen" (text in Chinese),
Kaogu, 1957, no. 6, pp. 23-26; The Archaeological Team of the Hopei Bureau of Culture, "Re-
connaissances and trial diggings on the site of
Yen-hsia-tu at Yi-hsien, Hopei Province" (text
in Chinese, abstract in English), Kaogu, 1965, no.
1, pp. 81-106; The Archaeological Team of the
Museum of Chinese History, "Report on the investigation of the site of the Lower Capital of the
State of Yen" (text in Chinese), Kaogu, 1962, no.
1, pp. 10-19, 54; Trésors d' art chinois, Paris,
1973, no. 113.

fig. 18

fig. 19

19A

20

Vase in the shape of a bronze *hu*
Red pottery covered with black slip; incised
ornament
Late Eastern Chou period,
ca. 3rd century B.C.; h. 35.8 cm.
Seattle Art Museum

The incised decoration, consisting of repeated geometric and animal motifs, is organized into horizontal bands. The tigerlike
animals with their heads turned backward,
repeated around the neck and the body, are
separated by bands of geometric design consisting of wavy lines, triangles, and dia-
monds. The two animal masks, applied to
the shoulder of the vessel, enhance its resemblance to bronze vessels of the Late Chou
period.

Basing himself on dealers' information,
Walter Hochstadter established the famous
site of Chin-ts'un, near Loyang (Honan
Province) as the place where vessels of this
type had come from. Among the many pieces
that were collected and recorded by Bishop
W. C. White as having come from this site,
not a single piece of this type occurs, but a
similar vase in the Honolulu Academy of
Arts is reported to have come from Loyang.

Published: Los Angeles County Museum, *Chinese
Ceramics from the Prehistoric Period through
Ch'ien Lung*, Los Angeles, 1952, no. 19; Walter
Hochstadter, "Pottery and stonewares of Shang,
Chou and Han," The Museum of Far Eastern
Antiquities, Stockholm, *Bulletin*, no. 24, 1952,
p. 91, figs. 65-66; Stanford University Museum,
Arts of the Chou Dynasty, Palo Alto, 1958, no. 86.

The attribution of the jars of this type to
Loyang, or, even more specifically, nearby
Chin-ts'un, may have been inspired by occasional parallels between their incised decoration and the animal decor on some
bronzes reputed to have come from this
famous clandestine excavation site. It must
be admitted, however, that if stylistic consideration alone had led to the attribution of
these vessels to Chin-ts'un, one of the few
other sites known before World War II, that
of Li-yü (northern Shansi), discovered in
1923, would have been a much more likely

provenance, for the parallels with bronzes from this site are much more numerous.

That recent excavations have now refuted the hearsay information of the dealers should therefore not come as a surprise. What is unexpected, however, is that the provenance of the pieces of this type should be sought in the immediate vicinity of Peking, so close to the home base of the dealers who supplied the erroneous information. Dark gray or black vessels with an incised decoration of animals, fish, and bands of geometric design have been found in a suburb of Tientsin, at Huai-jou, near Peking, and at I-hsien in Hopei Province.

The find of I-hsien, especially, is of interest, for this is the site of the Lower Capital of the Late Chou feudal state of Yen (see cat. no. 19). Several pieces of pottery found there turned out to be marked with unidentified regnal dates ("in the tenth moon of the tenth year," etc.) and with the names of potters, but none of these marks occur on the incised black ware.

An even larger number of *hu* vessels of the same type as excavated here was found at Huai-jou, where a total number of thirty pieces came from fifteen Eastern Chou tombs. These finds confirm Hochstadter's supposition that all of these pieces were once provided with covers, for none of the excavated pieces is ever without one. As a rule, a cover has three handles representing stylized birds placed in radial position. At Huai-jou the excavators established a typological sequence of five successive shapes of *hu*. The piece exhibited here appears to correspond with types no. 4 or no. 5 of the Huai-jou excavation. From this we may conclude that they probably date from the third century B.C. This dating does not seem to agree entirely with that of the excavators of tomb no. 29 near Tung-tou-ch'êng in the center of the northern outer wall of the Lower Capital. Judging only from drawings, the pieces found in this tomb appear to be the finest examples of this type of vessel. The *hu* jar found in this tomb corresponds in shape to type 5 of Huai-jou, but its excavators describe the tomb as

fig. 20

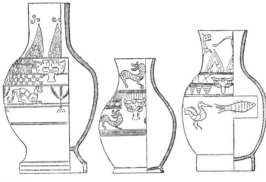

fig. 21

dating from the early Warring States period, more than a century earlier than the third century B.C., the date suggested for the Huai-jou jars of type 5.

Many of the vessels of this type seem to have come from tombs that contained no bronze vessels. It seems probable, therefore, that the pieces were thought of as substitutes for the much more costly bronze vessels, which served as a prototype for them.

References: Charles D. Weber, "Chinese pictorial bronze vessels of the Late Chou period," part 1, *Artibus Asiae* 28 (1966), 107-140; The Archaeological Team of Peking City, "Eastern Chou and Han tombs to the North of Huai-jou near Peking" (text in Chinese), *Kaogu*, 1962, no. 5, pp. 219-239; The Archaeological Team of the Bureau of Culture, Tientsin City, "The second excavation of a Warring States tomb at Chang-kuei-chuang in the eastern suburbs of Tientsin" (text in Chinese), *Kaogu*, 1965, no. 2, pp. 96-97; The Archaeological Team of the Hopei Bureau of Culture, "Report on the excavation of tombs at the Lower Capital of Yen during the years 1964-65" (text in Chinese), *Kaogu*, 1965, no. 11, pp. 548-561, 598.

20

The Arts of Ch'u

During the years 1936 and 1937 the local authorities at Ch'ang-sha, Hunan Province, ordered the leveling of an extensive area just outside the city walls in preparation for the building of a new municipal center. It was during the groundwork for this project that a number of ancient tombs were discovered that yielded a large number of the most extraordinary objects, quite unlike those found in the tombs of the north. The objects were the cultural relics of the ancient kingdom of Ch'u, which flourished during the Eastern Chou period. Since ancient times the southern kingdom of Ch'u had been renowned for its great late Chou literary masterpiece, the *Ch'u-tz'u,* or *Songs of the South,* written by the incorruptible statesman Ch'ü Yüan (traditional dates 332-295 B.C.), whose tragic suicide is commemorated all over China in the annual Dragon Boat Festival. It was not until the first discovery of these Ch'ang-sha tombs was made that it became evident that the creative genius of the Ch'u tribe had found expression in the fine arts as well.

The first exhibition in the West of Ch'ang-sha antiquities was held at Yale University in 1939; it was organized by John Hadley Cox, who had been on the scene when the first discovery at Ch'ang-sha was made. Soon the bronzes, jades, wooden statuary, and pieces of lacquerware that were unearthed in and around Ch'ang-sha in increasing numbers began to attract the attention of collectors all over the world. Unfortunately, the clandestine character of the excavations precluded the gathering of precise archaeological data. The result is that the discovery of even the most important antiquities to come out of China, such as the famous Ch'u silk manuscript (The Sackler Collections, New York) and the Cranes and Serpents sculpture in the Cleveland Museum of Art, is still largely shrouded in mystery. With the exception of the burials that were effectively sealed with charcoal and white clay, which acted as a preservative for cultural relics as well as human remains, many tombs have been completely saturated with ground water. When the bootleg excavators allowed the excavated lacquerwork to dry out after centuries of immersion in water, many fine pieces sustained irreparable damage through shrinkage of their wooden cores.

Controlled excavations, carried out during the last twenty years, have vastly increased our knowledge of the culture of the ancient kingdom of Ch'u. Not only large numbers of fine objects have been excavated and carefully preserved, but also the area from which finds have been reported has expanded to become almost coterminous with the often shifting borders of the ancient state. The immediate vicinity of Ch'ang-sha, the shores of the nearby Tung-t'ing Lake, and the valley of the Hsiang River still remain the area richest in archaeological finds. Of increasing importance, however, is Chiang-ling County in Hupei Province, where the Ch'u capital Ying, the birthplace of Ch'ü Yüan, seems to have been located. Farther to the northeast, in the Huai River valley, lies Shou-hsien, where the state of Ch'u had its capital during the final years of its decline in the third century B.C.

In this exhibition a number of objects have been assembled that are, like almost all objects in Western collections, of uncertain provenance, but that appear to have come from Ch'u tombs. A few pieces have been selected because the excavation of similar pieces has helped us to understand their original function or allowed us to reconstruct their complete shape. Additional pieces, each one matching recently excavated specimens, have been added to illustrate the archaeological context in which the others may have been found.

References: Noel Barnard and Douglas Fraser, eds., *Early Chinese Art and Its Possible Influence in the Pacific Basin,* vol. 1, New York: Intercultural Arts Press, 1972; David Hawkes, *Ch'u Tz'u, The Songs of the South,* Oxford: Clarendon Press, 1959; The Archaeological Institute of the Academia Sinica, *Ch'ang-sha fa-chüeh pao-kao,* Peking: Science Press, 1957; The Provincial Museum of Hunan, "The Ch'u tombs of Ch'ang-sha" (text in Chinese, summary in English), *Kaogu Xuebao,* 1959, pp. 41-60; Annette L. Juliano, "Three large Ch'u graves recently excavated in the Chiang-ling district of Hupei Province," *Artibus Asiae* 37 (1972), 5-17.

21
Drum stand in the shape of two birds and two tigers
Painted wood
Late Eastern Chou period, 4th-3rd century B.C. (?), several modern replacements and reconstructed drum; total height: 63 cm.
Museum of Fine Arts, Boston. 49.494

The drum stand consists of eleven separate parts. The bodies of the two birds are carved from a single piece of wood; the necks and heads of the birds fit into them with a mortice and tenon. These three parts are carved from the same kind of wood; they are covered with remnants of white, yellow, and red paint on a grayish black ground. The four legs fit into the figures of two crouching tigers, which have been provided with detachable, upturned tails.

The four legs are carved from a different kind of wood, perhaps the same as that from which the tails of the tigers are made. The legs are stained with a black, sootlike substance, which even covers a break. It is likely, therefore, that the legs and tails are modern replacements of missing original parts. On one of the tigers a thin gesso layer seems to have been applied with a broad, flat brush, an implement unknown in China in late Chou times.

Although the age and authenticity of the individual components of this piece are not equally firmly established, the ensemble is of considerable interest as it is the only example of this type outside China, except for the much larger Cranes and Serpents sculpture in the Cleveland Museum of Art. The Cleveland sculpture was the first of this type ever to be discovered at Ch'ang-sha. The Japanese archaeologists Umehara and Mizuno, who first published Cleveland's masterpiece in 1937, made only little headway in the problems concerning its name, function, original shape, and symbolic meaning. But even though the Cranes and Serpents was peerless in artistic quality, it was not entirely without parallel. John Hadley Cox established in 1938 that another sculpture of this type had been excavated, representing "a pair of birds, carved

21

from one piece of wood, their tails joined together." If the piece referred to is not the Boston sculpture, which appeared on the market more than ten years later, it may well have been the prototype used by a sculptor to restore or reconstitute it. Cox, in talking to the excavators of the tomb in which the Cranes and Serpents was found, was able to establish that the piece had served as a drum stand. Hollis correctly concluded that the birds should be placed back to back rather than facing one another, as Umehara and Mizuno proposed.

References: Howard C. Hollis, "Cranes and Serpents," The Cleveland Museum of Art, *Bulletin,* 25 (October 1938), pp. 147-151; Umehara Sueji and Mizuno Seiichi, "The twin cranes and serpents, a lacquered sculpture, said to have been excavated at Ch'ang-sha" (text in Japanese), *Bijutsu Kenkyu,* no. 72, 1937, pp. 487-491.

It is perhaps typical of the sad state of affairs in Chinese archaeology of the time that the knowledge of the existence of drum stands in the shape of birds and beasts was never passed on from their bootleg excavators to honest Chinese archaeologists. When the first new discovery of such a piece was made after World War II, therefore, an error was committed in reconstructing its original shape. This mistake would never have occurred if the excavators had known as much as the tomb robbers or the restorer of the Boston piece. When the large, seven-room tomb (tomb no. 1) at Ch'ang-t'ai-kuan, Hsin-yang County, Honan Province, was discovered in 1957, the excavators found, in addition to the now famous set of bells (see cat. no. 14) several other musical instruments. A stand consisting of two addorsed tigers was found near the remnants of two drums. There were also four leg-shaped supports, and, as these fitted into the sockets on the backs of the tigers, the excavators mistook them for drum supports and placed the reconstructed drum right on top of them, not realizing that an essential part, i.e., the birds, was missing.

It was only during the next year, when a second large tomb was found adjacent to

fig. 22

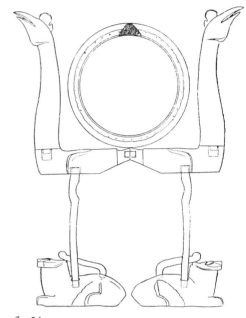

fig. 24

fig. 23

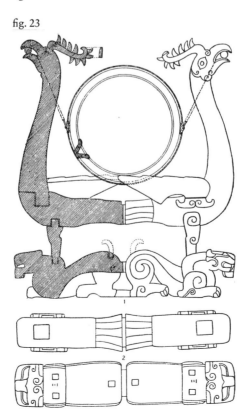

tomb no. 1, that a more complete stand, consisting of two birds standing on a pair of tigers, was excavated (fig. 22). The discovery led to a new effort at reconstructing the drum stand from tomb no. 1. Miss Yüan Ch'üan-yu proposed a reconstruction whereby a pair of birds of the type found in tomb no. 2 was placed on top of the addorsed tigers. A large drum was suspended from the crests of the birds by means of loops. Fearing that the drum might be too heavy to be hung from the birds' necks without additional support, Miss Yüan designed a central upright support fitting into the pair of sockets in the center of the tiger stand. A few years later Chia Ngo came up with an improved reconstruction of the drum stand from tomb no. 2 (fig. 23). He realized that the sockets in the hind part of the tigers were for detachable tails, not for an additional support. He also assumed that the drums were originally suspended from strings running through the beaks of the birds. That such an arrangement existed is evident from the magnificent painting on the coffin of a tomb excavated at Sha-tzu-t'ang near Ch'ang-sha in June 1961. On the coffin are painted two cranelike birds facing each other. A pair of musical stones, or jade pendants, is suspended from strings running through the open beaks, behind the pearls held in them. Between 1962 and 1965 three additional drum stands were discovered, all in the area of Chiang-ling, Hupei Province. These new discoveries added a considerable amount of information to what had been successfully reconstructed already, but they failed to solve all of the remaining problems.

The sculptures found at Ko-p'o-ssu, tomb no. 34 (fig. 24), and P'o-ma-shan, tomb no. 4, are comparable to the Boston piece. Although their measurements are similar, however, there is a marked difference in the length of the legs. Those of the Boston drum stand are at least 5-10 cm. shorter, which suggests that they may be later replacements. The sculpture found in the magnificent tombs at Wang-shan was found without legs. A reconstruction of this piece, published in the *Jimmin Chūgoku* of June 1973, inspired the Boston Museum to attempt a reconstruction of a drum. It was made especially for this exhibition by Robert G. Walker and Yasuhiro Iguchi.

The drums of the pieces found at Ko-p'o-ssu and P'o-ma-shan were reconstructed from fragments. They turn out to be somewhat smaller than the reconstruction proposed by Miss Yüan. Both were found to contain holes, probably for suspension, but the location of these holes in relation to the stand could not be established with certainty. In this respect the reconstruction remains tentative. The nails with which the skin was fastened to the drum were made of bamboo.

Two differences between the Boston sculpture and the excavated examples should be noted. One is that the bodies of the Boston birds are carved from one piece. Although in several other sculptures the birds, carved from separate pieces, have been carefully tenoned together, the piece from Ch'ang-t'ai-kuan tomb no. 2 was likewise carved from a single block. The Boston birds have closed beaks and are at present without crests and wings. It is difficult to see how a drum could be suspended from them. As long as the entire problem of the suspension of the drums has not been satisfactorily explained, however, this feature need not necessarily be seen as an argument against the authenticity of the Boston piece.

The birds on the drum stands from Chiang-ling all seem to represent the same species, evidently a member of the family of long-legged waders. The inventory of Ch'ang-t'ai-kuan tomb no. 1, written on bamboo slips found in the tomb, simply lists a "carved drum," but ancient Chinese literature occasionally mentions the expression "egret drum." There is even a story, quoted in the chapter on music in the *History of the Sui Dynasty,* which relates that "King Kou Chien of Yüeh [reigned 478-464 B.C.] beat the great drum at Thunder Gate to subdue the people of Wu. Later, when the Eastern Chin moved it to Chien-k'ang, a pair of egrets picked up the drum and flew away with it into the clouds." The birds of the stand from tomb no. 2 at Ch'ang-t'ai-kuan look more like phoenixes, and it is obvious that the birds of the stands do not always represent the same real or imaginary species. The ancient work on ritual *Chou Li* states more generally "short-haired animals [i.e., tigers] are good for bell stands, feathered ones are suitable for stands for musical stones."

To superimpose animals of a different class—birds and beasts, cranes and serpents, phoenixes and tigers—is a device well known in Chinese art of the south. For example, among the bronzes found at Shih-chai-shan (Yünnan Province) are several with representations of cormorantlike birds standing on top of curling snakes. Whether a symbolic meaning should be attached to this kind of juxtaposition is unknown. A not implausible explanation is that egrets and tigers each symbolize different types of musical tones. At this time too little is known about the religious culture of the Ch'u tribe to form a reliable interpretation of one of the most interesting types of Ch'u art that the excavations have revealed: its monumental wooden sculpture.

References: Yüan Ch'üan-yu, "On the problem of reconstructing the drum with tiger stand from a Ch'u tomb at Hsin-yang" (text in Chinese) *Wen Wu,* 1963, no. 2, pp. 10-12; Chia Ngo, "Further notes on the reconstruction of the drum and drum stand unearthed from the Ch'u tombs at Hsin-yang" (text in Chinese), *Wen Wu,* 1964, no. 9, pp. 23-26; The Cultural Committee for Hupei Province, "Brief report on the cleaning out of two Ch'u tombs at Chiang-ling, Hupei Province, and the tiger-and-bird stands excavated from them" (text in Chinese), *Wen Wu,* 1964, no. 9, pp. 27-32; Working Team of the Hupei Provincial Bureau of Culture, "A large number of important cultural relics excavated from three Ch'u tombs at Chiang-ling, Hupei Province" (text in Chinese), *Wen Wu,* 1966, no. 5, pp. 33-35; *Jimmin Chūgoku,* 1973, no. 6 (supplement), frontispiece; A. Bulling, "Studies and Excavations made in China in recent years," *Oriental Art,* n.s. 11, no. 4 (winter 1965), 235-242.

22
Carved wooden board
Lacquered wood, carved and reticulated
decoration
Late Chou period, ca. 3rd century B.C.;
1. 173.5, w. 31 cm., thickness 1.5-2 cm.
Field Museum of Natural History, Chicago

When this wooden board was acquired by
the Field Museum of Natural History in
1939, the dealer who sold the piece claimed
that it had come from the same tomb in
Ch'ang-sha as the celebrated Cranes and
Serpents sculpture in the Cleveland Museum
of Art. Although no eye witness account of
the excavation is available, this claim finds
support in the circumstance that the wings of
the Cleveland Cranes (which at the time of
the purchase by Cleveland had been replaced
by modern copies) were acquired from the
same Chinese source at the same time as the
carved wooden board. After selling the board
to Chicago, the dealer presented the original
wings to the Cleveland Museum.

Unclear as the board's ultimate provenance
remained for many years, so too was its original function. In the museum's inventory the
curator Martin Wilbur described it as "a lacquered wooden grille, believed to be an inner
lid to a coffin." Eleanor Consten, who first
published the piece, described it as follows:
"Lid of a coffin, Late Chou period, lacquered
wood, from Ch'ang-sha. As the ornament is
pierced, this must be the lid of an inner
coffin, which stood inside a second, tightly
closed sarcophagus. The ornament is a
further development of the interwining
dragon motif" (text in German). The only
other—rather fanciful—suggestion as to the
possible use of pieces of this type has been
made by William Watson, who labeled a recently excavated example of the same type
as a "wooden board of a musical instrument,
ch'in."

Published: Eleanor Consten, *Das Alte China*,
Stuttgart: Kilpper Verlag, 1958, pl. 67 (right),
caption p. 247; for William Watson's identification see his *Archaeology in China*, London: Parrish, 1960, pl. 92.

Several recent excavations at Ch'ang-sha
and elsewhere have yielded a considerable
amount of new information on the carved
wooden planks with pierced decoration,
which are a typical product of the high level
of craftsmanship and artistic imagination
attained by the artisans of the ancient state of
Ch'u. These planks, often called *ling-ch'uang*
(a term of which the accuracy is somewhat in
doubt) were not used as lids for the inner
coffin, as Wilbur and Consten thought, but
turn out to have been placed at the bottom of
the coffin, where they provided support for
the body. The highly stereotyped openwork
decoration is of two different types. One type
is strictly geometric; it consists of crosses,
triangular shapes, and TLV patterns resembling those found on bronze mirrors of a
later period. The other type has a more
elegant, but rigidly symmetrical decoration
of intertwining dragons, almost completely
dissolved into ornamental patterns. The
pierced design of at least two recently excavated pieces is virtually identical with that
of the plank in the Field Museum; these are
the pieces found in tomb no. 50 at Ch'ang-tê
and in tomb no. 26 at Yang-t'ien-hu, a suburb of Ch'ang-sha. Whereas the Chicago
piece has suffered badly from excessive moisture, however, the plank from tomb no. 26 at
Yang-t'ien-hu seems to have retained its
original coat of red and black lacquer, which
adds greatly to the beauty of the design.

Several other pieces, including one illustrated here (fig. 25), differ from the plank in
the Field Museum in only one detail. In the
Chicago piece, on both sides of the central
knot in the intertwining dragon design two
scrolls combine and terminate in a trefoil
shape resembling a *fleur de lis*, whereas in
pieces from Yang-t'ien-hu tomb no. 25 and
Ch'ang-sha tomb no. 124, this trefoil is replaced by a dragon's head. Especially as all
other details of the design are identical, it is
difficult to establish which of the two versions of the motif is the older. Whether it
represents "a design of intertwining dragons,
almost completely dissolved into ornamental
patterns" (Eleanor Consten) or "essentially

22

fig. 25

an ornament that has mysteriously acquired life" (Max Loehr) is a question to which these excavations have not yet supplied a definite answer.

The custom of providing the body with additional support at the bottom of the coffin seems to have survived in China into modern times. J. J. M. de Groot, describing burial customs current in Amoy toward the end of the nineteenth century, mentions a board placed in the coffin that is reminiscent of the *ling-ch'uang* of ancient times: "Everything is now covered with the before-mentioned loose board, fitting in the coffin at a little distance from the bottom. In this board are seven holes arranged like the stars of the Great Bear, or seven painted circles, sometimes with and sometimes without a small hole in the center of each. It is known as the 'seven stars' board" (*The Religious System of China*, vol. 1, Leiden: Brill, 1892, pp. 90-91). This custom goes back at least to the fourteenth century; in Ming tombs several boards of this type have been found. The earliest instance of the use of the "seven stars" board discovered thus far seems to be in the tomb of the parents of the famous Prince of Wu, Chang Shih-ch'êng (died 1367), a salt trader who governed Soochow and Hangchow during the last years of the Yüan period and the rise to power of Chu Yüan-chang, the founder of the Ming dynasty. Chang's parents were buried at Soochow in 1365. At the bottom of both coffins is a board with seven perforations together forming the constellation Ursa Major.

References: Tombs in which reticulated wooden planks have been found have been published in the following archaeological journals: 1) Ch'ang-sha, Yang-t'ien-hu, tomb no. 25: *Wen Wu*, 1954, no. 3, pp. 53-54; *Kaogu Xuebao*, 1957, no. 1, pp. 93-103. 2) Ch'ang-sha, Yang-t'ien-hu, tomb no. 26: *Wen Wu*, 1956, no. 12, color plate. 3) Ch'ang-tê, Tê-shan, tomb no. 50: *Kaogu*, 1963, no. 9, p. 469, fig. 18 (perhaps identical with *Kaogu*, 1959, no. 4, p. 207, fig. 1. 4) Ch'ang-sha, Patriots' Park, tomb no. 3: *Wen Wu*, 1959, no. 10, pp. 65-70, fig. 13. 5) Ch'ang-sha, Yang t'ien-hu, tomb no. 14: *Wen Wu*, 1956, no. 12, color plate. 6) Ch'ang-sha, tomb no. 125: *Ch'ang-sha fa-chüeh pao-kao*, pl. 6, no. 4 (fragment of a piece almost identical with no. 5); 7) Ch'ang-sha, tomb no. 406. *Ch'ang-sha fa-chüeh pao-kao*, pl. 6, no. 4; for a discussion of the name *ling-ch'uang* see Yeh Ting-hou, "Discussion of the name of the plank with carved decoration excavated from a Ch'ang-sha tomb," *Wen Wu*, 1956, no. 12, pp. 23-25; The Soochow Museum, "Brief report on the cleaning out of the tomb of Lady Ts'ao, the mother of Chang Shih-ch'êng of Wu, Soochow," *Kaogu*, 1965, no. 6, pp. 289-300.

23

23
Human figurine
Wood with remnants of textile clinging to it
Late Eastern Chou period,
ca. 3rd century B.C.; h. 50 cm.
Museum of Fine Arts, Boston, Charles B.
Hoyt Collection. 50.1956

The figurine has an armless and shapeless body, the back of which has suffered from exposure to water or fire, or both. Only the features of the face have been smoothly carved, for the entire body consists of a roughly hewn tapering shaft. Near the lower end a leather band has been attached to the statuette.

24
Human figurine
Wood with traces of polychromy
Late Eastern Chou period,
ca. 3rd century B.C.; h. 59.7 cm.
Seattle Art Museum, Eugene Fuller Memorial
Collection

25
Human figurine
Wood with traces of polychromy
Late Eastern Chou period,
ca. 3rd century B.C.; h. 57.1 cm.
Collection of Mr. and Mrs. Eugene Bernat

26
Human figurine
Wood with traces of vermillion and black paint
Late Eastern Chou period,
ca. 3rd century B.C.; h. 58.3 cm.
Collection of Mr. and Mrs. Myron S. Falk, Jr.

The figurines exhibited here as nos. 24-26 all came from a single set, which originally seems to have consisted of more than fifteen pieces, and which was dispersed over private collections and museums in this country in 1949. The three statuettes are quite different from the figurine exhibited as no. 23, for on all three the costumes are indicated in carving as well as in painting. Most of the pigments, however, have disappeared because of the exposure of the pieces to moisture. Of none of the pieces in the set the original hands seem to have been preserved. These hands were tenoned into rectangular mortices that have been cut into the sleeves of most of these figurines.

One of the earliest Eastern Chou tombs discovered near Ch'ang-sha brought to light the first of the tall, cylindrical wooden statues of men and women in a stiff, erect pose, which have now come to be recognized as a typical creation of the woodcarvers of the Ch'u kingdom. Examples of this type of mortuary sculpture were included in the first exhibition of Ch'ang-sha material organized by Yale University in 1939. The well-pre-

24   25   26

fig. 26

served examples, especially, aroused great interest because of their detailed rendering of costumes and face tattooing.

Published: Laurence Sickman and Alexander Soper, *The Art and Architecture of China,* 2nd ed., Harmondsworth: Penguin Books, 1960, pl. 10.

During the last twenty years tombs in the area around the city of Ch'ang-sha (Yang-chia-wan, Yang-t'ien-hu [fig. 26], and Ssu-mao-ch'ung) have yielded considerable numbers of wooden figures of a similar type. Although partially despoiled of its mortuary furniture by a clandestine excavation in the winter of 1948, still one of the finest tombs excavated in the Ch'ang-sha area is the one assigned the number 406. It yielded a total number of thirty wooden figurines, all of which had been deposited in the western part of the space between the coffin and the tomb wall, close to the feet of the deceased (fig. 34).

The drawing of this tomb shows the figurines closely stacked on top of one another and covered by three spears. It is not entirely certain that this was their original location, for the bootleg excavators who preceded the archaeologists may well have disturbed the furniture of this inundated grave site. In other tombs, especially Yang-chia-wan no. 6, figurines were piled in all three compartments surrounding the coffin.

The figurines found in tomb no. 406 are of two different types. Some of them are lifelike, in which case the details of the costume have been carved and painted. These pieces resemble nos. 24-26 exhibited here. Other figurines, however, are of a more stylized appearance and closely resemble the figurine displayed here as no. 23. The details of the body are totally neglected; they have a flat back with a groove running from head to foot like a spinal cord. To these figures cling fragments of silk, as in the case of the Boston figurine. It is most likely, therefore, that the details of the body are not indicated because it merely acted as a core of a figure dressed in silk clothes. The groove on the excavated examples suggests that these dressed dolls may have been used as puppets, which were tied to a stick in order to be held up high. Shang Ch'êng-tso saw in Ch'ang-sha another puppet of this type, which carried a leather band around the chest.

The damage to the back of the Boston figurine, probably the result of burning, recalls an unusual phenomenon observed by John Hadley Cox during his stay in Ch'ang-sha. "In exceedingly rare cases," he wrote, "fire occurred when the ceiling beams (of a tomb) were lifted, and the excavators were nearly scared out of their wits, feeling certain that guardian spirits of the tomb were retaliating for the sacrilege."

By far the closest resemblance to the pieces exhibited as nos. 24-26 is displayed in a set of seven figurines excavated from a tomb at Yang-chia-wan in July 1953. Three of these show a triangular slip of the undergarment emerging from below the long robe, a feature shared with the pieces of the set shown here.

The other puppets at Yang-chia-wan displayed the schematic treatment of the body, which suggests that these pieces were dressed in clothes.

So far only very few figurines have been found in Late Eastern Chou tombs of which the hands have been preserved. One set, consisting mostly of kneeling figures, formed an orchestra. Other figurines, found at Yang-chia-wan in 1954, show a man holding a miniature version of the scoop exhibited here (no. 32) and another man holding a semicircular, spadelike instrument. Perhaps the two men represent cooks or gardeners.

Wooden figurines continued to be carved after the Ch'u kingdom had lost its independence. In the tomb at Ma-wang-tui, dating from the Western Han period, and containing the extraordinarily well preserved body of a noblewoman, no less than 162 wooden figurines were found packed together in the space between the coffin and the walls of the grave. These Han figurines, however, display a more advanced style of carving, quite different from the solemn, angular charm of the earlier examples.

References: Gallery of Fine Arts, Yale University, *An Exhibition of Chinese Antiquities from Ch'ang-sha Lent by John Hadley Cox,* New Haven, 1939, pp. 4, 5; The Archaeological Institute of Academia Sinica, *Ch'ang-sha fa-chüeh pao-kao* [Report of the excavations at Ch'ang-sha], Peking: Science Press, 1957, pp. 25-26, 60, pls. 28-29; *Wen Wu,* 1954, no. 3, p. 54; The Provincial Museum of Hunan, "The Ch'u tombs of Ch'ang-sha," *Kaogu Xuebao,* 1959, no. 1, pp. 41-60; *Ch'üan-kuo chi-pên chien-shê kung-ch'êng-chung ch'u-t'u wên-wu chan-lan t'u-lu* [Illustrated catalogue of cultural relics excavated at construction sites in the entire country], preface by Chêng Chên-to, Peking, 1954, vol. 2, pl. 165; The Hunan Provincial Museum et al., *Ch'ang-sha Ma-wang-tui i-hao Han-mu fa-chüeh chien-pao* [Brief report on the excavation of tomb no. 1 of the Han period excavated at Ma-wang-tui, Ch'ang-sha], Peking: Wen Wu Press, 1972; Shang Ch'êng-tso, *Ch'ang-sha ku-wı wên-chien-chi,* Nanking: Chinling University Press, 1939, ch. 1, pp. 37a-b.

27

Model of a house
Buff stoneware, incised, cut, and modeled
Han dynasty, 2nd century B.C.-2nd
century A.D.; h. 24.1 cm., l. 18 cm.
Yale University Art Gallery

This model of a house, brought back from
Ch'ang-sha by John Hadley Cox, conveys an
excellent impression of rural life in southern
China during the Han period. Vertical slits
and diamond-shaped openings have been
cut out in the walls to permit a maximum of
ventilation in a hot and humid climate. In the
backyard are various animals; two servants
inside are grinding grain, and a third person
is sitting in the doorway.

Published: Gallery of Fine Arts, Yale Univer-
sity, *An Exhibition of Chinese Antiquities from
Ch'ang-sha*, New Haven, Conn., 1939, p. 14, fig.
7; George J. Lee, *Selected Far Eastern Art in the
Yale University Art Gallery*, New Haven: Yale
University Press, 1970, no. 118.

The two architectural models in this exhibition, the watchtower from Honan (cat.
no. 48) and this house from Ch'ang-sha,
illustrate the contrasting life styles of northern and southern China during the Han
period. In the north, often exposed to the
hazards of lightning attacks by the barbarians on horseback, people had to be on the
alert, and the balconies were manned by
lookouts and armed guards, with crossbows
and arrows. In the south the forces of nature
were the main hazard. The slope of the roof
was steeper to expedite the removal of water,
and especially in the Canton area, the house
was often placed on elevated pole foundations to guard against floods. Different kinds
of trellis work allowed the necessary
ventilation.

Judging from the models found in tombs
in and around Ch'ang-sha as well as farther
south, the style of architecture exemplified in
the Yale model was common all over southern China during the Han period. Similar
models have been found at Yüeh-liang-shan,
a suburb of Ch'ang-sha (fig. 27), at Canton,
and in the large Kwangsi tomb at Ho-fu (see
cat. no. 55). From this last tomb came the

27

only known model of a house in bronze,
complete with a roof of corrugated bronze
shielding the house and the open gallery in
front of it from the rain.

References: *Ch'üan-kuo chi-pên chien-shê kung-
ch'êng-chung ch'u-t'u wên-wu chan-lan t'u-lu*
[Illustrated catalogue of cultural relics excavated
at construction sites in the entire country], preface by Chêng Chên-to, Peking: 1954, vol. 2, pl.
185; *Kuang-chou ch'u-t'u Han-tai t'ao-wu* [Clay
models of houses of the Han period excavated
at Canton], Peking: Wen Wu Press, 1958; The
Archaeological Team of the Autonomous Region
of the Chuang Tribe, Kwangsi, "A wooden burial
chamber of the Western Han dynasty at Ho-fu,
Kwangsi" (text in Chinese), *Kaogu*, 1972, no. 5,
pp. 22-30.

fig. 27

28

Round box with cover
Wood and cloth, covered with painted
lacquer
Late Eastern Chou period, ca. 3rd
century B.C.; h. 10 cm., diam. 26.5 cm.
Museum of Fine Arts, Boston, Keith McLeod
Fund. 68.696

Whereas most lacquer boxes of this type
have suffered irreparable damage shortly
after excavation because of shrinkage of the
wooden core on which the lacquer was
applied, this box seems to have survived the
process of drying out remarkably well. The
well-preserved design on the lid as well as on
the walls of the box and lid has been described by Max Loehr as follows: "The central medallion, framed by three borders of
diversified design, is occupied by a very complicated configuration of connected rocaille-
like elements. At close inspection this
vivacious configuration proves to be the body
of a single dragon with fantastic, organically
indefinable extensions and flourishes. Except
for the head, his body is rendered as though
in profile view, with limbs crossing over the
body or underneath it. The extraordinary
thing is that this creature is partly organism
and partly ornament, yet in all its ambiguity
possesses a semblance of vitality. A more
compact version of the ornamental dragon
figure appears on the wall of the same
lacquer box lid. The dragon is essentially an
ornament that has mysteriously acquired
life."

The box is known as the Laughing Dragon
Box; it was named after the open-mouthed
dragon scratching its neck with its right front
claw, which appears on the central medallion
of the lid. Like most other examples of early
Chinese lacquer in Western collections, the
box is said to have come from Ch'ang-sha
and is dated in the Late Eastern Chou period.

Published: Chiang Hsüan-yi, *Changsha: the Chu
tribe and its art,* Shanghai: Art and Archaeology
Society, 1950, vol. 2, pl. 24a-c; Max Loehr, "The
Fate of the Ornament in Chinese Art," *Archives
of Asian Art,* no. 21 (1967-68), p. 13, figs. 9, 10;
"Centennial Acquisitions: Art Treasures for

Tomorrow," *Boston Museum Bulletin* 68 (1970),
32-33, no. 15.

Excavations carried out in and around
Ch'ang-sha since 1950 have brought to light
a large number of round lacquer boxes.
Whereas in the past the contents of boxes
found in clandestine digs were often dispersed, the toilet articles often found in them
are now carefully registered and analyzed.
However, in spite of the large number of
boxes that have been excavated at Ch'ang-sha
in recent years, not a single piece has been
discovered that is decorated with a design
resembling that of the Laughing Dragon Box.

Two extremely poor illustrations accompanying an article dealing with the problems
of conservation of this type of lacquer suggest a possible answer to this problem (fig.
28). The article, written by Chang Tzu-ch'i,
describes a semicircular fragment of thin
wood, decorated on both sides with a design
in lacquer. The piece was excavated in 1951
from a tomb at the village of Chu-chi in
Shou-hsien County, Anhwei Province. The
tomb was built of wood and dated from the
Warring States period. As far as can be made
out from the illustrations, the design on this
circular object, probably the lid of a box, is
closely related to that of the Laughing Dragon
Box, especially that on the wall of the lid.

The village Chu-chi is probably identical
with Chu-chia-chi, where during the early
thirties a large number of fine bronzes was
found. The affiliation of this important site
with the state of Ch'u is proved by the inscriptions on bronzes that were found there.
One of these refers to King Yu of Ch'u, who
is known to have reigned from 237 to 228
B.C. Shou-ch'un, near the present Shou-hsien,
was the last capital of the Ch'u kingdom, in
decline before it was conquered by the state
of Ch'in in 222 B.C. The political history of
the area during the last centuries of the
Eastern Chou period is rather chaotic and
consists of a succession of wars, changes in
allegiance, and shifting centers of government and power. It would be incautious,
therefore, to connect any of the finds in this
area with a specific state, except in such cases

as the tomb of the Duke of Ts'ai (see cat. no.
14), where definite epigraphical evidence is
available to link the find with the governing
house of Ts'ai. The type of burial and the
type of lacquerware found in it seem to
argue in favor of the supposition that the
tomb at Chu-chi village, from which this
fragmentary piece came, dates from the de-
clining years of the Ch'u state.

Although more evidence will be needed to
prove this point, it seems possible that the
Laughing Dragon Box comes from the same
area. Unfortunately, the box underwent drastic restoration on the inside, probably in
order to prevent shrinkage of the wooden
base. We do not know, therefore, whether
the Laughing Dragon Box was once decorated on the inside, as is the case with the
fragment from Chu-chi village. If that fragment were part of a box, we may assume its
diameter to have been 18 or 19 cm., which is
considerably smaller than the Laughing
Dragon Box.

References: Chang Tzu-ch'i, "Experiences with
the conservation of painted lacquer fragments"
(text in Chinese), *Wen Wu,* 1955, no. 12, pp. 107-
114; Li Ching-tan, "Report on the preliminary
investigation of the Ch'u tombs at Shou Hsien"
(text in Chinese), *T'ien-yeh K'ao-ku Hsüeh-pao*
(Shanghai), 1 (1936), 213-279.

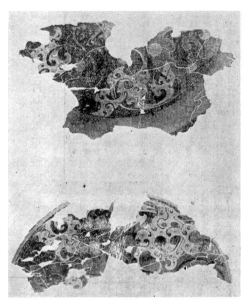

fig. 28

28

28

28

28

29

29

29
Seal
Silver, dark patina
Late Eastern Chou period,
ca. 3rd century B.C.; h. 3.1 cm.
Collection of Dr. Paul Singer

The small seal is shaped like a slightly taper-ing miniature obelisk placed on a rectangular base, the top of which slopes on all four sides. A round hole pierces the obelisk. The vertical sides are decorated with crossed rec-tangles. On the bottom is engraved the seal consisting of two unidentified graphs in sunken lines.

Published: Paul Singer, *Early Chinese Gold and Silver,* New York: China Institute of America, 1972, no. 17.

Seals described as being cast in bronze, not silver, have been found in several tombs of the Late Eastern Chou period in the Ch'ang-sha area. Closest in shape is a piece found in tomb no. C 7 at Sha-hu-chiao, Ch'ang-sha (fig. 29). In addition to the four characters on the bottom it has one graph engraved on the side. Another seal of the same type, found in Ch'ang-sha, has the same round hole pierc-ing the shaft, probably for attachment to a cord. In connection with a seal carved in stone and engraved with an inscription con-taining the name "Ch'ang-sha," discovered in tomb 18 at Hou-chia-t'ang, Ch'ang-sha, which had been previously excavated by grave robbers, Lo Tun-ching of the Hunan Cultural Committee raised and answered in the affirmative the question whether it was worthwhile to excavate tombs that had been previously robbed.

In his book on Chinese connoisseurship van Gulik briefly mentioned pre-Han seals. "A few of these early seals have been pre-served," he wrote, "but whether or not their legends were engraved at a later time is a moot problem; they mostly give official titles." Although the excavations at Ch'ang-sha have not yet produced a large number of pre-Han seals, there now seems to be a suffi-cient amount of authenticated material to begin the study of the early history of seal carving in China.

References: Li Chêng-kuang and P'êng Ching-yeh, "Excavation of ancient cemeteries in the Sha-hu-chiao region, Ch'ang-sha" (text in Chinese), *Kaogu Xuebao,* 1957, no. 4, pp. 33-68; The Provincial Museum of Hunan, "The Ch'u tombs of Ch'ang-sha" (text in Chinese, summary in English), *Kaogu Xuebao,* 1959, no. 1, pp. 41-61; Lo Tun-ching, "Are ancient burials that have been robbed worthwhile excavating?" (text in Chinese), *Wen Wu,* 1956, no. 10, pp. 37-39; R. H. van Gulik, *Chinese Pictorial Art as Viewed by the Connoisseur,* Rome: Is. M.E.O., 1958, p. 419.

fig. 29

30

"Hundred nipple" mirror
Bronze, dark patina
Western Han period, ca. 1st century B.C.;
diam. 15.9 cm.
Collection of Dr. Paul Singer

The central boss has the shape of a mountain top surrounded by eight smaller peaks. The larger of the two fields of the mirror is encircled on both sides by striations and arcs, which are formed by the raised borders completing the star-shaped fields into circles. Curvilinear bands connect the nipples in the main field. Four rosettes add to the number of nipples; they may have inspired Chinese antiquarians to name this type the "hundred nipple" mirror.

Examples of this type, all with minor variations, are not uncommon in Western collections. Illustrated examples include pieces in the David-Weill and Hallwyl collections, the Museum of Far Eastern Antiquities, Stockholm, and the Museum of Fine Arts, Boston.

References: Osvald Sirén, *A History of Early Chinese Art,* vol. 2, London: Benn, 1930, pl. 62; A. Bulling, *The Decoration of Mirrors of the Han Period,* Ascona: Artibus Asiae Publishers, 1960, pp. 32-35.

Ancient Chinese mirrors had been the subject of considerable research in the Western world long before recent excavations began to supply a large amount of information on localized finds. The first mirror antedating the Han period was brought to Europe in 1922 by the Swede Orvar Karlbeck. It was he who assembled much of the bronze material in European collections, which inspired his compatriot Bernhard Karlgren to formulate the first systematic classification of ancient Chinese bronze mirrors. Like Bishop White (see cat. no. 12), Karlbeck always tried to establish the provenance of the material he acquired. He passed this information on to Karlgren, who used it in a most cautious way, always relying on the provenance of groups of objects rather than on that of individual pieces.

In an article in which he compares the results of recent excavations in the field of

pre-Han mirrors with the data he gathered years ago, Karlgren is quick—perhaps a little too quick—to point out that "nothing has happened to invalidate the chronological scheme." This may be largely true as far as the dating of mirrors is concerned, but it does not take into account the great gains made in our knowledge of the regional distribution of these mirrors. Perhaps there is one aspect of his use of Karlbeck's provenance data that Karlgren, in spite of all his scholarly caution, may not have fully realized. Although he avoided the most obvious pitfalls by considering only groups of objects, and not individual pieces, what he reconstructed from these data was not so much the regional distribution of Chinese mirrors as the network of dealers who had supplied the material. His horizon was limited to the areas where Karlbeck and the dealers who supplied him were active. Most of Karlbeck's activities as a "Treasure Seeker in China" (the title of his memoirs) took place before the clandestine excavations in and around Ch'ang-sha began, and he did not venture into this area. The result is that only the recent excavations could have revealed that the province of Hunan, and especially the area around Ch'ang-sha, was one of the principal centers for the manufacture of mirrors, although Shou-hsien, the last capital of the Ch'u state, had been recognized as another center years ago.

Mirrors are precious objects that travel easily, and as a consequence, they are often found far from the place where they were originally made. The mirror of the "hundred nipple" type exhibited here is an example of this phenomenon. The frequency with which it has been found at Ch'ang-sha suggests that this may be the area of its original provenance (fig. 30). However, closely related examples have turned up in tombs as far apart as Huai-jou County, Hopei Province, and Ch'êng-tu, Szechwan. A modified version with much more pronounced knobs was found in a grave at Lo-yang. Although its provenance remains, therefore, somewhat uncertain, this type of mirror is a character-

fig. 30

istic component of the tomb furniture of Western Han tombs in the region formerly belonging to the Ch'u kingdom.

References: Bernhard Karlgren, "Huai and Han," Museum of Far Eastern Antiquities, Stockholm, *Bulletin*, no. 13, 1941; idem, "Some pre-Han mirrors," ibid., no. 35, 1963, pp. 161-169; *Ch'ang-sha fa-chüeh pao-kao*, Peking: Science Press, 1957, pl. 67, fig. 2; The Hunan Cultural Committee, "Brief report on cleaning up of Warring States, Han, T'ang and Sung tombs at Huang-ni-k'êng" (text in Chinese), *Kaogu*, 1956, no. 6, pl. 10, no. 3; Hunan Provincial Museum, ed., *Hu-nan ch'u-t'u t'ung-ching t'u-lu*, Peking: Wen Wu Press, 1960, pl. 56; The Loyang Archaeological Team, Institute of Archaeology, Academia Sinica, "Excavations of Western Han tombs in the western suburbs of Loyang" (text in Chinese, summary in English), *Kaogu Xuebao*, 1963, no. 2, pp. 1-58, pl. 7, figs. 1, 8; for a mirror excavated in Szechwan see *Kaogu*, 1958, no. 2, p. 23, fig. 10, and for one from Huai-jou see *Kaogu*, 1962, no. 5, p. 231.

30

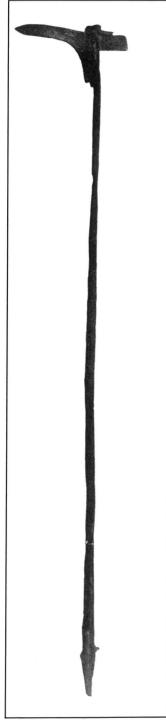

fig. 31

31

31
Ko halberd
Bronze, dark green patina
Late Eastern Chou period,
ca. 3rd century B.C.; w. 27.9 cm.
Collection of Dr. Paul Singer

In the Ch'u kingdom of the Late Eastern Chou period one of the most common mortuary gifts was a *ko* halberd of the slender, elongated type that had evolved from the broader and heavier halberds of the Shang and Early Chou periods. Large numbers of halberds of this type have been found in tombs in and around Ch'ang-sha as well as elsewhere within the old kingdom, enabling the archaeologists to establish a continuous typological sequence for this weapon.

Although the use of the *ko* halberd was by no means limited to the state of Ch'u, the excavations in this area have contributed two valuable pieces of information not available from sites elsewhere in China. Because the Ch'u method of burial has often proved to be most conducive to the preservation of wooden articles, several tombs have yielded examples of *ko* weapons of which the wooden shaft had been preserved. One piece, excavated with the halberd as well as with the accompanying bronze ferrule, had a wooden shaft measuring 144 cm. in length (figs. 31-32).

One of the most interesting finds of very recent date (February 1971) is that of tomb no. 1 at Liu-ch'êng-ch'iao in the eastern part of Ch'ang-sha. Among the fine pieces recovered from this tomb is a *ko* with the shaft still attached and in almost perfect condition.

fig. 32

The shaft, measuring 140 cm., almost the same length as the piece mentioned above, was lacquered except for the section where it was held. The ferrule was made of wood. An interesting feature of several weapons in this find is that the shaft consists of wood; it is square in section but has been wound with the skin of bamboo to make it round. This technique is already mentioned in the ancient *Rituals of Chou*. The bamboo is covered with a fine lacquered decoration, which closely resembles that on the Cranes and Serpents sculpture in the Cleveland Museum of Art.

Although a large number of *ko* have been found, only a few isolated cases are known in which the objects in the tomb have survived to the extent that even the strip of silk used to wind the halberd to the lacquered bamboo shaft has been preserved. A fine example, comparable to the halberd from the Singer collection shown here, is a piece found in tomb no. 1 at Wang-shan, Chiang-ling County in 1965.

The starlike figures on the blade are produced by a controlled variegation of the bronze surface, but the technical process by which this effect is achieved has not yet been satisfactorily explained. It also occurs frequently on swords (see cat. no. 38).

References: Historical Museum, Peking, *Ch'u wên-wu chan-lan t'u-lu* [Illustrated catalogue of an exhibition of Ch'u cultural relics], Peking, 1954, pl. 81; Working Team of the Hupei Provincial Bureau of Culture, "A large number of important cultural relics excavated from three Ch'u tombs at Chiang-ling, Hupei Province" (text in Chinese), *Wen Wu,* 1966, no. 5, pp. 33-55; The Hunan Provincial Museum, "Tomb no. 1 at Liu-Ch'êng-ch'iao, Ch'ang-sha," *Kaogu Xuebao,* 1972, no. 1, pp. 59-72.

32
Scoop
Bronze
Late Eastern Chou or Early Western Han period, ca. 4th-2nd century B.C.; l. 17.9 cm.
Collection of Dr. Paul Singer

The bronze scoop consists of an oval receptacle resembling a small winnow, to which a hollow, rectangular shaft has been attached at a sharp angle. Implements of this type frequently appear in tombs of the Eastern Chou to Western Han period. Occasionally fragments of wood are still sticking into the shaft, but up to the present time not a single piece seems to have been found from which the original length of the wooden handle can be reconstructed. Scoops of this type have been found not only in and around Ch'ang-sha but also in Sung-tzu County, Hupei Province, and in the vicinity of Canton. An inscribed example in the Tien-tsin Historical Museum was excavated at Chu-chia-chi near Shou-hsien, Anhui Province (fig. 33). Although this implement is obviously a characteristic product of Ch'u culture, its use seems to have spread beyond the borders of this Eastern Chou feudal state.

References: Chang Hsin-ju, "Bronze vessels discovered at Peiling, Liu-yang County, Hunan" (text in Chinese), *Kaogu,* 1965, no. 7, p. 374; The Canton Cultural Committee, "Brief report on the excavation of the Western Han wooden chamber burial no. 003 at Huang-hua-kang, Canton" (text in Chinese), *Kaogu,* 1958, no. 4, pp. 32-40; The Provincial Museum of Hunan, "The Ch'u tombs of Ch'ang-sha" (text in Chinese, summary in English), *Kaogu Xuebao,* 1959, no. 1, pp. 41-60; The Archaeological Institute of the Academia Sinica, *Ch'ang-sha fa-chüeh pao-kao,* Peking: Science Press, 1957, pl. 18, fig. 4, p. 39; Historical Museum, Peking, *Ch'u wên-wu chan-lan t'u-lu* [Illustrated catalogue of an exhibition of Ch'u cultural relics], Peking, 1954, pl. 10; Jung Kêng, *The Bronzes of Shang and Chou,* Peking: Yenching University, 1941, vol. 2, p. 466, fig. 886.

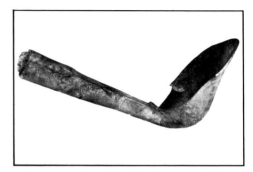

fig. 33

32

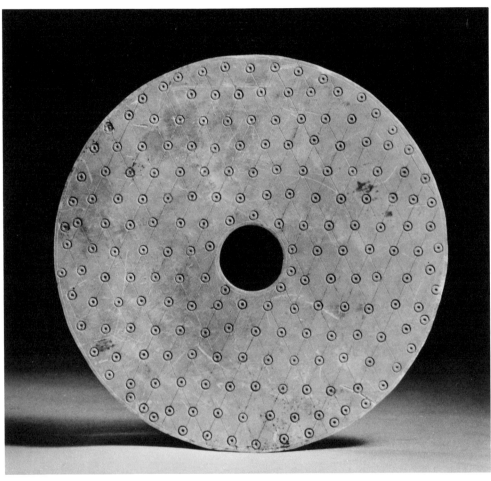

33

33
Pi disc
Whitish soapstone with light brown discolorations
Western Han period, ca. 2nd century B.C.;
diam. 16 cm.
Collection of Dr. Paul Singer

The round stone disc is covered with a design of thin straight lines running parallel across the piece in two different directions and intersecting at a 45 degree angle. The intersections are marked by small circles with a hole in the center. Pieces of this type occur in several variations; sometimes the back is entirely plain, sometimes it is covered with the crossing lines without the small circles.

Excavations at Ch'ang-sha have produced several *pi* discs (fig. 35) of a type similar to that exhibited here. It occurs in tombs that can be determined by their structure and other furniture as dating from the early part of the Western Han period (ca. 2nd century B.C.). From the large number of excavations at Ch'ang-sha, which yielded a variety of *pi* discs in jade, soapstone, serpentine, and occasionally in glass, a certain pattern in the use of these objects can be observed. Tombs of the Late Eastern Chou period sometimes contain more than one disc of this type, the largest number coming from one tomb being five or six. Pairs of discs were placed flanking the head and the knees of the man buried in Ch'ang-sha tomb 406, while a fifth piece was placed in front of the skull (fig. 34). A sixth piece was standing straight in the narrow space between the innermost and second coffin, just behind the head.

Although there is some uncertainty as to the original position of the pieces in this tomb (see cat. no. 26), other finds confirm that the most common location of *pi* discs in tombs was close to the head. The placement of discs in pairs, flanking the head and knees of the man buried in tomb 406 (although partially reconstructed on the basis of oral information) seems to illustrate the famous words of the philosopher Chuang-tzu (late 4th century B.C.) who on his deathbed instructed his disciples: "Heaven and earth will be my inner and outer coffin, the sun and the moon my twin *pi* discs, the stars and planets my beads, and all the products of nature my mortuary gifts; therefore, are the articles required for my burial not at hand?"

Judging from the position in which the *pi* discs are often found in early Han graves, it appears that the custom of placing these pieces close to the head survived the fall of the Ch'u kingdom. Of the use of twin *pi* discs, evidently referred to as customary by Chuang-tzu and found in Late Chou tombs, there is no evidence in Ch'ang-sha tombs of the Han period. The eleven discs mentioned in the *Report on the excavations at Ch'ang-sha* came from exactly the same number of separate burials.

References: The Archaeological Institute of Academia Sinica, *Ch'ang-sha fa-chüeh pao-kao* [Report on the excavations at Ch'ang-sha], Peking: Science Press, 1957, pp. 65-66, 83-84, pl. 45; *Kaogu*, 1957, no. 4, pl. 10, fig. 4.

fig. 35

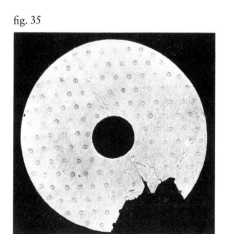

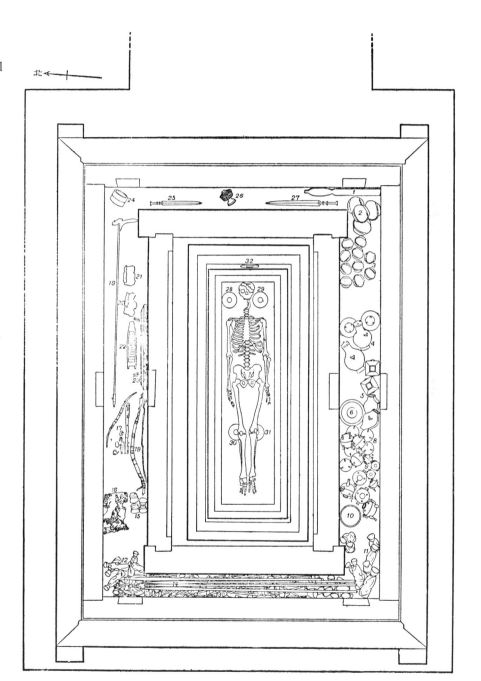

fig. 34

34

34
A pair of dragon-shaped ornaments
Light green jade with carved, engraved, and
reticulated decoration
Late Eastern Chou period,
ca. 3rd century B.C.; l. 20.5 cm.
Collection of Mr. and Mrs. Myron S.
Falk, Jr.

Carved silhouettes of dragons, crouching or coiled, sometimes with their heads turned, have been found in tombs dating from the Late Eastern Chou period. The heads always stand out in silhouette and are accentuated by means of thin lines, which follow the contours. The body is covered with the typical Eastern Chou spiral, or comma, ornament. On the two pieces exhibited here this ornament has been carved in low relief; on some of the recently excavated examples it is merely engraved into a flat surface.

Pieces of this type have been found at Chiang-ling, Hupei Province, at Ch'ang-tê, Honan Province, and at Shou-hsien, Anhwei Province (fig. 36). The location of these finds and the context in which they have been found suggest that this type of jade dragon may be a typical creation of the Ch'u artists, slightly different from the stretched-out or S-shaped dragons that occur in burials in the Central Plain and other northern areas.

References: Hunan Provincial Museum, "Burials of the Warring States period at Tê-shan, Ch'ang-tê, Hunan Province" (text in Chinese), *Kaogu*, 1959, no. 12, pp. 658-662; Werner and Bedřich Forman, *Ancient Relics of China*, Peking: The People's Art Publishing House, 1962, pl. 21; The Cultural Committee of Hupei Province, "Brief report on the cleaning out of two Ch'u tombs at Chiang-ling, Hupei Province, and the tiger-and-bird stands excavated from them" (text in Chinese), *Wen Wu*, 1964, no. 9, pp. 27-32.

fig. 36

35a

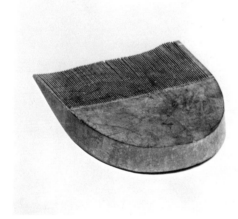

35b

This pair of combs came from a round lacquer box (now also in the Singer collection), which was said to have been excavated at Ch'ang-sha. In addition to the combs it contained two hair pieces, a variety of wood and reed articles and several textiles. Three of the textiles (a bonnet and a pair of mitts) were sold separately to the Museum for the Arts of Decoration of the Cooper Union, New York.

Fine-toothed and large-toothed combs, made out of a single piece of wood or out of two pieces of wood glued together, have been found in Ch'ang-sha tombs in considerable numbers (figs. 37-38). One of the combs, found in Ch'ang-sha City, did not come from a toilet box, like most other pieces, but was evidently carried in the pocket. It had a wooden box with a sliding lid and an interior section shaped to fit the comb. The fine-toothed comb exhibited here has been perfectly preserved: the teeth are still resilient and springy. These combs are quite similar to those used in China up to the present time.

References: *Archaeological Treasures Excavated in the People's Republic of China* (exhibition catalogue) Tokyo/Kyoto National Museum, 1973, nos. 35-36 (from Ma-wang-tui, Ch'ang-sha); Historical Museum, Peking, *Ch'u wên-wu chan-lan t'u-lu* [Illustrated catalogue of an exhibition of Ch'u cultural relics], Peking, 1954, nos. 32-38; Jean A. Mailey and Calvin S. Hathaway, "A bonnet and a pair of mitts from Ch'ang-sha," *Chronicle of the Museum for the Arts of Decoration of the Cooper Union*, 2, no. 10 (December 1958), 315-346; Noel Barnard, *Scientific Examination of an Ancient Document as a Prelude to Decipherment, Translation and Historical Assessment—the Ch'u Silk Manuscript*, Canberra: Department of Far Eastern History, Institute of of Advanced Studies, The Australian National University, 1972, pp. 65-67.

fig. 37

fig. 38

35a
Large-toothed comb *(shu)*
Wood, lacquered black
Late Eastern Chou period, ca. 3rd century
B.C.; l. 6.4 cm.
Collection of Dr. Paul Singer

35b
Fine-toothed comb *(pi)*
Reddish brown wood
Late Eastern Chou period, ca. 3rd century
B.C.; l. 7 cm.
Collection of Dr. Paul Singer

36
Willow-leaf shaped sword *(liu-yeh chien)*
Bronze
Western Chou period, ca. 10th century B.C.;
l. 25.4 cm.
Royal Ontario Museum, Toronto, Bishop
William Charles White Collection

This short sword is forged as one single
piece. The blade section has two cutting
edges and is nearly three-fourths of the total
length of the sword. The other one-fourth,
which does not have cutting edges, serves as
the tang. The tang is a flat, thin plaque that
widens gradually from the broken end toward the section of the blade. There are four
little projections (one is broken now) evenly
cast on either side of the tang. The two
cutting edges start at the widest section of
the sword, the heel of the blade, and run into
a joint at the sword-point, which now has a
rounded appearance, probably due to some
damage from either patination or age. The
body of the blade is rhomboid, with the center of the body rising slightly to form a mid-
ridge line. A decoration in relief appears just
below the conjunction of the tang and the
blade and apparently is derived from part of
the eye and ear motif originally used in a
complete *t'ao-t'ieh* design, but simplified and
stylized for use on the sword. Immediately
below the eye-ear motif is a slim, long, triangular pattern in simple, sunken lines.
There are two broken sections, one on the
blade and the other on the tang.
Published: S. Umehara, "A short sword inlaid
with turquoise of the Yin period" (text in Japanese), *Kōkogaku Zasshi* 41, no. 4 (1956), 62-67.

This is one of four similar swords acquired
by the late Bishop White in China. They were
all reportedly from Honan Province—the
center of Shang and early Chou cultures. In
1956 Sueji Umehara briefly mentioned these
swords in his discussion of a possibly late
Shang date (twelfth century B.C.) for Chinese
swords of this particular type (short, leaf-
shaped, guardless, decorated in Shang-Chou
motifs, etc.). In the same year, in his *Chinese
Bronze Age Weapons* (pp. 76-77), Max

36

fig. 39

Loehr expressed a similar belief that the earliest type of bronze sword in China was of the "leaf-shaped" kind, but he preferred a later dating than Umehara. Chou Wei, a Chinese pioneer in the field of ancient Chinese weapons, made noteworthy contributions in the pre-World War II period to the study of Chinese swords. Chou Wei points to the possibility that the earliest sword in China proper could have been inspired by spearheads. Later the spearhead-shaped swords were developed into the leaf-shaped kind (Chou Wei, pp. 113 and 116). Unfortunately no scholar was able to obtain concrete support from scientifically excavated evidence.

In 1959 an archaeological team that had been working along the Fêng River area in greater Sian City gave a simple, one-sentence announcement of the discovery at Chang-chia-p'o of a "willow-leaf"-shaped bronze weapon with two perforations on its tang (Fêng Hsi, p. 256). This extremely important and very exciting discovery of the earliest evidence so far of an excavated bronze sword in China did not immediately receive its deserved attention from specialists in China and abroad. In China Kuo Pao-chün made a brief comment on this Chang-chia-p'o sword in 1961, but dated it incorrectly to the end of the Western Chou period (eighth century B.C.). The authoritative book, Archaeology in New China, compiled by the Academy of Science in the same year, did not mention the sword at all. It was Lin Shou-chin of the Institute of Archaeology, Peking, who really delved into this material and published two impressive articles on Chinese swords in 1962 and 1963.

Scholars in the West were also slow in responding to the discovery of the Chang-chia-p'o sword. Chang Kuan-chih did not mention it until 1968, when he revised his book The Archaeology of Ancient China. The Chou China published in 1963 by Chêng Tê-k'un did contain the information but gave an incorrect measurement for the length of the sword (31.5 cm. instead of 27 cm., Chou China, p. 245).

This Chang-chia-p'o sword (fig. 39) was more carefully described by the Institute of Archaeology, Peking, in its formal report Fêng Hsi fa-chüeh pao-kao. The sword was found in tomb no. 206, lying at the side of the skeleton, at the waist, with its point toward the feet. This short sword (l. 27 cm.) has been thought to be the only example ever excavated in China. But the most recent information coming from China indicates that the same type of bronze sword was discovered at Ling-t'ai, Kansu Province, as well. Ling-t'ai is about 150 kilometers to the northwest of Sian City, at the border of Kansu and Shensi provinces (see Ch'ên Ch'ien, p. 24).

The Chang-chia-p'o sword can be safely dated to the eleventh-tenth century B.C. Because other bronze works that came out of the same tomb are consistently of the early Western Chou period, this early date, unique shape, and the very location (Chang-chia-p'o was possibly part of the Western Chou capital Fêng or Kao) of the sword make it extremely important for the understanding of the origin and the development of bronze swords in China proper.

Compared with the one exhibited here, the Chang-chia-p'o sword seems to be more mature in shape, proportion, and in the structure of the tang section. The two holes on the tang would certainly help to secure a handle. The blade of the Chang-chia-p'o sword is also broader than the Toronto one and therefore is more functional. The disappearance of any decoration on the blade section of the Chang-chia-p'o sword is an interesting difference between the one excavated and the one shown here, as well as the sword in the Museum of Far Eastern Antiquities, Stockholm (cat. no. 37), the sword illustrated in Shang-chai chi-chin lu and the sword published by Sueji Umehara in Kōko-gaku Zasshi. We see the decorated swords as still under the influence of previous weapons such as the type ko or mao, whereas the excavated sword from Chang-chia-p'o is a much more independently developed type.

References: Sueji Umehara, Yin Hsü: Ancient Capital of the Shang Dynasty (text in Japanese), Tokyo: Asahi Shinbunsha, 1964, pp. 35, 36, fig. 11; Max Loehr, Chinese Bronze Age Weapons, Ann Arbor: University of Michigan Press, 1956; Chou Wei, Chung-kuo Pin-ch'i-shih kao, Peking, 1957; Institute of Archaeology, Peking, K'ao-ku-hsüeh chi-ch'u, Peking, 1958, p. 96, fig. 16 (5); the Fêng Hsi Archaeological Team, Institute of Archaeology, Peking, "Report on the excavations at Fêng Hsi, Sian, from 1955 to 1957 (text in Chinese), Kaogu, no. 10, 1959, pp. 525-527; Institute of Archaeology, Peking, Fêng Hsi Fa-chüeh Pao-kao, Peking, 1962; Kuo Pao-chün, "Yin Chou ti ch'ing-t'ung wu-ch'i," Kaogu, no. 2, 1961, p. 115, fig. 20 (left); Institute of Archaeology, Peking, Archaeology in New China (text in Chinese), Wen Wu Press, 1962, pp. 51-54; Lin Shou-chin, "The origin of bronze swords of the Chou period" (text in Chinese), Wen Wu, no. 11, 1963, pp. 50-55; Lin Shou-chin, "Preliminary study of bronze swords of the Eastern Chou period" (text in Chinese), Kaogu Xuebao, no. 2, 1962, pp. 75-84; Chêng Tê-k'un, Chou-China, Cambridge, Mass., 1963, p. 239, fig. 27 (5), p. 245; Ch'ên Ch'ien, "The sword of the King Kou-chien of Yüeh State" (text in Japanese), People's China Monthly, 1973, no. 6 (supplement), p. 24; Liu T'i-chih, Shan-chai Chi-chin lu (text in Chinese), Shanghai, 1934, vol. 11, pp. 3a-3b; M. Hayashi, Chūgoku Inshū jidai no buki [Chinese weapons of the Yin and Chou periods], Kyoto, 1972, p. 215.

37

Two Bent Weapons with Face as Ornament
Bronze, remains of ivory ornaments
Western Chou period, ca. 11th-10th century
B.C.; a: l. 23.2 cm.; b: l. 21.6 cm.
Collection of Dr. Paul Singer

The two weapons are virtually identical, though not a pair. They are cast with the hilt and the blade together in one piece. There is no sword guard on either weapon; instead one finds at the heel of both sides of the blade a slightly sunken space in a flat, stiff "U" shape. This design perhaps is a "device for letting in and securing hold of both of the plates of the hilt," as Max Loehr puts it. On one of the two weapons shown here there is on each side a rectangular plaque of ivory still intact inside the "U" section. Paul Singer believes the vague traces on one of the two ivory plaques represents the decoration of a *t'ao-t'ieh* mask. Both tangs are a little narrower than the width of the "U" section but are of the same thickness as the base of the "U" sections. Originally, the length of the tang section could have been a bit longer than it is now, and there could have been one or two more holes in it. The cutting edges of the two weapons are dull and show cracks. On both sides of the blade of both weapons, a low mid-ridge runs from the rather round tip up right to the chin of the pictograph-like ornament of a human face. The faces are executed in simple, sunken lines. Although they differ slightly from each other, stylistically they are similar. The width of the blade section always reaches its maximum at the level of the two ear-tips of the face. From there upward or downward the width of the blade declines gradually. Both of the weapons exhibited have been mysteriously bent. Paul Singer thinks the bending took place prior to the burial and that there might have been some symbolic meanings, e.g. defeat, sacrifice, etc., for such an unusual phenomenon.

Published: Paul Singer, "The Unique Object in Chinese Art," *Oriental Art* 7, no. 1 (1961), 32-34, figs. 1-2; Max Loehr, *Relics of Ancient China from the Collection of Dr. Paul Singer,* New York: Asia Society, 1965, p. 85, fig. 37B, p. 153.

37

fig. 40

Chinese bronze weapons of the type exhibited here are rare and were little known previously. Max Loehr was the first to introduce them in detail and classified them as "daggers" of the early Chou period (eleventh-tenth century B.C.). The two examples studied by him are reportedly (probably based on tomb robbers' information) from Hsün-hsien, Honan Province—not far from the famous Yin ruin at An-yang. Of the two Loehr "daggers," the one with loops just below the "U" section is the same type as the so-called bronze knife in the collection of the Museum of Fine Arts, Springfield, Massachusetts; the loopless one is similar to the two displayed here. Close comparison reveals that the looped type is of more advanced design and decor than the loopless type.

So far among the numerous archaeological reports from China, we have not come across any bronze weapon that has the same structure and decoration as the five pieces mentioned above. However, recently unearthed relics do give us help in a better understanding of these unique objects. First of all, since the great discovery of a so-called willow-leaf-shaped sword at Chang-chia-p'o, Shensi Province, from an early Chou (eleventh century B.C.) tomb, there is little doubt that swords did exist in China proper as early as the eleventh century B.C. (cat. no. 36). Basically the short sword (l. 27 cm.) from Chang-chia-p'o has an outline similar to the two shown here—small size, tang and blade cast in one piece, perforations in the tang section, guardless, leaf-shaped, etc. But the excavated sword does not have the unique "U" section and the human-faced ornament. In a way the exhibited swords still bear the characteristics of spearheads, to be used for piercing rather than for hacking and cutting. Especially the two loops at the heel of the blade are usual for Chinese weapons of the spearhead type (*mao*) during the late Shang period. Nevertheless, the very nature of the short, flat tang section of the five pieces hardly could lead one to believe that they could have been designed for the same usage as the spearheads. These facts seem to show that in China there

was a transitional period when the Chinese were somehow inspired to adopt certain weapons, such as the head from a spear, for hand combat. Later on when this kind of converted spearhead became more popular, an independently developed short sword like the one excavated at Chang-chia-p'o appeared. Or both the Chang-chia-p'o type and the spearhead type could have been invented around a similar period but in different areas.

Secondly, the decoration of a human face on a piece of bronze weapon is not unknown in the late Shang period. The human face on the ceremonial axe in this exhibition (cat. no. 10) is a good example. However, rarely would one encounter such a stylized, symbolic human-face ornament—almost like a pictograph of the Shang time—as seen in the two weapons here. So far the closest comparison perhaps comes from a *ko* halberd excavated in tomb no. 1721 at Shang-ts'un-ling, Honan Province (fig. 40). At the heel of the blade section there is a decor in low relief of a human face. The interesting thing here is not that it looks like the Singer decoration. Rather, it is the unusual placement of a human face at the heel of the blade of a weapon with the eyes looking toward the sharp point. The author of the report on the Shang-ts'un-ling tombs expressed surprise at finding such a rare ornament. (*Shang-ts'un-ling,* p. 53). In the same tomb, no. 1721, a so-called spinal-ridged sword was also found that is considered the second earliest example excavated till now. As Loehr has already pointed out, both the representation and the execution of the human face on this kind of weapon are quite distinctively Chinese, if not the typical Shang and Chou Chinese. They are distinctively different from those marks that appear on bronze swords of the Pa and Shu peoples of today's Szechwan Province or the Tien people of Yünnan Province; both types are much later than the kind shown here—not to mention the various bronze swords from non-Chinese areas that used to be considered the origin of the Chinese sword.

Thirdly, the custom of burying bent

weapons together with the deceased is little known from literary references in China, and no scientifically excavated evidence was available until recent times. In 1964 several hundred tombs of the Western Chou period were excavated at P'ang-chia-kou, in the greater Lo-yang area, Honan Province. According to the report, tomb no. 139 yielded quite a number of bronze weapons, but strangely enough most of them are either bent or broken. Judging from the illustrations, they seem to have been bent in the same manner as the two shown here or the one bent dagger now in the collection of The Museum of Far Eastern Antiquities, Stockholm. Significantly, the author of this report, the Lo-yang Museum, mentioned that this is not the sole occurrence at all (p. 28): this phenomenon was frequently encountered in this area. The author also reported that in the neighboring Shensi Province such damaged weapons had been discovered in tombs of Western Chou date. Unfortunately no explanation or speculation was offered in the report as to why the weapons were bent. For those of us far from Shensi and Lo-yang, we can only guess that the victors probably bent the weapons.

References: Loyang Museum, "Re-excavation of five Western Chou tombs at P'ang-chia-kou, Loyang" (text in Chinese), *Wen Wu,* 1972, no. 10, p. 31, figs. 32-39; Museum of Fine Arts, Springfield, Mass., *The Raymond A. Bidwell Collection of Chinese Bronzes and Ceramics,* Springfield, 1965, pl. 21; Max Loehr, *Chinese Bronze Age Weapons,* Ann Arbor: University of Michigan Press, 1956, cat. nos. 85-86; Chou Wei, *Chung-kuo Pin-ch'i-shih Kao* [Preliminary history of weapons in China], Peking, 1957, pp. 113-116; the Institute of Archaeology, Academy of Science, Peking, *The Cemetery of the State of Kuo at Shang-ts'un-ling* (text in Chinese, with English abstract), Peking, 1959, p. 35, fig. 31, p. 53, pl. 54; Szechwan Provincial Museum, *Szu-ch'uan Ch'uan-kuan-tsung Fa-chüeh Pao-kao,* Peking, 1960; Sun T'ai-ch'u, "The fourth excavation at Chin-ning, Yünnan Province" (text in Chinese), *Kaogu,* 1963, no. 9, pp. 480-485; Olov Janse, "Notes sur quelques épées anciennes trouvées en Chine," *Bulletin of Museum of Far Eastern Antiquities,* no. 2, 1930, pl. 11, fig. 7.

38

Sword of King Ho-lu (?) of Wu State
Bronze with greenish and brownish patina,
12-character inscription inlaid in gold
Eastern Chou period, ca. late 6th to early
5th century B.C.; l. 49.2 cm.
The Sackler Collections

The sword is covered with greenish and
brownish patina, but its shape and structure
can still be clearly seen. The hilt has the
shape of a tapering tube and its entire surface
is without decoration. To its end is attached
a disk-shaped pommel, with the other end
formed by a thin rhombic sword guard that
serves to protect the hand and reinforces the
connection between the hilt and the blade.
At one time the hilt must have been wrapped
in cloth or silk to approximately the same
thickness as the diameter of the pommel. The
now empty cavity in the center of the pommel was originally ornamented with a stud,
probably of jade. The cross-section of the
blade makes a flat rhombus. The lower half
of the blade, toward the point, is slightly
narrower than the other half. The mid-ridge
is low and the surface on either side is comparatively flat and broad. The two cutting
edges curve to join at the sword-point;
although this part is coated with thick
patination we may assume the original shape
was close to that of the sword from the
Singer collection (cat. no. 39).

The characters of the inscription are inlaid
in gold evenly in two lines on the same side
of the blade. All characters are rendered in a
slim, elongated style. They should be read
from the right line down toward the guard
and then in the same way for the left line. All
characters are readable and can be translated
into modern Chinese, with the exception of
the fourth and the fifth characters in the right
line. According to the sentence structure of
the time the fourth character is undoubtedly
the name of the king (*wang*, the third character). The fifth character may or may not be
part of the king's name. The composition of
the fourth character, at first glance, looked
somewhat like the word *shuai* ("to lead,"
Mathews, no. 5910) in Shang oracle bone

writings and some Western Chou scripts (see
Ting Fu-pao, *Shuo-wên-chieh-tzu ku-lin*,
Taipei; Commercial Press, 1959 reprint, p.
5936 a-b). However, after archaeological discoveries of a bronze sword and a bronze
basin of the King Ho-lu of the State Kung-
Wu were recently published in China, this
fourth character on the Sackler sword seems
more likely to be *Kuang* ("bright," Mathews,
no. 3583) rather than *shuai*. Kuang was the
personal name of the King Ho-lu, which appears on most of the bronze objects made on
his order. The writing style as well as the
structure of the character *Kuang* cast on the
king's basin very much resembles the fourth
character of the Sackler sword (see Kuo-
Mo-jo, "The dating of a royal tomb of the
Ts'ai State recently excavated at Shou-hsien,
Anhui," *Kaogu Xuebao*, no. 1, 1956, pp.
3-4, pl. 8). In September 1964 a bronze
sword again bearing the name Kuang of the
King Ho-lu was unearthed in Yüan-p'ing,
Shansi Province. This character *Kuang* is
slightly damaged by patina, but the main
body of the word is still clear and it is convincingly similar in writing to the *Kuang* on
the basin.

The fifth character of the Sackler sword
consists of a radical *yen* (Mathews, no. 7357)
and a *pu* (Mathews, no. 5379). The identification of this character is not clear at this
moment, but it does not prevent our understanding the inscription as a whole. We thus
read it as: "Kung-Wu wang Kuang [?] i chi-
chin tzu tso yung chien" [King Kuang of the
State of Kung-Wu forged this sword with
auspicious metal for his own usage]. "Kung-
Wu" was the state name preferred by the
inhabitants of the kingdom which other
states called Wu, as we can see in the *Shih-
chi* by Ssu-ma Ch'ien. The compound *chi-
chin* here actually means "bronze."

One can see that the second character, *Wu*,
and the last character, *chien* (sword), are
represented a bit differently from the more
familiar ones, but there should be little doubt
about our reading of the words. A variation
of writing in Chinese had existed widely
among most of the states before the third

38

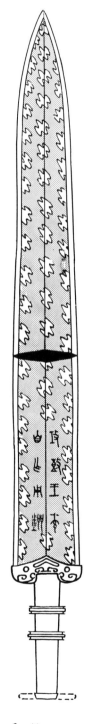

fig. 41

century B.C. Starting in 221 B.C. a movement to standardize Chinese characters was forcefully carried out under the order of the first emperor of the newly established Ch'in dynasty (221-209 B.C.). The slight difference in structure of the characters *Kuang, Wu,* and *chien* on the Sackler sword in comparison with other words of the same meaning is an indication of such local variation of the pre-standardization period, or before the third century B.C.

If the identification discussed above is correct, then this historically important sword of the King Ho-lu of Kung-Wu could shed new light on the few other bronze swords also belonging to the royal families of the same state, which are listed below:

(A) Recently excavated:
1. Sword of Prince Ku-fa (King Chu-fan) (*Wen Wu,* 1960, no. 7, p. 71-72).
2. Sword of King Ho-lu (*Wen Wu,* 1972, no. 4, pp. 69-72, pl. 2) (fig. 41).
3. Sword of King Fu-ch'a (*Chinese Literature* [Peking], 1972, no. 3, pp. 92-96).

(B) Recorded in private catalogues:
1. Sword of King Yüan (King Chu-fan?) (Liu T'i-chih, *Hsiao-chiao-ko chin-wen t'a-pen,* Shanghai, 1935, ch. 10/100 a-b).
2. Sword of Son of Prince Chi-cha (Tsou An, *Chou chin-wên ts'un,* Shanghai, 1906, ch. 6/2; 94; Ch'êng Yao-t'ien, "T'ao-shih wei chien k'ao," *T'ung-i-lu* (author's preface in 1803), An-hui ts'ung-shu ed., vol. 2, 1933 reprint, pp. 37 a-b, pl. 20).
3. Sword of King Fu-ch'a (Yü Hsing-wu, *Shang-chien-i ku-ch'i-wu t'u-lu,* Peiping, 1940, ch. 1/41 a-b).

Of the six swords listed, the excavated ones are very valuable first-hand material. Chronologically, they represent three generations of royal swords of the Kung-Wu State; from King Chu-fan (reigned 560-548 B.C.) to his son King Ho-lu (reigned 514-496 B.C.) and to Ho-lu's son King Fu-ch'a (reigned 495-473 B.C.). Typologically speaking, the one belonging to King Chu-fan is especially important. It has a strong "spinal ridge" (using Lin Shou-chin's terminology) forming a line in the middle of the blade, from the guard all the way to the point. We agree with the opinion expressed by Lin Shou-chin of the Institute of Archaeology, Peking, that this type of sword is probably the prototype for the next evolution of swords shaped like that of the Sackler Collection shown here. And that the excavated sword of Chu-fan is itself in turn a continued development from the guardless swords such as those unearthed at Shang-ts'un-ling, San-men-hsia City, Honan Province. Again, typologically, the sword of King Fu-cha, which was unearthed at Linchu, Shantung Province, indicates a third stage of swords in this Chu-fan-Sackler tradition. Kuo Mo-jo tried solely from a linguistic approach to identify a sword that has an inlaid inscription of "King Yüan of the State of Kung-Wu . . ." as actually the sword of King Chu-fan. Scholars, e.g., Max Loehr and Lin Shou-chin, have voiced reservations about Kuo's linguistic reconstruction of the link between the word *Yüan* and the words *Chu-fan.* If we set aside the linguistic arguments, we should see not only that the writing style of the inscription is apparently earlier than those of the Sackler sword but also that the sword of King Yüan has the typical structure of the "spinal ridge" in the middle of the blade section, a design similar to that of the excavated sword of King Chu-fan mentioned above. Therefore, it is fairly reasonable to assume that the sword of King Yüan is possibly one generation earlier than the Sackler type even though we are not sure who King Yüan was.

References: Chen Erh, "A story about swords," *Chinese Literature* (Peking), 1972, no. 3, pp. 92-96; Ch'ên Mêng-chia, "Research on a group of Ts'ai bronzes recently found at Shou-hsien, Anhui Province" (text in Chinese), *Kaogu Xuebao,* 1956, no. 2, p. 111; the Institute of Archaeology, Peking, *The Cemetery of the State of Kuo at Shang-ts'un-ling,* Peking: Science Press, 1959, pls. 35, 46, 54; Kuo Mo-jo, *Liang Chou Chin-wên-ts'u Ta-hsi K'ao-shih* (text in Chinese), Tokyo: Bunkyudō Shoten, 1935, pp. 154b-155a; Lin Shou-chin, "Bronze daggers and swords of the Eastern Chou period" (text in Chinese), *Kaogu Xuebao,* 1962, no. 2, pp. 75-84; R. H. Mathews, *Chinese-English Dictionary,* Cambridge: Harvard University Press, 1969; Max Loehr, *Chinese Bronze Age Weapons,* Ann Arbor: University of Michigan Press, 1956, p. 196; Tai Tsun-têh, "Eastern Chou bronzes unearthed at Chih-yü, Yüan-p'ing" (text in Chinese), *Wen Wu,* 1972, no. 4, pp. 69-72, pl. 2; M. Hayashi, *Chūgoku Inshū jidai no buki* [Chinese weapons of the Yin and Chou periods], Kyoto, 1972, pp. 216-224.

39

Bronze sword with wooden case
Warring-States period, early 4th century
B.C.; sword: l. 42.2 cm., case: l. 64.8 cm.
Collection of Dr. Paul Singer

The sword is in perfect condition, with its
two edges still very sharp. The design of the
handle here is both aesthetically and func-
tionally the most mature of all Chinese
swords. The round, solid hilt has two high
rings *(hou)* cast evenly between the pommel
and the guard. In this way silk ropes could be
wound around the hilt more firmly, as is
demonstrated in this well-preserved example,
still intact since the fourth century B.C. The
sword guard, forged over the conjunction of
the hilt and the blade, is thicker and stronger
than that of the Sackler sword—showing a
concern for the strength of the joined section.
The structure of the sword blade is delicate.
Its middle ridge rises high, running from the
guard down to the point. The blade space on
either side of the ridge shows a slight curve.
Like most Eastern Chou bronze swords, the
lower two-fifths are a bit narrower than the
upper part of the blade. Neither decoration
nor inscription has been found on the sword.

The wooden sword case *(chien-tu)*, though
warped now, is still complete in most details.
The original scabbard did not survive except
for a few pieces of bamboo and a green jade
shape. All these and the sword are lying on
hanks of yellow silk covering the bottom of
the case. The case is made of one block of
wood. Its cover bears simple, parallel carved
lines as decoration; there are also traces of
black paint.

Published: J. D. La Plante, *Arts of the Chou
Dynasty,* Stanford: Stanford University Press,
1958, cat. no. 100; T. K. Chêng, *Archaeology in
China: Chou China,* Toronto: University of
Toronto Press, 1963, p. 245, pl. 31e; Max Loehr,
*Relics of Ancient China from the Collection of
Dr. Paul Singer,* New York: Asia Society, 1965,
p. 162, no. 118 (no illus.).

Bronze swords, complete with the hilt-
rope, the scabbard, and a wooden case, have
been found on several occasions by archaeologists in China. Significantly they all be-

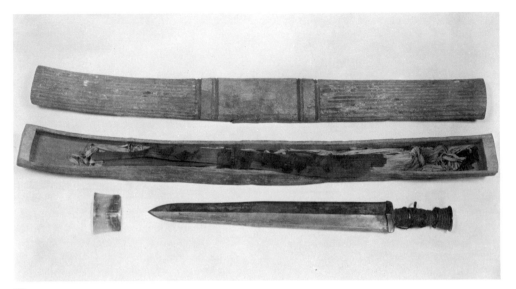

39

fig. 42

longed to the Ch'u culture of the fifth and fourth century B.C. of today's greater Ch'ang-sha area. Among them the set that was unearthed in June 1954 in tomb no. 15 at the southern suburb (Tso-chia-kung Shan) of Ch'ang-sha City is most interesting to compare to the one shown here (fig. 42). The excavated case is also made from a single block of wood and is of similar size—only 7.2 cm. longer than the Singer one. Its cover is treated almost exactly the same as this one: with simple, parallel lines carved all over it except in the center section. According to the archaeological report, there is evidence that silk ropes were used to tie the case together. Presumably the Singer sword case was also tied up in that way. The excavated sword itself was found in perfect condition placed in a black lacquer scabbard that was also in good condition. The sword still had its hilt wound in braided cord, and its two cutting edges have remained sharp. In all other details the Singer sword and the excavated one are the same, except that the latter is much longer, measuring 62 cm. in length. If there is any explanation for the difference between a sword of 42.2 cm. and one 62 cm. long, it should be the one offered by *K'ao-kung-chi,* the earliest Chinese literary reference of bronze swords of the Eastern Chou period. *K'ao-kung-chi,* which was compiled anonymously no later than the second century B.C., divided the Eastern Chou swords into three classes, according to their lengths. The longest swords, with the blade's length five times longer than the hilt, were forged for men of the higher class. Swords with a blade length four times the length of the hilt were for men of the middle class, and when the blade was only three times longer than the hilt, it was for the lower class fellow. While the length of the Singer wooden case is very close to that of the one excavated, the difference of length between the Singer sword and the excavated one may very well be because of each owner's different social status, as suggested by the *K'ao-kung-chi.* According to Professor Shang Ch'en-tso, the hanks of yellowish silk in the sword case exhibited

here are what have been referred to in the Chinese classic *Li-chi* as *fu-jao* (wrapping cloth for swords). The use of the *fu-jao* and the case had certain ceremonial significance in ancient China.

Theoretically, since Chinese bronze swords of this type are of very advanced design, one would surmise that they were produced relatively later than the others shown here (cat. nos. 36-38). However, Chinese archaeological data have shown that this type was fully developed as early as the time of the King Ho-lu of Wu, ca. late sixth to early fifth century B.C., if not even earlier (cat. no. 38). Aesthetically speaking, Chinese swords of later times, especially after the Han dynasty, have never surpassed swords of this type.

References: Wu Ming-shêng, "A wooden coffin tomb of the Warring-States period at Tso-chia-kung shan, Ch'ang-sha" (text in Chinese), *Wen Wu,* no. 12, pp. 5-19; Cultural Relics Committee of the Hunan Province, "Three large graves with wooden chambers excavated at Ch'ang-sha, Hunan" (text in Chinese), *Kaogu Xuebao* 1957, no. 1 pp. 93-96, pl. 2, fig. 6; Peking Historical Museum, *Ch'u Wen-u Chan-lan T'u-lu,* Peking, 1954, pl. 71; Hunan Provincial Museum, "Tomb no. 1 at Liu-ch'eng-ch'iao, Ch'ang-sha" (text in Chinese), *Kaogu Xuebao* 1972, no. 1, pp. 59-72, pl. 14; Ch'eng Yao-t'ien, "T'ao-shih wei chien k'ao," *T'ung-i-lu,* Shanghai: Anhui ts'ung-shu ed., 1933 reprint, ch. 9, 1a-b; Shang Ch'eng-tso, *Ch'ang-sha ku-wu Wen Chien Chi* [Records of cultural relics from the greater Ch'ang-sha area], Nanking: Chin-ling University Press, 1939, ch. 2, 7a-8b; Cultural Department of Hupei Province, "Important cultural relics unearthed from three tombs of the Ch'u State at Chiang-ling, Hupei" (text in Chinese), *Wen Wu,* 1966, no. 5, p. 41, fig. 7.

40

40

Lintel and pediment of a tomb
Five hollow ceramic tiles, painted in ink and colors on a white ground
Han period, end of 1st century B.C.-1st century A.D.; total h. 73.8 cm., w. 240.7 cm.
Museum of Fine Arts, Boston. 25.10-13, Denman Waldo Ross Collection; 25.190, gift of C. T. Loo.

The entire piece, trapezoid in shape, is made up of a pediment, consisting of two triangular and one rectangular piece, and a lintel, consisting of two parts. The center of the rectangular piece is decorated with the modeled head of a ram. The lintel has been cut on both sides after firing, probably in order to secure it to the walls. The entire piece was once covered with a white ground on which the figure scenes had been painted in ink and colors. Especially the rectangular slab has suffered from moisture; it has lost almost all of its painted surface.

A field trip to Lo-yang made by Professor Otto Fischer of Basel University, shortly after these tiles had been acquired by the Boston Museum, led to the discovery of their exact provenance. In August 1926 Fischer visited the antique dealer Liu Ting-fêng in Lo-yang, Honan Province, and received from him a photograph of the tiles, taken shortly after their excavation, as well as a detailed account of the circumstances under which the tiles had been discovered. Liu told Fischer how he had personally excavated (it is more likely that he supervised the excavation of) a large burial mound about eight *li* to the west of Lo-yang, beyond the (Hsi) Chien River, about ten years earlier. For about one year Liu spent his nights secretly digging into the mound until he finally reached the tomb chambers "many meters below the surface," and succeeded in bringing the mortuary objects out. According to Liu's description there were "four oblong chambers, built at varying distances from one another." Each of the chambers had an entrance door with three door posts surmounted by two lintels and with a pediment consisting of three pieces on top. Liu had found no inscription in the tomb. In the chambers he had found a large number of vases and vessels, made of simple gray terra cotta without any decoration or glaze whatsoever. One of the gate pediments was painted on both sides. The five parts of which it consisted were removed and later sold to a dealer in Shanghai, from where they first went to America and then to Paris.

Perhaps because of the language barrier a misunderstanding may have arisen concerning the exact location of the tomb. Instead of "eight *li* to the west of the present Lo-yang, beyond the (Hsi) Chien River" Liu may have referred to a village in the same area that had the words *pa li*, i.e., "eight miles" in its name. A recent Chinese book on Han painting gives the village Pa-li-t'ai, to the west of Lo-yang, as the provenance of the tiles. The Boston *Portfolio of Chinese Paintings* contains the information that the village was named Pa-ch'ing-li. None of these names appear on detailed maps of the area.

Information supplied by C. T. Loo in 1924 allows us to follow the tiles on their subsequent travels around the world. During these years of travel and storage the square central slab with the ram's head became separated from the other pieces. It lost practically all of its painting, much of which had still been quite clearly visible at the time when Liu Ting-fêng had the above-mentioned photograph taken. The slab was identified as part of the pediment shortly after the other tiles had been acquired by the Boston Museum; C. T. Loo presented it to the museum in the same year.

The French sinologue Paul Pelliot and Dr. Denman Waldo Ross, trustee and benefactor

40

40

of the Museum of Fine Arts, were the first to grasp the artistic and archaeological importance of these tiles. John Ellerton Lodge, the curator of the Department of Asiatic Art, did not share their views and wrote to C. T. Loo: "At present, of course, they have the value of rarities, but such a value, as you know, is not likely to be permanent. Other things of the same kind and in a better state of preservation are almost certain to be found." Displaying wise judgment, Dr. Ross refused to take that risk; his generous offer to buy the tiles for the museum decided the outcome of the negotiations. It would take more than thirty years for John Lodge's prediction to come true.

References: Kojiro Tomita, *Portfolio of Chinese Paintings in the Museum (Han to Sung Periods)*, Boston, 1933, pls. 1-8; Otto Fischer, *Die chinesische Malerei der Han-Dynastie,* Berlin: Neff Verlag, 1931, pp. 82-83; Ch'ang Jên-hsia, *Han-hua i-shu yen-chiu,* Shanghai: Shanghai Publishing Co., 1955, caption, pl. 19.

Since 1950 a large number of Han tombs have been excavated in the vicinity of Lo-yang. At Shao-kou, to the northwest of Old Lo-yang, more than five hundred tombs were excavated as early as 1952. It was not until 1957, however, when another group of 170 tombs were excavated in that area, that Chinese archaeologists found a tomb that contained a painted pediment of the same type as the Boston tiles.

Built in a combination of large hollow tiles and smaller bricks, the tomb, to which the excavators assigned the number 61, consists of a large main chamber, two side chambers, and two smaller rooms, connected with the side chambers. The pediment, supported by a central post, acts as a partition between the front and rear sections of the main burial chamber (fig. 43). Like the Boston tiles, the newly discovered pieces are painted on both sides, but the design on the three upper tiles, which constitute the pediment, has been pierced before it was painted. The obverse shows on the triangular sections two symmetrical groups of animals (deer, horses, bears) and supernatural beings. The

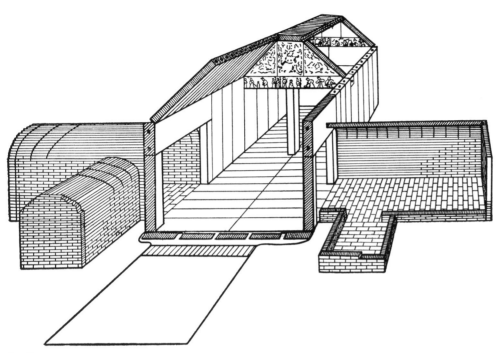

fig. 43

fig. 44

central slab is decorated with a partly effaced design of a somewhat similar type; it includes representations of the Four Directional Animals: phoenix, dragon, tortoise, and tiger (fig. 44). On the reverse, genii riding dragons flank the representation of a gate surmounted by lattice work and five *pi* discs.

The lintel has painted figure scenes on both sides. At least one of these has been definitely identified as an illustration of the story "Three warriors killed by two peaches," recorded in the minor classic *Yen-tzu Ch'un-ch'iu* and sometimes illustrated on Han stone reliefs. Although the style of figure painting is quite closely related to that of the Boston tiles, the newly discovered paintings are remarkable for the dramatic gestures and grotesque facial expressions of some of the figures. In this respect the paintings breathe a spirit that is quite different from the serene mood of the Boston tiles.

Although the newly found pediment has been a topic of considerable discussion in several Chinese journals and even of heated debate in Western publications, not much attention has been given to the new light that the discovery of tomb no. 61 throws on such problems as the function, iconography, style, and date of the Boston tiles.

The Boston pediment depicts a tiger and bear in fierce combat. Although the composition is carefully balanced, the symmetry is much less rigidly maintained than it is on the pediment of tomb no. 61. On each of its triangular sections, the Boston tiles show an official, accompanied by two grooms. In each lower corner crouches a chained animal, a bear on the right and a tiger on the left. These animals seem to be kept in reserve for the actual combat, which was once depicted on the central slab, but which has now become almost totally invisible. The hindlegs of the bear and the tail of the tiger can still be seen on the triangular slabs, and the old photograph taken by Liu Ting-Fêng clearly shows the attacking tiger. Even in the old photograph, however, the bear is already barely discernible. Above each of these attacking animals was the figure of a seated man. Right below the modeled head of a ram in high relief was painted a *t'ao-t'ieh* mask with a ring. Usually, these rings occur in pairs on gateways (as on the reverse of the pediment in tomb no. 61), but the single piece on the Boston tile seems to have been painted there without any thought of its original function.

Otto Fischer was the first to suggest that the scene on the Boston pediment represents an animal fight in the Shang-lin (Superior Forest), an animal park of the Han emperors. This suggestion has been adopted, somewhat hesitatingly, it seems, by Kojiro Tomita. The only scholar to reject this identification has been Carl Hentze. Stressing the symbolic meaning of these animals, he rejected the possibility that such secular, circuslike amusements would have been depicted in a tomb. Assuming that the ram's head faced the south, as it does in most tombs, Hentze pointed out that the tiger is shown to the left of the ram, i.e., in the west, the direction traditionally associated with the tiger.

A recent study by Edward H. Schafer contains a wealth of new information on the animal parks of the Han dynasty, and some of the facts revealed by him tend to reconcile the views of Hentze with the original identification. First of all, it should be pointed out that the animal fight was more than vulgar bear teasing, and was, to a large extent, ceremonial in character. The animal park was a small replica of the realm, and the animals were, therefore, kept in locations corresponding to the directions with which they were associated. Among the livestock in the park, bears and tigers are mentioned specifically. During the Han period there was even a special cage for tigers. As bear and tiger were thought to epitomize strength and valor, a combat between these two animals must have represented the peak of beastly ferocity.

Perhaps most important for our understanding of the iconography of the Boston tiles is that the Lo-yang tiles have an emblematic, symbolic design on the pediment and apparently unrelated figure scenes on the lintel. If the same division of themes applies to the Boston tiles, the men and women who

are shown conversing or otherwise engaged, accompanied by their retinue of servants, are not just visitors to the imperial game preserve but historical characters who make their appearance in illustrations of anecdotes of the same type as "Three warriors killed by two peaches." Unfortunately, however, besides a woman carrying a baby on her back and a servant kneeling with a jar, there are no distinct iconographical clues that would enable us to identify these scenes. A suggestion has been made by Susan Bush that one of the scenes could represent the story of the filial son Lao-lai-tzu, who performed childish pranks in front of his parents. Unfortunately, however, the two persons thought to be his aged parents are both shown holding spears, which would hardly be in keeping with their status and age.

An additional obstacle to the identification of the scenes is their extremely poor state of preservation. The obverse of the lintel was cleaned by William Young of the museum's research laboratory, but the reverse still awaits further treatment. Judging from infrared photographs there does not seem to be much hope that further cleaning might reveal details that could lead to the identification of the scenes. Since there is a preponderance of women on one side and a group consisting mostly of men on the other side of the lintel, one could perhaps suggest that these represent, respectively, Famous Women and Filial Sons. As long as no definite identifications can be made, however, such a clear division of themes remains highly speculative.

The structural resemblance between the two pediments is so close that it seems most likely that both pieces performed the same architectural function. There are, however, a few discrepancies that require further explanation. In tomb no. 61 the ram's head is found inside the tomb on the pediment over the main entrance. This evidence, combined with the oral testimony of Liu Ting-fêng that the Boston pediment was part of the entrance gate of the tomb, would suggest that the Boston tiles may indeed have been part of the entrance gate. The extremely poor state

of preservation of the painting could be the result of continuous contact with sand or clay. On the other hand, it seems rather unlikely that the outside of a tomb would have had any painted decoration at all. In all probability we should not take the words of Liu Ting-fêng literally. From the way he described the tomb as consisting of "four oblong chambers built at varying distances from one another" we could assume that the pediment served as a partition between two parts of a tomb chamber, which Liu considered to be separate rooms. The indentation in the center of the lintel indicates that it was let into the head of the supporting central column. The notches on both ends suggest, not that the ends of the lintel were supported by columns (as Liu seems to suggest), but that they were let into the walls of the tomb. That the entire pediment fitted into a recessed groove in the walls and ceiling of the tomb may be assumed from the fact that there is a noticeable difference between the colors of the edges of the pediment and its other parts.

Perhaps one of the most important aspects of the discovery of tomb no. 61 is that it finally gives us additional evidence for establishing the date of the Boston tiles. Ever since John Ellerton Lodge first questioned the Han date of the tiles, there has been a tendency among scholars to assign the paintings to the end of the Han period or slightly later. The excavators of tomb no. 61, on the other hand, have many more data at their disposal. On the evidence of the hundreds of Han tombs they have investigated, Chinese archaeologists have established that in the Lo-yang area tombs constructed in a combination of hollow tiles and bricks represent a transitional type between earlier tombs, built entirely of hollow tiles, and later tombs, built entirely in brick. Considering also the tomb furniture, they arrived at a date for tomb no. 61 that lies in the first half of the first century B.C. Even with maximum allowance for the differences between the Boston tiles and the pediment from tomb no. 61, it seems possible that the latest possible date of the Boston piece would be the first century A.D. and perhaps even earlier.

References: Jonathan Chaves, "A Han painted tomb at Loyang," *Artibus Asiae* 30 (1968), 5-27; A. Bulling, "Historical Plays in the Art of the Han Period," *Archives of Asian Art* 21 (1967-68), 20-38 (reviewed by A. C. Soper, "All the World's a Stage," *Artibus Asiae* 30 (1968), 249-259); Edward H. Schafer, "Hunting Parks and Animal Enclosures in Ancient China," *Journal of the Economic and Social History of the Orient* 11 (1968), 318-343; Carl Hentze, "Schamanenkronen zur Han-Zeit in Korea," *Ostasiatische Zeitschrift,* n.s. 9 (1933), 160; The Archaeological Team, Bureau of Culture, Honan, "Excavations of a Western Han tomb with wall paintings at Lo-yang" (text in Chinese), *Kaogu Xuebao,* 1964, no. 2, pp. 107-125; Kuo Mo-jo, "An investigation of the wall paintings in a Western Han tomb at Lo-yang" (text in Chinese), *Wên-wu ching-hua,* no. 3, Peking: Hsin-hua shu-tien, 1964, pp. 27-29.

41-42

Ornamental plaques

Glass, covered with an allover design in glass paste and cold pigments

Han period, 2nd century B.C.-2nd century A.D.; each plaque 5.8 x 4.5 cm. (approx.)

A set of 35 pieces: Collection of Dr. Paul Singer

A set of 42 pieces: Museum of Fine Arts, Boston. 47.1057a-ap

The Boston plaques, thin as wafers and arranged in rectangular panels, are covered with barely distinguishable overall designs representing clouds and figures in glass paste relief with the addition of cold pigments. It is not clear how much of the decoration is original. The figures on the Boston plaques do not appear to date from as early a period as the Han dynasty. The Singer set has no added decoration. Each small plaque is pierced with four holes, one in each corner, through which a thread or thin wire was passed to hold the plaques together. As the sets of the Singer collection and the Boston Museum came on the market at approximately the same time and through the same dealer, it is surmised that they may at one time have belonged together.

Of all recent discoveries in China none seems to have been more successful in capturing the imagination of people throughout the world than the find of the two jade suits in the tombs at Man-ch'êng in 1968 (fig. 45). Few people realize, however, that the existence of such jade suits was known to the Chinese throughout history from descriptions in ancient Chinese literary sources. One of these was published in English more than eighty years ago by the Dutch sinologue J. J. M. de Groot in the first volume of his monumental *Religious System of China*. A passage from the *Hsi-ching tsa-chi* (Miscellaneous records of the Western Capital; see cat. no. 45) reads in de Groot's translation: "The sovereigns of the Han Dynasty were in the habit of sending their dead into the tomb with robes adorned with pearls and with boxes of jade stone. These boxes looked like

coats of mail, chains being carved out upon them and inlaid with gold. The boxes used in the case of the emperor Wu (140-87 B.C.) were all inlaid on the lid with figures of dragons, phoenixes and tortoise-dragons. Hence they were called at that time 'dragon-boxes of jade'." De Groot can hardly be blamed for his failure to amend his corrupt text from "chains being carved out upon them and inlaid with gold" to "sewn together with gold thread," for at that time no Westerner had laid eyes upon a Han tomb or its mortuary furniture.

From the number of references to "jade clothes sewn with gold thread" and "jade boxes" in Han and later literature, it is quite evident that such suits were much more widely used than would seem to be suggested by this exceptional find at Man-ch'êng and by a third piece found at Hsü-chou, Kiangsu Province, in 1970. Moreover, from a passage in the section on ceremonies in the *Later Han History* it is apparent that jade suits varied in accordance with the rank of the deceased. The principal difference was to be found in the threads with which the jade pieces were sewn together. Only the emperor was entitled to have his jade suit sewn with gold thread. The highest ranking princes and feudal lords were entitled to silver thread, princesses to mere copper wire. This sumptuary rule is first mentioned two centuries after the funeral of Liu Shêng and Tou Wan. That both of them were buried in jade suits sewn with gold thread should, therefore, not be seen as a contravention of a law that may not even have existed at the time. It is a well-established fact, however, that sumptuary laws were often rendered ineffective by extravagance, inspired by the Confucian precept of filial piety. The jade suit found at Hsü-chou was sewn together with silver thread.

That it took so long before an actual example of a jade suit was discovered and restored is undoubtedly because the bootleg excavators of the past lacked archaeological skill and training, as well as the time, patience, and opportunity to salvage a complete

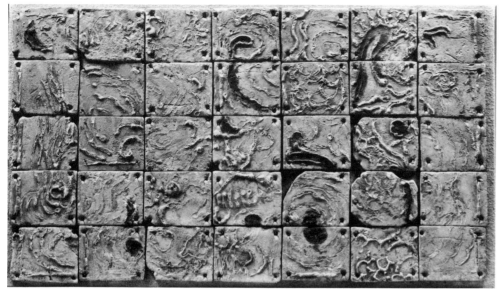

41

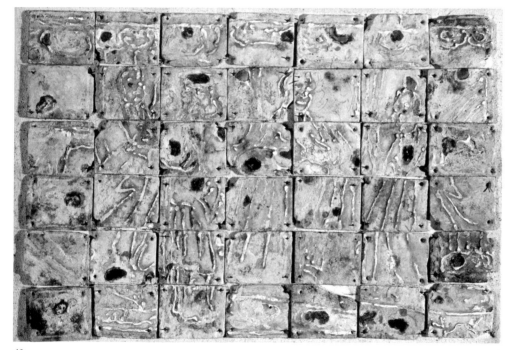

42

fig. 45

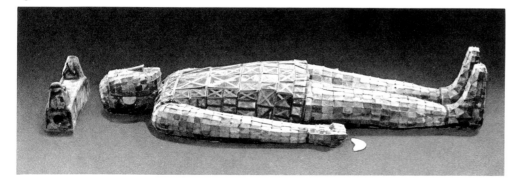

suit. Instead, they merely scooped up the jade plaques and sold them to the dealers, together with other archaeological odds and ends.

The glass plaques shown in this exhibition may have been part of a similar suit worn by a prominent Chinese of somewhat less exalted rank than a prince or feudal lord. Although sumptuary laws do not specifically mention the use of glass, it would seem to be the logical substitute for the in all probability more expensive jade, as it does not require the laborious sawing and drilling of the latter. Moreover, the Chinese word *yü*, which we translate as "jade," is often used as a generic term, covering a much wider range of materials including glass as well as marble. The glass paste and cold pigments may have been a less expensive substitute for the engraving that decorated the jade suit of Emperor Wu.

From the detailed description of the structure of the jade suits published by the Archaeological Institute of Academia Sinica, it appears that Liu Shêng's suit was made out of 2,498 plaques, whereas that of Tou Wan consisted of 2,160 pieces. The thin plaques vary in size, the largest rectangular plaque measuring 4.5 by 3.5 cm., the smallest 1.5 by 1 cm. The suit was made in twelve separate parts, two for the head, two for the body, and one for each of the arms and hands as well as the legs and feet (fig. 46). Apparently each part was made to measure. This, at least, is what we may conclude from the restored suit of Liu Shêng, which shows an unmistakable *embonpoint*, suggesting that in addition to being fond of wine and women (a matter of official record), he may also have been a gourmand.

In one other respect the glass plaques may have been cheaper to use than those of jade. Their size is considerably larger than that of the largest jade pieces. In view of the complex technique of tying the plaques, of which the excavators of the Man-ch'êng suits have given a careful description, the use of larger plaques must have constituted a very considerable saving, not only in the number of

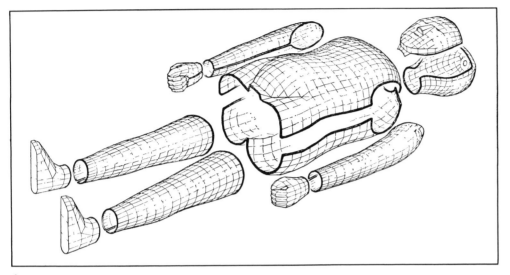

fig. 46

pieces needed but especially in labor spent on sewing them together.

The philosopher and alchemist Ko Hung wrote in his *Pao-p'u-tzu:* "If gold and jade are put in the nine orifices the result is that the corpse will not decompose." Although he wrote three or four centuries after Liu Shêng's death, Ko Hung must have repeated a much older belief, for a study of the Man-ch'êng jade suits reveals that the same method was adopted for the burial of Liu Shêng. By placing jades in mouth and ears and on the eyes, as well as by dressing the corpse in jade the Chinese hoped to prevent the decomposition of the corpse. The Taoist historian T'ao Hung-ching (A.D. 452-536) believed in these preservative properties of jade and gold when he wrote "When an ancient grave is dug up and the corpse is found looking as if it were still alive, then there is bound to be a great amount of gold and jade inside as well as on the corpse. The laws of the Han dynasty required that kings and princes be buried in clothes decorated with pearls [perhaps, beads] and in jade boxes in order to prevent the decomposition of the body." Archaeology has now supplied convincing proof to the contrary: the bodies of Liu Shêng and Tou Wan had turned into dust almost without leaving a trace. Deprived

of the support of the bodies inside, the suits had completely collapsed.

The custom of providing the rich and members of the nobility with jade suits continued throughout the Han period, as is indicated by scattered references to them in biographies, contained in the official histories of the Han Empire. Shortly after the fall of Han in 222 the ruler of Wei prohibited further use of costumes adorned with pearls and jade boxes. There is no evidence that this order was disobeyed. From this we may conclude that the custom of placing the dead in jade suits began and ended during the reign of the imperial house of the Han.

References: The Man-ch'êng Excavation Team of the Archaeological Institute of Academia Sinica, "Brief record of the excavation of the Han tombs at Man-ch'êng" (text in Chinese), *Kaogu,* 1972, no. 1, pp. 8-18; Department of Arts and Crafts, The Archaeological Institute of Academia Sinica, "The conservation and restoration of the "Jade costumes sewn with gold thread" from the Han tombs at Man-ch'êng" (text in Chinese), *Kaogu,* 1972, no. 2, pp. 39-47; Ku Yen-wen, "Han tombs at Mancheng," *New Archaeological Finds in China,* Peking: Foreign Languages Press, 1972, pp. 13-19; J. J. M. de Groot, *The Religious System of China,* Leiden: Brill, vol. 1, 1892, pp. 273-374 and vol. 2, 1894, p. 401.

43

Po-shan-lu ("hill censer")
Gilt bronze
Eastern Han period, ca. 2nd century A.D.;
h. 13.3 cm.
Anonymous loan

The censer consists of a round receptacle
with a conical cover in the shape of a mountain with many peaks. The stem on which
the censer stands has four petals. It is supported by a dragon, coiled around the center
of a circular dish, which acts as the base of
the piece. The entire censer is made of gilt
bronze, which until a recent cleaning, was
still covered with the earth from which it
had been excavated many years ago. The
cleaning revealed that the stylized mountain
landscape is inhabited by animals, among
which can be recognized a tiger, a monkey,
and a tortoise.

44

Po-shan-lu ("hill censer")
Bronze, covered with green patina
Eastern Han period, ca. 2nd century A.D.;
h. 9.7 cm.
Ashmolean Museum, Oxford, Sir Herbert
Ingram Collection. 1956.901

The pierced lid of globular shape is surmounted by a small figure of a phoenix and
is attached to the receptacle by means of a
hinge. The four petals and the modeled
dragon resemble those of cat. no. 43.

45

Po-shan-lu ("hill censer")
Bronze, covered with green patina
Western Han period,
late 2nd-1st century B.C.; h. 24 cm.
William Rockhill Nelson Gallery of Art,
Kansas City, Missouri

A figure of a man, kneeling on the back of a
recumbent dragon, holds in his raised right
hand the bowl-shaped receptacle of the incense burner. The bowl is covered with a
removable top in the shape of a mountain
inhabited by immortals and animals, which

43

103

are shown reticulated or standing out in low relief.

This very fine piece, formerly in the collection of Mrs. Christian Holmes, resembles closely a slightly larger piece of the same type (h. 28.6 cm.) in the Museum of Lü-shun (the former Port Arthur), Liao-ning Province.

Published: Royal Academy of Arts, London, *International Exhibition of Chinese Art,* London, 1935, no. 394; *Ryojun Hakubutsukan Zuroku,* Tokyo: Zauhō Press, 1943, pl. 17, fig. 8.

The origin of "hill censers" in bronze or pottery can be traced to the Western Han period, as was pointed out by Berthold Laufer, the first Western scholar to make a study of these pieces. The type seems to have been developed out of the Late Chou vessels of the *tou* class, which have a tall stem and a spreading foot similar to those of many hill censers.

Berthold Laufer collected large amounts of archaeological material from the Han period during his years of residence in Sian between 1901 and 1904. However, in keeping with the traditions prevailing among Chinese as well as Western scholars of that time, he did not collect information on the site where and the circumstances under which these pieces were found. Instead, he concentrated on research based on literary sources, a task in which he achieved considerable success. Thirty-eight years later, Archibald Wenley, still adopting the same approach, was able to correct some of the conclusions that Laufer had reached in his pioneer study.

One of the principal points made by Laufer and Wenley is that the name *po-shan-lu* does not seem to date from the time in which the hill censer made its first appearance. Inscribed examples use such circumlocutions as a "bronze tripod of one peck capacity with a tray below" and fail to mention the name by which these pieces came to be known later. Wenley quotes literary works of the fourth century as the first to mention the name. The term occurs twice in the *Hsi-ching tsa-chi* (Miscellaneous records of the Western Capital), a work purporting to be of Han date but considered by many to be

a sixth century fabrication. Since information from this dubious source has been repeatedly confirmed by recent excavations (see cat. nos. 42, 46), the possibility that the term *po-shan-lu* could date back to the Han period should perhaps not be ruled out altogether.

Another point that has led to considerable speculation in the past is the interpretation of the symbolism expressed in these pieces. Laufer, who translated its name as "brazier of the vast mountain," was the first to suggest that the mountain represents P'êng-lai, the mythical abode of the Taoist immortals. The belief in this distant island played an important role in the folklore of the Han period. Chavannes saw in the central peak, surrounded by lower peaks on the cardinal points, a possible representation of the axial mountain Sumeru, the pivot of the universe in Indian cosmology.

One traditional Chinese explanation is that the *po-shan-lu* represents Mount Hua. According to the philosopher Han Fei-tzu (third century B.C.), King Chao of Ch'in challenged the Spirits of Heaven in a game of *liu-po* on Mount Hua. In reference to this event the mountain was renamed (Liu-)Po-shan. Instead of the translation "vast mountain" we should, therefore, perhaps opt for "gambling mountain." Whatever the exact symbolism of the *po-shan-lu* may be, it is evident that it represents a mountain where man can meet the Spirits of Heaven or pitch his skill against that of the gods, a mountain inhabited by spirits and by such animals as those associated with the Four Directions.

Recent excavations have brought to light new material that supplements the information previously gathered from literary sources alone. Laufer's conclusion that the hill censer was an invention dating from about the time of the Han Emperor Wu-ti (140-86 B.C.), though not definitely confirmed by excavations, was probably very near the truth. None of the few tombs dating from the early years of the Western Han dynasty seems to contain a hill censer. The first datable examples of the *po-shan-lu* came from the re-

cently excavated tombs at Man-ch'êng, in which were buried Wu-ti's elder brother Liu Shêng (died 113 B.C.) and his wife Tou Wan. Among the twenty-eight hundred objects recovered from these lavishly furnished tombs are two hill censers. The example from Liu Shêng's tomb, made without a dish, has an inlaid decoration in gold, somewhat similar to but slightly later than that of a hill censer in the Freer Gallery of Art, Washington, D.C.

The *po-shan-lu* from Tou Wan's tomb is closely related to the piece from Kansas City exhibited here. It is supported by the same type of man seated on an identical dragon. The decoration on the reticulated hill-shaped cover is bolder, but this may be the result of the most important difference between the two pieces—the difference in size. The example from Tou Wan's tomb (fig. 48) measures 32.4 cm. in height, exceeding the size of comparable pieces in other collections by at least one-third.

Another important difference between the

fig. 47

po-shan-lu from Tou Wan's tomb and that of the Nelson Gallery is that the latter lacks the round dish. One would be inclined to assume that the dish of the Nelson Gallery piece was lost, if it were not that the same part is missing from the piece of exactly the same type in the Lü-shun Museum. Especially during the Western Han period *po-shan-lu* were sometimes made without a dish, as the gold-inlaid piece from Liu Shêng's tomb proves. It is quite possible, therefore, that during this early period the dish was sometimes added and sometimes omitted.

Although these two splendid examples provide us with definite proof of the existence of hill censers during the Western Chou period, the number of firmly datable examples is not yet large enough to enable us to reconstruct the typological development of the *po-shan-lu* during the Han and later periods. It is surprising how small the number is of pottery hill censers found in Han tombs excavated in the vicinity of Loyang. Among the more than one thousand burials at the cemetery of Sha-kou on the southern slope of Mount Mang, excavated in 1953, only three hill censers were found. The 217 tombs excavated near Ch'i-li-ho yielded only two hill censers.

The censers in the Ashmolean Museum and the private collection have two distinct features, which may be compared with inscribed or recently excavated examples. The first is the quatrefoil on the stem. This typical Han motif occurs on several other hill censers in bronze. One of these is a piece excavated in 1956 by farmers from a tomb in the Nan-yang area (Honan Province). Although the find has not been extensively published, the information available suggests that the tomb may date from the early Eastern Han period. This piece is quite similar to a hill censer of unknown provenance in the Oshita collection, Takatsuki *(Shina Kodō Seika, Japan,* vol. 6, no. 507). Another example in a Japanese collection bears an inscription containing a date corresponding to 64 B.C. *(Sekai Kōkogaku Taikei,* vol. 7, fig. 102).

44

fig. 48

The second distinguishing feature is the coiling dragon supporting the stem of the censer. Many hill censers with a spreading foot have the shape of a dragon engraved or cast in it, but the two pieces exhibited here are among the few in which the dragon has been fully modeled.

Among the recently excavated pieces illustrated in Chinese archaeological literature there is only one example of a hill censer that combines these two features. In January 1958 the archaeologist Liu Kuei-fang was sent to the village of Fang-pei-ts'un (I-hsien, Shantung Province) to investigate reports of the excavation by farmers of a tomb in that area. He found a large number of Han mortuary objects, which had been dug up by the farmers, but the actual mound had already been leveled, and there was no way to ascertain the structure and date of the tomb. Among the objects recovered from it were three pieces of gilt bronze and more than a dozen bronzes. Though not gilt like some of the other pieces, a bronze hill censer, measuring 29 cm. in height (fig. 47), is closely related to the pieces on exhibition. The coiling dragon is modeled in the round; it supports a stem decorated with a quatrefoil. The lid of the censer is provided with a hinge and is surmounted by the figure of a phoenix.

Since a gilt bronze foot measure found in this same tomb corresponds in size to the standard dimension adopted in the sixth year of the Chien-ch'u era (A.D. 81), Liu Kuei-fang is inclined to date the find in the later years of the Eastern Han period (ca. 2nd century A.D.). If we assume that the modeling of the dragon represents an advance from the engraved representation of this animal on a spreading foot, pieces provided with this feature could well date from the second century of our era.

References: Ku Yen-wen, "Han tombs at Man-cheng," *New Archaeological Finds in China*, Peking: Foreign Languages Press, 1972, pp. 13-19; Liu Kuei-fang, "Gilt bronze vessels and other cultural relics unearthed from an ancient tomb at I-hsien, Shantung" (text in Chinese), *Wen Wu*, 1956, no. 12, pp. 34-38; Cultural Bureau Shan-tung Province and Shantung Provincial Museum, comp., *Shantung Wên-wu Hsüan-chi* [Selected cultural relics from Shantung], Peking: Wen-Wu Press, 1959, fig. 147; Liu Hsing-ch'ang and Chang Chu-chao, "Investigation of a Han tomb at Po-li-hsi-ts'un, Nan-yang, Honan" (text in Chinese), *Kaogu*, 1957, no. 6, pp. 42-43; for information on the name and meaning of *po-shan shan-lu* see Berthold Laufer, *Chinese Pottery of the Han Dynasty*, Leiden: Brill, 1909, pp. 174-198; A. G. Wenley, "The Question of the Po-Shan-Hsiang-Lu," *Archives of the Chinese Art Society of America* 3 (1948-49), 5-12.

46
Lamp in the shape of a ram *(yang-têng)*
Bronze with an engraved design, covered by
green patina
Western Han period, 2nd-1st century B.C.;
h. 9.5 cm.
William Rockhill Nelson Gallery of Art,
Kansas City, Missouri

Bronze lamps in the shape of a recumbent
ram seem to be among the most common
types of mortuary gifts in bronze of the Han
period. The lamp from the Nelson Gallery,
with its robust modeling and subtle engraving, is one of the finest among a large number
of comparable pieces, including examples in
the Musée Guimet, Paris, the Rietberg Museum, Zürich, and the Singer collection.
Another fine example in the Berlin State
Museums disappeared in the aftermath of
the Second World War.

Of all these lamps the hollow back is a
hinged cover, which can be turned upward
to act as a receptacle for a lamp. In spite of
the considerable number of pieces of this
type in Western collections, no firm date can
be attached to any of them. An exception is a
now lost example, of which a woodcut illustration is published in the archaeological
catalogue *Chin-shih-so* (chin, vol. 3). The
lamp bears an inscription containing a date
corresponding to 49 B.C. The date is preceded by the words: "Great riches, honor and
prosperity should give you lasting hap-
piness." This inscription is in keeping with
the auspicious symbolism associated with the
ram. As the Chinese graph for ram, *yang*,
resembles the word *hsiang*, i.e., "auspicious,"
the ram was considered an animal of good
fortune, fit to be placed in effigy in the tombs
of the dead (see also cat. no. 40).

Published: Royal Academy of Arts, *International
Exhibition of Chinese Art,* London, 1935, no.
572; Martin Feddersen, *Chinesisches Kunstge-
werbe,* Braunschweig: Klinkhardt & Biermann,
1955, p. 141; M. R. Allen, "Early Chinese
Lamps," *Oriental Art* 2 (1950), 139, fig. 12.

It comes somewhat as a surprise that the
large number of excavated tombs dating
from the Han period yielded only a few

46

fig. 49

isolated examples of the *po-shan-lu* and even fewer lamps in the form of a ram. One of the very few lamps found in recent years was excavated from a Han tomb at Tung-kuan, Ch'ü-fu County, Shantung Province. This lamp, which measures 10.3 cm. in height, is of exactly the same type as the pieces in Western collections. The most remarkable, as well as the only datable example comes from the tomb of Liu Shêng (155-113 B.C.; see cat. nos. 42 and 45). The ram from this tomb (fig. 49) lacks the engraved decoration and the goatee and is almost double the size (h. 18.5 cm.) of the Nelson Gallery piece.

Practically all funerary objects from the tombs of Liu Shêng and Tou Wan are remarkable for their combination of large size and high quality. It is obvious, therefore, that the tradition according to which the status of the deceased was reflected in the size, number, and quality of the mortuary gifts existed already during Han times. As the brother of the Emperor Wu Ti (141-87 B.C.), Liu Shêng was certainly entitled to funerary gifts of the finest quality and the largest size. Comparable objects in Western collections, such as the *po-shan-lu* in the Freer Gallery of Art, the *po-shan-lu* from the Nelson Gallery (cat. no. 45), and this lamp in the shape of a ram, although all of superb quality, are invariably smaller than their counterparts in these two tombs. It is reasonable to conclude, therefore, that the bootleg excavators of the past failed to find a tomb of comparable importance.

It is possible that this is the result of the effective measures taken to prevent illegal entry into these tombs. The *Hsi-ching tsa-chi* (Miscellaneous records of the Western Capital), a historical source of uncertain date and often doubted veracity, states that when, during the Han dynasty, the tomb of King Ai of Wei (third century B.C.) was broken into, it was discovered that this tomb was protected by molten iron, which had been poured over it. It took three days of boring and chiseling before the tomb could be entered. Such a fanciful story is apt to be dismissed as archaeological folklore. As it turns out, however, it was exactly by this method that the tombs of Liu Shêng and his wife were protected. The iron was not poured over the tomb itself, but the doors at the ends of the passages leading to them were sealed off by pouring molten iron between two parallel brick walls. By this method a wall of iron was created in order to ensure that these grandees of the Han Empire could rest in peace forever.

References: Shantung Provincial Museum, *Shantung wên-wu hsüan-chi,* Peking: Wen Wu Press, 1959, figs. 144-145; Ku Yen-wen, "Han tombs at Mancheng," *New Archaeological Finds in China,* Peking: Foreign Language Press, 1972, pp. 13-19; J. J. M. de Groot, *The Religious System of China,* vol. 2, Leiden: Brill, 1894, p. 397.

47
Phoenix lamp
Bronze, green patina
Western Han period, dated in accordance
with 28 B.C., h. 18.9 cm.
Royal Ontario Museum, Toronto, Bishop
W. C. White Collection. 933.12.124

The bronze lamp consists of a shallow, round dish held in the beak of a phoenix standing on the back of a tortoise; with neck outstretched, the bird is poised for flight. On the rim of the dish is an engraved inscription stating that this phoenix lamp was made as the second of a series intended for use in the imperial palace; it gives a date corresponding to 28 B.C. and the weight of the lamp as one catty (sixteen ounces) and fourteen ounces. A *po-shan-lu* with the same type of animal support is in the Avery Brundage Collection.

The phoenix lamp is said to have come from Ch'ang-an (Sian), and, as Bishop William Charles White and Maude Rex Allen have pointed out, it was there that the Han palace was located, in which lived in seclusion the legendary beauty Chao-chün. Steadfastly refusing to bribe the court painter commissioned to do the portraits of all the ladies in the imperial harem, Chao-chün was portrayed in a most unflattering way, with the result that the emperor gave her in marriage to a chieftain of the Huns. Bishop White and Mrs. Allen believe the phoenix lamp may have been used in the women's apartments of the palace by the princesses who were the companions of this famous heroine; but the inscription, part of which is difficult to understand, unfortunately does not seem to bear out this romantic thought.

Published: *Illustrated London News,* April 4, 1936, pl. 1; Maude Rex Allen, "Early Chinese Lamps," *Oriental Art* 2 (1950), p. 139, no. 16; *Chinese Art in the Royal Ontario Museum,* Toronto, 1972, no. 64; René-Yvon Lefebvre d'Argencé, *Ancient Chinese Bronzes in the Avery Brundage Collection,* San Francisco: M. H. De Young Museum Society, 1966, pl. 55, p. 120.

Although inscribed Han bronzes have been known and admired since Sung times, excavations in recent years have brought to light a considerable amount of new material. Closest in date to the Toronto phoenix lamp is a hoard of nine vessels, found in September 1962 at the village of Ta-chüan-ts'un, Yu-yü County, Shansi Province. Five of the vessels were inscribed with a date corresponding to 26 B.C., only two years later than the Toronto phoenix lamp. One of these was a huge (diam. 65.5 cm.) cauldron on legs in animal shape, with a gilt and painted decoration of animals, including an elephant and a camel. From an artistic point of view the most important piece is a vessel for warming wine of the cylindrical shape formerly called *lien* with a vivid animal decor in relief.

Another Han bronze hoard of extraordinary interest was found at San-chiao-chên in the western suburbs of Sian, not far from the place where once stood the celebrated A-fang Palace. The twenty-two pieces, found in December 1961, include basins, jars, tripods, and bells. In accordance with Han customs, most have inscriptions indicating their weight and, in the case of vessels, their volume. The inscriptions often mention a serial number, the name of the maker, and the date of manufacture. One of the tripods bears an inscription with a date corresponding to 51 B.C., but most pieces seem to have been made in 19 and 18 B.C. Of special interest for the study of Han standards of weight and cubic measurements is a comparative table drawn up by the excavators. It lists the weight and volume as indicated by the inscriptions, the weight in catties and ounces according to modern Chinese standards, and the weight and volume of each unit of measurement. For the weight some of the slight discrepancies may be attributed to a different degree of corrosion of the metal; but this, of course, does not apply to the cubic measurements. A phoenix lamp from the tomb of Tou-wan (see cat. nos. 41-46) represents the same motif in an earlier form (fig. 50).

fig. 50

References: Kuo Yung, "Western Han bronze vessels excavated at Yu-yü County, Shansi Province," *Wen Wu,* 1963, no. 11, pp. 4-12; The Cultural Committee of Sian City, "A Western Han bronze hoard discovered at Kao-yao-ts'un, San-chiao-chên, Sian," *Kaogu,* 1963, no. 2, pp. 62-70.

47

48

Model of a watchtower
Pottery covered with a green iridescent glaze
Han period, 2nd century A.D.; h. 88 cm.
William Rockhill Nelson Gallery of Art,
Kansas City, Missouri

The tower consists of three stories, each of which is provided with a balcony and large overhanging eaves, supported at the corners by diagonally slanting brackets. All corners of the eaves are decorated with large quatrefoils, two of which have been added to the ridge of the roof as acroteria. On each balcony have been placed three figures; some of these obviously represent soldiers on guard duty, as they are armed with crossbows. Like most other architectural models of this type, this tower consists of three separate pieces placed on top of one another.

This exceptionally fine model was acquired by the Nelson Gallery in 1934 as part of a set of twenty-one pottery models of houses, farm implements, and cooking stoves, as well as figurines representing men and animals. As all are covered with an identical glaze, the claim that all these pieces belong together is most likely to be correct. At the time of the sale the dealer gave the city of Shan-hsien, Honan Province, as its provenance.

Published: Kadokawa Shoten, ed., *A Pictorial Encyclopedia of the Oriental Arts, China,* vol. 1, New York: Crown Publishers, 1969, color pl. 35.

Shan-hsien, on the south bank of the Yellow River, close to the border with Shansi Province and the confluence with the Wei River, has long been known for its Han tumuli. The provenance given by the dealer for this large mortuary set was therefore not an unlikely one. However, not until Chinese archaeologists made an important discovery in the spring of 1972 could definite confirmation of the provenance of the Kansas City set be obtained.

Although the discovery is of such recent date that even a preliminary report has not yet appeared, the inclusion of some pieces found in the course of this excavation in the Chinese archaeological exhibition in Japan

allows us to draw certain conclusions. At least three Han tombs, dating from the middle of the second century A.D., were discovered near Chang-wan in Ling-pao County, Honan Province. Tomb no. 3 yielded a pottery model of a house (fig. 51), which, although larger in size and provided with a slightly extended first floor section, is virtually identical with the Nelson Gallery model. The bracketing system, the quatrefoil decoration, as well as the armed soldiers are all of exactly the same type. Moreover, Ling-pao County is only a short distance from Shan-hsien. It is, therefore, quite possible that the two models are not only from the same period but even from the same workshop.

The excavation of large pottery models of towers has confirmed the impression that this type of architecture is largely restricted to the northern regions of China, although a few have turned up as far south as Kiangsu. During the same period the houses in southern tombs reflect the architecture of those areas where the need for armed protection against raiding nomads did not exist, and where the semitropical and monsoon climate required architecture of a different type (see cat. no. 27).

References: *Archaeological Treasures Excavated in the People's Republic of China* (exhibition catalogue), Tokyo/Kyoto, National Museum, 1973, no. 105; *Asahi Graph,* June 20, 1973, p. 71.

fig. 51

48

49
Seated man (tomb figurine)
Pottery covered with a green iridescent glaze
Han period, 2nd century A.D.; h. 19.5 cm.,
w. 13.3 cm.
William Rockhill Nelson Gallery of Art,
Kansas City, Missouri

The seated man is clad in a flowing robe with wide sleeves; he wears a tall headdress. His hands are extended as if he is applauding. This gesture has been interpreted as an indication that the figurine may represent a singer or a musician, clapping to the beat of the music.

The figurine is part of a mortuary set, consisting of twenty-one pieces, all of which were acquired by the Nelson Gallery, Kansas City, in 1934. The set was said to have been excavated near Shan-hsien, Honan Province (see cat. no. 48).

Published: Kadokawa Shoten, ed., *A Pictorial Encyclopedia of the Oriental Arts, China,* vol. 1, New York: Crown Publishers, 1969, pl. 135.

Tomb no. 3 at Ling-pao, which yielded the close parallel to the Nelson Gallery's model of a house (cat. no. 48), also provided a convincing answer to the question as to what kind of activity this musician, or singer, is engaged in. The piece bears a striking resemblance to one of two figurines on a pedestal found in tomb no. 3. Between the two figures is a rectangular board, or table, upon which are laid out six sticks. This number indicates that the two men are engaged in a game of *liu-po* ("sixes") (fig. 52). During the Warring States and Han periods, this game enjoyed considerable popularity, but it later lapsed into complete oblivion, except in Korea, where it seems to have survived in a somewhat modified form. The rules of the *liu-po* game are no longer known, but one learns from ancient literary sources that it was played with six sticks and twelve checker pieces.

In the mortuary set from Ling-pao two of the checker pieces are still in the game; they are placed upon a square board next to the six sticks. Just as our game of chess uses the

secular metaphor of kings and warfare, the game of *liu-po,* in keeping with the spirit of the times, seems to have employed cosmological symbolism. This is not apparent from the game as it is represented here but can be seen much more clearly on the sculptural representation of the *liu-po* game found last year in a Han tomb at Ma-chü-tzu, Wu-wei County, Kansu Province. In that tomb two seated male figurines, carved in wood, were found with a *liu-po* board placed between them. The patterns on the board resemble the so-called TLV patterns on Chinese mirrors and sundials, which employ a similar cosmic symbolism.

Whether the gestures of the *liu-po* players from the Ling-pao tomb are meant to express gamblers' passion or specific hand signals connected with this game is not known. A rubbing from a stone slab in a Szechwan tomb shows two celestial beings striking a similar pose (see Michael Sullivan, *An Introduction to Chinese Art,* Berkeley: University of California Press, 1961, pl. 45). The wooden figures from Wu-wei make gestures that are quite different; one of them is shown in the act of placing a checker piece on the board.

Although a complete inventory of the Ling-pao tombs has not yet been published, there can be little doubt that the mortuary set in Kansas City and the recently excavated pieces from Ling-pao are all products of the same period and region, possibly even of the same workshop. Perhaps further comparative study of the Ling-pao and Shan-hsien sets will reveal other examples of what seems to be a typical illustration of the difference in results gained by clandestine digging and scientific excavation. It is not known with certainty whether the Kansas City set of twenty-one pieces represents the total inventory of the Shan-hsien tomb. The possibility exists that the dealer sold other objects from the same tomb piecemeal prior to the sale of the set. In view of the perfect condition of the most fragile pieces of the set, it does not seem likely that the tomb has sustained heavy damage. The loss of the other figure and the

stand belonging to the *liu-po* set may therefore perhaps be attributed to surreptitious or hurried excavation. In all probability the rare *liu-po* set was not recognized for what it really represented and was broken up into two "musicians" and one "stand." The complete piece of this type of mortuary sculpture brought to light by the recent excavations at Ling-pao is of great documentary value for the study of ancient Chinese games.

It is possible that mortuary sets of *liu-po* players were a specialty of west Honan. Another complete set is in the British Museum; it was described by William Watson as "figures of men playing a game." In the display in that museum a figure of a guard has been placed next to the set as a kibitzer, a pastime that has not shared the fate of the rules of the *liu-po* game itself.

References: *Archaeological Treasures Excavated in the People's Republic of China* (exhibition catalogue), Tokyo/Kyoto, National Museum, 1973, no. 102; *Asahi Graph,* June 20, 1973, pp. 70-71; The Kansu Provincial Museum, "Brief report of the excavation of three Han tombs at Ma-chü-tzu, Wu-wei County" (text in Chinese), *Wen Wu,* 1972, no. 12, pp. 9-23; for information and literaure on *liu-po* see Schuyler Camman, "Significant Patterns on Chinese Bronze Mirrors," *Archives of the Chinese Art Society of America* 9 (1955), p. 56, note 28; William Watson, *Handbook on the Collections of Early Chinese Antiquities,* London: British Museum, 1963, pl. 47.

fig. 52

49

50

50

Dancer (tomb figurine)
Gray pottery, painted in white and red
Eastern Han period, ca. A.D. 100; h. 15.2 cm.
Collection of Dr. Paul Singer

The figure strikes a dancing pose with the right hand raised, the face turned to the right, and the left hand resting on the raised right thigh. Judging from the style of hairdo the figurine probably represents a woman. Modeled by hand and shaped with the spatula, this figurine is a typical example of the lively realism that characterizes mortuary sculpture of the Han period.

Published: Max Loehr, *Relics of Ancient China from the Collection of Dr. Paul Singer,* New York: Asia Society, 1965, no. 142; for a similar piece see Kobayashi Taiichirō, *Kantō kozoku to meiki dōgu,* Kyoto: Ichijō Shobō, 1947, pls. 62-63.

51

Standing man (tomb figurine)
Gray pottery with traces of white and red paint
Eastern Han period, ca. A.D. 100; h. 8.1 cm.
Collection of Dr. Paul Singer

The figure stands with his right hand raised as if signaling to someone in the distance. The right arm looks as if it were cut off, but this treatment of the arm, which can also be observed in cat. no. 50, seems to be common among figurines of this type. In his left hand he holds a bird, possibly a duck. Perhaps the figurine is meant to represent a beater of a hunting party, signaling to his master that he has found the bird.

The two figurines exhibited here both come from the collection of Emanuel Gran, a longtime resident of Shanghai. This Old China Hand conceived of the idea of bypassing the local art market by posting a man at the Shanghai railway station. This man would approach farmers as they arrived in town, carrying the antiques they had excavated from their land in order to dispose of them in the city. By buying these pieces the collector acquired many groups of objects of

fig. 53

fig. 54

51

the same provenance (see also cat. no. 14). Such pieces are quite rare in collections that have been acquired piece by piece from different sources.

That these two small figurines must have the same origin is evident from the fact that two almost identical pieces were found together in a tomb at the village of Ku-lu-kou, Hsin-an County, Honan Province (figs. 53-54). In spite of a slight difference in height (the dancer from Ku-lu-kou measures only 10.4 cm.), there can be little doubt that these two pieces both came from a similar tomb. The figure of the huntsman was probably produced by means of a mold, in which case there is a likelihood that more pieces of this type will be found. The dancer, on the other hand, was individually modeled. The close similarity between these two pieces suggests that they date from the same period and that they may have come from the same area or even the same workshop. Unfortunately, the tomb at Ku-lu-kou village was damaged to the extent that no firm conclusions as to its date could be drawn from the ruins. On the basis of the style of the objects found in the collapsed structure the excavators have dated the find in the middle of the Eastern Han period. This conclusion is confirmed by the excavation of tomb no. 23 at Shao-kou near Lo-yang, where figurines resembling the dancer were found.

References: The Archaeological Team of the Honan Bureau of Culture, "A Han tomb at Ku-lu-kou, Hsin-an County, Honan Province" (text in Chinese), Kaogu, 1966, no. 3, pp. 133-134, 137; The Loyang Area Archaeological Team, Lo-yang Shao-kou Han-mu [Han tombs at Shao-kou, Lo-yang], Peking: Science Press, 1959, pl. 38.

52

Vase
Bronze with incised decoration, green and brown patina
Han period, 1st century B.C.-
1st century A.D.; h. 23.3 cm.
Collection of Dr. Paul Singer

The bulbous body of the vessel, supported by a flaring foot, has three broad bands of horizontal concave fluting around the shoulder, which curves into a long, slender, and cylindrical neck. The vessel is decorated with an incised design of animals, represented in an undulating landscape against a striated background. The bands of animal decor alternate with bands of sawtooth and diamond patterns.

Published: Max Loehr, *Relics of Ancient China from the Collection of Dr. Paul Singer*, New York: Asia Society, 1965, no. 122.

53

Miniature *pien-hu*
Bronze with incised decoration
Han period, 1st century B.C.-
1st century A.D.; h. 7.8 cm.
Collection of Dr. Paul Singer

The incised decoration consists of sawtooth and diamond patterns and a representation of confronting animals placed against a striated background. The cover, chain, and handle, which are often attached to pieces of this type (see cat. no. 55) are missing from this unusually small example of a well-known class of vessels.

54

Covered tripod bowl
Bronze with incised decoration
Han period, 1st century B.C.-
1st century A.D.; h. 7.8 cm.
Collection of Dr. Paul Singer

The globular body is decorated with an incised design of bands showing animals in an undulating landscape alternating with diamond patterns and plain bands. The two loops on the plain band around the shoulder and one in the center of the cover may once have been connected with a chain.

55
Pien-hu
Bronze with cast and incised decoration
Han period, 1st century B.C.-
1st century A.D.; h. 21.6 cm.
The Sackler Collections

The shape of this *pien-hu* differs from most other vessels of this type in that the regular spreading foot has not been cast as a single part but has been divided into two separate feet of equal size. Apart from the sawtooth and diamond patterns and the plain depressed bands that follow the curve of the body on each side, the entire body is covered with a profusion of dragons, tigerlike animals, and birds, executed in a design consisting mainly of incised lines and striations. The bodies of some of the animals have been cast in relief. A curved handle, ending on both sides in a dragon's head, is attached to the vessel and the cover by means of a chain that connects the two loops on the shoulder with those on the cover.

Although a closer inspection of the vessels exhibited here reveals minor stylistic variation in the representation of the animals, there can be no doubt that all of them belong to a distinctive local style that differs in several respects from the Chinese bronze styles prevalent in the metropolitan area of northern China during the Han dynasty. That the design is entirely, or almost entirely, executed in incised lines constitutes a definite departure from the traditional Chinese technique of cast decoration. The frequent use of bands of geometric design to separate or frame the animal scenes is another characteristic of this style that sets it apart from the Han bronzes found at Loyang and Sian.

As to the area with which this style of bronze vessels should be associated, the first archaeological clues were somewhat contradictory. The discovery by Japanese archaeologists at Lo-lang (North Korea) of a cover of a toilet box decorated with an incised

52

53

design in the same style seemed to point to a northern provenance for these bronzes. In the most recent American study in which the problem of the provenance of these pieces is discussed, *The Freer Chinese Bronzes* (p. 589), a statement by Umehara has been mistranslated, quoting this scholar as having said that a number of bronzes of this type had been found at a single site in 1923. In reality, however, the Japanese archaeologist merely mentioned that a number of pieces came into Japanese collections during the twenties and thirties. As far as their provenance is concerned the Freer Gallery catalogue continues "Word of mouth information current among dealers and collectors, however, has for some time attributed these pieces to Ch'ang-sha, Hunan Province, in the ancient state of Ch'u; and there is some evidence to support this view." One of the parallels cited by the Freer catalogue in support of a Ch'ang-sha provenance is a vase of the type of cat. no. 52, excavated by Olov R. T. Janse from a tomb at Lach-tru'o'ng in the province of Thanh-hoa (North Vietnam).

References: John Alexander Pope et al., *The Freer Chinese Bronzes,* Washington, D.C.: Freer Gallery of Art, 1967, vol. 1; Olov R. T. Janse, *Archaeological Research in Indo-China,* Cambridge, Mass.: Harvard University Press, 1947, vol. 1, introduction, fig. 10.

The earliest controlled excavations in the Ch'ang-sha area seemed to confirm the attribution suggested by the dealers and again put forward in the Freer catalogue. A bulbous, long-necked vase, practically identical with the Singer piece, was excavated at Yüeh-liang-shan near Ch'ang-sha during the early fifties. At about the same time a cylindrical covered box was excavated at Chiang-chia-shan near Hêng-yang, some distance to the south of Ch'ang-sha (fig. 57). Except for these two pieces, however, the extensive archaeological excavations carried out in and near Ch'ang-sha over the last twenty years do not seem to have yielded a single additional example of a bronze with incised animal and geometric design.

Whereas Ch'ang-sha tombs added little to

54

fig. 55

our knowledge of this type of Han bronze, excavations carried out elsewhere in the southern provinces of China yielded a rich harvest of parallel pieces. The best documented, exactly datable piece comes from a tomb in the village of P'ing-pa, Ch'ing-chên County, Kweichow Province, where between 1956 and 1958 a team from the Kweichow Provincial Museum excavated a large number of Han tombs. Of special interest is tomb no. 15 of this cemetery. Among the many objects recovered from this well-preserved tomb was a bronze vase of the same type as cat. no. 52. It is slightly larger (h. 26.8 cm.) than the vase in the Singer collection, but it has the same spreading foot, the same bands of fluting, and the same thickened lip (fig. 55). Although the animal scenes are quite different from those on the Singer vase, consisting of a band of animals in pursuit rather than animals in the melee represented on most of the other pieces, the bands of geometric design are the same. As in the Singer vase the lower half of the bulbous body has been left plain. The excavators of the P'ing-pa tomb noted the resemblance of this vase to the one from Yüeh-liang-shan, Ch'ang-sha, mentioned above. They also stated that this type of animal design is the most common on bronzes found in Kweichow.

Of great importance for establishing the date for this group of bronzes is the find in the same tomb of a winged lacquer cup carrying an inscription dated in accordance with A.D. 3. The lacquer was made in a workshop at Kuang-han, in the present Province of Szechwan. A plain bronze *pien-hu* from tomb no. 13, undated but probably from the same period, has the same depressed bands as the *pien-hu* from the Sackler Collections.

Especially since the date of these tombs is established only by the date on pieces of lacquerware imported from as far away as Szechwan, one could argue that the find of the bronze vase in tomb no. 15 does not give us any firm evidence of the southern provenance of this type of bronze. After all,

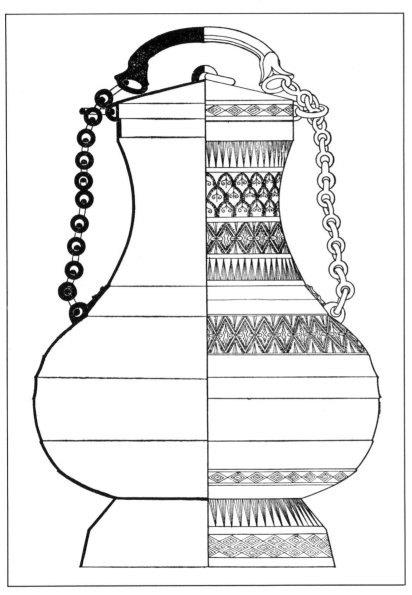

fig. 56

fig. 57

Szechwan lacquer was also found in North Korea, where a bronze of the same type also turned up. The P'ing-pa excavation is not an isolated instance, however; an excavation carried out in an eastern suburb of Canton in 1960 produced a rectangular table on low legs with an incised design of felines and birds, bordered by bands of geometric design. This piece obviously belongs to the same type of bronze.

In addition to the bronzes with a mixture of geometric animal designs, engraved into the surface, there is a closely related series of vessels in which the animal design has been entirely or almost entirely replaced by two distinct geometric patterns, which do not occur on the pieces exhibited here and described above. One of these patterns consists of interlocked lozenges framing a vertical design resembling the (much later) Buddhist *vajra* ("thunderbolt.") The other is a design described in the Freer catalogue as "feather tips." This design may be as old as the second century B.C., as is indicated by a *po-shan-lu*, datable to 126 B.C., which displays this motif (*Shan-chai chi-chin-lu*, vol. 28, p. 51).

A recent discovery (July 1970) of a completely intact, large tomb in Ho-fu County, Kwangsi Province, seems to solve the mystery of the provenance of the many pieces of this type in collections outside China, notably in the Freer Gallery of Art, Washington, D.C., the Art Institute of Chicago, and the Sumitomo Collection, Kyoto. One of the pieces found in the Ho-fu tomb is a vase (fig. 56), extremely close in shape, decoration, and size to a vase in the Freer Gallery of Art (no. 66.14). That the so-called feather tips design may have quite a different origin is suggested by a lamp in the shape of a phoenix, excavated from the same tomb. It has an allover, incised design of feathers, but this design is entirely different from the "feather tips" seen on vases and boxes of a non-zoomorphic shape.

Since the incised design is found only sporadically at Ch'ang-sha—whereas it is much more common in areas to the south of

55

the heartland of the Ch'u tribe—it seems reasonable to assume that these bronzes are the product of a local bronze style, the center of which should be sought farther south. That several pieces in Western collections have come to us with a dealer's provenance from Ch'ang-sha attached to them does little to invalidate this supposition. Although an alleged provenance from Ch'ang-sha never came to be the equal of one from An-yang, the site was well known during the late thirties and forties, and pieces in unsual styles that deviated from the better-known types from northern China often must have been labeled as having come from Ch'ang-sha without sufficient justification.

Further evidence to strengthen the case for a southern provenance of these bronzes is of a more indirect character. The similarity of the incised motifs to those found on the earthenware of Canton and vicinity suggests that both are the product of the same southern local culture (see cat. no. 56).

References: *Ch'üan-kuo chi-pên chien-shê kung-ch'êng-chung ch'u-t'u wên-wu chan-lan t'u-lu* [Illustrated catalogue of cultural relics excavated at construction sites in the entire country], preface by Chêng Chên-to, Peking, 1954, vol. 2, pls. 181-182; The Kweichow Provincial Museum, "The excavation of Han tombs at P'ing-pa, Ch'ing-chên County, Kweichow Province" (text in Chinese), *Kaogu Xuebao*, 1959, no. 1, pp. 85-103; The Cultural Committee of Canton City, "Brief report on the excavation of a Han tomb at Sha-ho in the eastern suburbs of Canton" (text in Chinese), *Wen Wu*, 1961, no. 2, pp. 54-57; The Archaeological Team of the Autonomous Region of the Chuang Tribe, Kwangsi, "A wooden burial chamber of the Western Han at Ho-fu, Kwangsi," (text in Chinese), *Kaogu*, 1972, no. 5, pp. 22-30.

56

Covered basin

Stoneware, incised ornament covered with an olive green glaze burnt brown in some areas. Western Han period, 2nd-1st century B.C.; h. 13.6 cm., diam. 23.5 cm.
Yale University Art Gallery

The bowl-shaped basin has a wide collar with pierced vertical slits. The body is covered with an incised crosshatch pattern. The cover repeats the same pattern with a border of triangles and an appliqué ring with three small figures of recumbent rams.

Several vessels of a similar type exist in other American collections. A piece in the Art Institute of Chicago has a bronze rim on the collar and birds instead of rams on the lid. A simpler version with an almost plain body is in the Honolulu Academy of Arts. The Yale vessel is known to have been brought from Ch'ang-sha by John Hadley Cox; the Honolulu piece is attributed to the same site.

Published: George J. Lee, *Selected Far Eastern Art in the Yale University Art Gallery,* New Haven: Yale University Press, 1970, nos. 119-120; *Archives of the Chinese Art Society of America 6* (1952), p. 65, fig. 4 (Chicago); *The Ceramic Art of China,* London: Oriental Ceramic Society and Victoria and Albert Museum, 1971, no. 15 (Honolulu).

Noting the difference in shape of the lid of a similar basin excavated at Yüeh-liang-shan near Ch'ang-sha (fig. 58) in the early fifties, George Lee concluded that the cover and basin of the Yale vessel do not belong together. In the meantime, however, several other pieces of this type have been found. In view of its similarity to these and pieces of the type in the Art Institute of Chicago, it no longer seems necessary to maintain Lee's assumption.

There is an interesting parallel between the ceramics of the type shown here and the bronze vessels with incised decoration (see cat. nos. 52-55). Finds in the early fifties seemed to confirm the attribution of these ceramics to the Ch'ang-sha area, but since that time no other pieces of this type seem to have been found there. Similar pieces, on the other hand, turned up in tombs in and around Canton, an area some distance to the south of the heartland of the Ch'u kingdom.

The covered basins of the type shown here are a good example. The vessel excavated at Yüeh-liang-shan near Ch'ang-sha, which prompted George Lee to separate cover and vessel of the Yale piece, was not followed by other finds in the same area. In Canton and in Kuang-tung Province, on the other hand, at least three pieces of this type have been found. One vessel, found without its lid, appeared in tomb no. 43 at Lung-shêng-kang in an eastern suburb of Canton in the winter of 1953. Except that the body is left plain, it comes close to the Yale piece in shape but is slightly larger (h. 17 cm., diam. 26 cm.). Very close in resemblance is a vessel excavated at Chin-lan-ssu, Tsêng-ch'êng County, Kuang-tung Province. At Nan-shih-t'ou, in a southern suburb of Canton, a plain-bodied piece of the same type was found together with a round, covered ceramic box (fig. 59) decorated with a design closely related to the "feather tips" on bronze vessels from the south (see cat. no. 55).

There are other connections that point in the same direction. A globular, covered ceramic box found in tomb no. 2 at Hsiang-lan-kang, Canton, has a cover with three recumbent rams. Its body is decorated with the same kind of crosshatch pattern as that found on the Yale vessel. Other ceramic pieces from the same tomb display the familiar triangular pattern found on pottery as well as on the bronzes. One piece in the same find has an incised design of a bird and a dragon quite closely related to those found on the bronzes with animal decoration.

From all these parallels, which could easily be multiplied, it appears that the ceramics and bronzes of the types described in cat. nos. 52-57 all come from the same general area. Although this area does include Ch'ang-sha and vicinity, it stretches from there to the south and not, as in the case of other typical forms of Ch'ang-sha art, toward the plain of the Huai valley farther north. The center of this form of ceramics and bronze industry is,

fig. 58

56

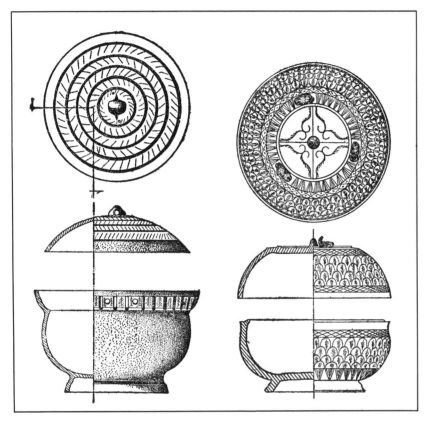

fig. 59

therefore, most likely to be sought farther south instead of in the Ch'u kingdom itself.

The increasing number of finds enables us to follow the typological development of this type of covered vessel through the entire Han period. The later pieces, made during the Eastern Han period, have one typical elaboration: the pierced decoration, first applied to the collar only, now spreads to the foot, creating a lighter base with a pierced crosshatched design.

References: *Ch'üan-kuo chi-pên chien-shê kung-ch'êng-chung ch'u-t'u wên-wu chan-lan t'u-lu* [Illustrated catalogue of cultural relics excavated at construction sites in the entire country], preface by Chêng Chên-to, Peking, 1954, vol. 2, pl. 188, no. 3; The Cultural Committee of Canton City, "Brief report on the cleaning up of the coffin burial no. 2 at Hsiang-lan-kang, Tung-shan, Canton" (text in Chinese), *Wen Wu,* 1958, no. 4, pp. 57-60; The Cultural Committee of Canton City, "Brief report on the cleaning out of a Western Han wooden coffin burial at Nan-shih-t'ou in the southern suburbs of Canton" (text in Chinese), *Wen Wu,* 1955, no. 8, pp. 85-94; The Cultural Committee of Canton City, "The Eastern Han wooden coffin burial no. 43 at Lung-shêng-kang, Canton (text in Chinese), *Kaogu Xuebao,* 1957, no. 1, pp. 141-153; for a fine example of the Eastern Han type see *Wen Wu,* 1961, no. 2, p. 49, fig. 8.

57
Covered box
Gray stoneware covered with an olive green
ash glaze mostly burnt brown
Western Han period, 2nd-1st century B.C.;
h. 21 cm.
The Sackler Collections

The three-legged, cylindrical box, with two simple ring handles on the body and one on the slightly domed lid, does not seem to have its exact counterpart in any of the excavations referred to in the previous entry. On the other hand, the type of ware, the color of the glaze, and the type of incised design clearly demonstrate that it belongs to the same category of ceramics. The crosshatch pattern on the body and the triangles on the rim of the lid are similar to those found in the Canton tombs. The design on the lid, resembling hairy leaves, is very close to that found on a jar excavated from the P'ing-pa tomb in Kweichow Province mentioned in cat. no. 55. A similar design occurs on a vase in the Metropolitan Museum of Art, attributed to Ch'ang-sha.

References: Fujio Koyama et al., *Sekai Tōji Zenshū,* Tokyo: Kawade Shobō, 1955, pl. 64.

57

Early Green
Stoneware

During the Late Chou period the area around Shao-hsing (Chêkiang Province) was part of the state of Yüeh. Later it was known as Yüeh-chou and gave its name to one of its most famous local products, *Yüeh* ware, a class of gray-bodied, high-fired ceramics covered with a grayish or yellowish green glaze, which were the precursors of the later celadons. Although it is known in the Western world as *Yüeh-yao*, present-day Chinese scholars prefer to use this name only for a certain type of T'ang and later ware, using the less specific term "green glazed ware" for all earlier wares of this color.

Long before *Yüeh-yao* had become a prized collector's item in the West and in Japan, one of its ancient kiln sites had already been discovered by the British missionary and scholar Bishop Arthur E. Moule, who had paid a visit to the kiln sites at Lake Shang-lin as early as 1890. During the thirties a number of Japanese consular officers, soon followed by James Marshall Plumer of the Chinese Maritime Customs and the English connoisseur A. D. Brankston, located several other kiln sites near Hangchow. These included the old kilns at Chiu-yen, some thirty miles to the north of that ancient city. During the twenties and thirties large numbers of ceramics of the *Yüeh* type began to appear on Western markets, and the contents of numerous tombs were thus dispersed over Western and Japanese collections.

One of the first to fully appreciate the beauty of *Yüeh* wares was Sir Herbert Ingram, whose collection, generously bequeathed to the Ashmolean Museum, Oxford, some twenty-five years after it had been brought together, is the most important assemblage of this type of ceramics outside China. Although the shards collected at different kiln sites made it to some extent possible to identify certain pieces as products of specific *Yüeh* kilns, the history of the development of *Yüeh* ware during the Six Dynasties period remained unclear, as there were hardly any firmly datable specimens among the many pieces in Western collections.

Investigations by Chinese scholars conducted since 1950 have shed much light on the history of *Yüeh* ware, especially during the earlier periods. Even more useful than the exploration of most of the already known and the discovery of several new kiln sites has been the excavation of a large number of tombs dating from the Six Dynasties period. These tombs, found in an area extending from Nanking and Ch'ang-sha to Foochow and Canton but mainly concentrated in the immediate vicinity of Nanking, yielded large numbers of *Yüeh* ware ceramics. During the Six Dynasties period tombs were sometimes built of bricks or tiles, on one, or several, of which a date has been stamped with a mold. Although occasionally discrepancies seem to occur, the dates on the tiles usually give us a reliable indication of the date for the tomb itself as well as for the mortuary gifts deposited in it.

How much progress has been made in this respect since the founding of the People's Republic of China can be demonstrated with the following example. Before the Second World War only one single datable tomb had been excavated under controlled circumstances (see cat. no. 68). In recent years Chinese archaeologists have brought to light hundreds of tombs, of which at least fifty can be dated by the inscriptions on tiles found in them. Many other tombs can now be dated with a considerable degree of accuracy by comparing their structure and interior decoration as well as the typology of the mortuary ceramics deposited in them with those of exactly datable tombs. All these discoveries have made it possible to assign much more precise dates to individual pieces and to reconstruct the typological development of such typical mortuary gifts as loop-handled jars and chicken-spouted ewers (see cat. nos. 65-66). It has also become possible to establish regional differences in style.

In this exhibition the advance in our knowledge of *Yüeh* wares is illustrated by two juxtaposed groups of ceramics. The first group consists of pieces that must have been excavated from tombs dating from the late third century and the fourth century A.D.

Although almost all the examples in this group are of different provenance and of slightly different date, the context in which pieces closely resembling these have been found in the course of recent excavations suggests that this selection comes close to an original assemblage of ceramics in a tomb of this period. To illustrate some of the regional differences in style, this group of ceramics, mainly from the Nanking and northern Chêkiang area, has been placed in juxtaposition with a group of pieces known to have been found together in one tomb in the Foochow area. Recent excavations confirm this oral information and permit us to date this Foochow group with greater accuracy than was possible at the time they were first discovered.

References: For the history of the discovery of the kiln sites before World War II see G. St. G. M. Gompertz, *Chinese Celadon Wares,* London: Faber and Faber, 1958, pp. 4-21; a useful survey of recent investigations is found in Fêng Hsien-ming, "Important finds of ancient Chinese ceramics since 1949," *Wen Wu,* 1965, no. 9, pp. 26-56, abstracted and translated by Mrs. Hin-cheung Lovell, London: Oriental Ceramic Society, 1966; a comparison of the major *Yüeh-yao* collection in the Western world with pieces recently excavated and exhibited in China: Mary Tregear, "Early Chinese Green Wares in the Collection of the Ashmolean Museum, Oxford," *Oriental Art,* n.s. 13, no. 1 (spring 1967), 29-35; The Kiangsu Cultural Committee, comp., *Nan-ching ch'u-t'u Liu-ch'ao ch'ing-tz'u* [Six Dynasties green ware excavated at Nanking], Peking: Wen-Wu Press, 1957.

58
Crouching lion
Gray stoneware, covered with a dull, olive green glaze (*Yüeh-yao*)
Chin period, 4th century A.D.; h. 7.9 cm., l. 12.8 cm.
Museum of Fine Arts, Boston, Charles B. Hoyt Collection. 50.1054

Of all the ceramic types current in *Yüeh-yao* none is more common than the mold-produced figure of a lion with a hollow body and a tube protruding from its back. Examples of this type, all displaying minor variations, exist in many private and public collections (British Museum; Buffalo Museum of Science; Center of Asian Art and Culture, San Francisco; Santa Barbara Museum; Lord Cunliffe Collection; Royal Ontario Museum, Toronto; etc.), but of none of these pieces can the provenance be traced. Gompertz *(Chinese Celadon Wares*, pl. 7B) has suggested that the piece in the Cunliffe Collection may have come from the Chiu-yen kilns, some thirty miles to the southeast of Hangchou.

The function of the tube on the back is unclear. Some scholars have considered this type of piece to be a candlestick, others have called it a water vessel or water dropper. Three lions of a similar type form the base of a large candlestick in the Hoyt Collection, Boston Museum (50.1050).

Following the example set by R. L. Hobson *(Eumorfopoulos Catalogue,* vol. 1, no. 447), others have labeled pieces of this type "T'ang" or "T'ang or earlier." Elsewhere the more correct attribution to the Six Dynasties period is given, but no effort has been made to date these pieces more closely within this period.

Published: *Far Eastern Ceramic Bulletin,* no. 12 (December 1950), pl. III, fig. 1; Museum of Fine Arts, Boston, *The Charles B. Hoyt Collection, Memorial Exhibition,* Boston, 1952, no. 206.

Recent excavations have confirmed the widespread use of this type of *Yüeh-yao.* Finds of similar pieces range from San-mao-ts'un, I-chêng county in Kiangsu to P'ing-pa

58

fig. 60

in Kueichow Province and Kuei-hua-kang in the northwest suburbs of Canton. A fine example was excavated at Tan-yang, Kiangsu Province, in 1966 (fig. 60). None of these specimens can be dated exactly, but the piece found at San-mao-ts'un comes from a grave containing a chicken coop of the "Quonset" type, associated with finds dating from ca. A.D. 300, and tomb no. 4 at Kuei-hua-kang is dated by its excavators in the Western Chin dynasty (A.D. 265-313). Its position in close proximity to tomb no. 4 (from which came a plate with winged cups and spoon, cat. no. 60) suggests that these may be graves in which members of the same family have been buried.

References: Cultural Commission of Canton City, "Brief report on the cleaning out of Chin tombs in the northwest suburbs of Canton City" (text in Chinese), *Kaogu,* 1955, no. 5, pp. 43-49; Nanking Museum, "A Chin tomb at the village of San-mao, I-chêng county, Kiangsu Province" (text in Chinese), *Kaogu,* 1965, no. 4, pp. 209-211; Fang Wei-fan, "Kueichow Province, strengthening its cultural protection activities, cleans out a large number of ancient tombs" (text in Chinese), *Wen Wu,* 1957, no. 9, p. 80; *Historical Relics Unearthed in New China,* Peking: Foreign Languages Press, 1972, pl. 120.

59
Model of a chicken coop
Gray stoneware covered with a grayish green glaze (*Yüeh-yao*)
Chin period, ca. A.D. 300; l. 12.8 cm., h. 6 cm.
Museum of Fine Arts, Boston, Charles B. Hoyt Collection. 50.2265a

Models of chicken coops began to make their appearance in tombs of the Han period, but the type that resembles our Quonset hut seems to be typical of the Six Dynasties period and of the Nanking and northern Chêkiang areas. The earliest datable example was found at Piao-yang, Kiangsu Province, in a tomb dated in accordance with A.D. 272. The type occurs in numerous small variations; the piece exhibited here shows a close resemblance to one found in the tomb dating from A.D. 302 excavated near Nanking (see cat. no. 62; fig. 61). Another example, placed on four miniature piles, was found in the tomb of General Chou Ch'u (see cat. no. 68), dating from A.D. 297. These finds suggest that these chicken coops enjoyed a certain measure of popularity as mortuary gifts around the beginning of the fourth century of our era.

References: Commission for the Protection of Cultural Relics of Nanking City, "Brief report on the cleaning out of a tomb of the Chin Dynasty at Shih-chia-hu, Pan-chiao village near Nanking" (text in Chinese), *Wen Wu,* 1965, no. 6, pp. 37-44; Lo Tsung-chên, "Report on the excavation of a tomb of the Chin Dynasty at I-hsing, Kiangsu Province" (text in Chinese), *Kaogu Xuebao,* 1957, no. 4, pp. 83-106; The Nanking Museum, "A tomb from the first year of Fêng-huang at Piao-yang, Kiangsu" (text in Chinese), *Kaogu,* 1962, no. 8, pp. 412-413.

60
Plate with two winged cups and spoon
Gray stoneware with a grayish green glaze (*Yüeh-yao*)
Chin dynasty, first half of the 4th century A.D.; diam. 14.7 cm.
Collection of Dr. Paul Singer

This plate is another typical example of *ming-ch'i* (literally, "spirit objects"), replicas of real utensils, unfit for use in daily life and made solely for burial with the dead. The two winged cups, which still retain the classical Han shape, and the curved spoon were made to adhere to the round plate.

Among the several examples of this type of mortuary gift discovered in recent years none seems to have come from a tomb that can be dated exactly. During excavations carried out near Ch'ing-chiang, Kiangsi Province, in the spring of 1959, a very similar piece was discovered in a tomb attributed by the excavators to the Western Chin period (A.D. 265-313) (fig. 62). Previously, another piece of the same type had been found in tomb no. 3 at Kuei-hua-kang in a northwest suburb of Canton. By comparing its structure with other tombs in the same area, the excavators concluded that it must have been built in the Western Chin period or slightly later.

References: Archaeological Team, Kiangsi Provincial Museum, "Chin Dynasty tombs at Ch'ing-chiang, Kiangsi" (text in Chinese), *Kaogu,* 1962, no. 4, pp. 186-192; Cultural Commission of Canton City, "Brief report on the cleaning out of Chin tombs in the northwest suburbs of Canton City" (text in Chinese), *Kaogu,* 1955, no. 5, pp. 43-49.

fig. 61

fig. 62

59

60

61
Jar
Gray stoneware covered with a grayish green glaze (*Yüeh-yao*)
Chin period, ca. 300 A.D.; h. 21.1 cm., diam. 29 cm.
Museum of Fine Arts, Boston, Edward S. Morse Memorial Fund. 38.958

The heavy jar has a wide mouth and a broad shoulder, which tapers toward the foot. Two loop handles and an animal mask with a ring in its mouth are molded and applied to the shoulder on both sides. Around the shoulder is a stamped band of lozenge patterns and punch marks.

Published: Thomas Dexel, *Die Formen chinesischer Keramik,* Tübingen: Wasmuth, 1955, pl. 276.

A tomb containing a tiger vessel and a model of a kitchen stove, resembling the pieces exhibited here, was found to contain also a vessel that, except for a slight difference in size (h. 20.2, diam. 24.4 cm.), is virtually identical with the Boston jar. The three pieces came from a tomb discovered at Mai-kao-ch'iao near Nanking in February 1965 that dates from A.D. 308. The excavation of tomb no. 1 at Ting-chia-shan near Nanking yielded yet another piece of approximately the same type but slightly larger than the Boston jar (h. 23 cm.). This tomb dates from A.D. 285 (fig. 63). It seems reasonable to assume, therefore, that the Boston jar is of approximately the same period as these two datable finds.

References: Commission for the Protection of Cultural Relics of Nanking City, "Cleaning out a tomb of the Western Chin dynasty at Mai-kao-ch'iao, Nanking" (text in Chinese), *Kaogu,* 1966, no. 4, pp. 224-227; The Kiangsu Cultural Commission, comp., *Nan-ching ch'u-t'u Liu-ch'ao ch'ing-tz'u* [Green ware of the Six Dynasties period excavated at Nanking], Peking: Wen-Wu Press, 1957, fig. 3; *Nan-ching Liu-ch'ao-mu ch'u-t'u wên-wu hsüan-chi* [Selected cultural relics excavated from Six Dynasties tombs at Nanking], Shanghai: The People's Art Publishing Co., 1957, pl. 17.

61

fig. 63

62

Model of a kitchen stove
Gray stoneware covered with a grayish green
glaze (*Yüeh-yao*)
Chin period, first half of the
4th century A.D.; l. 17.7 cm.
Collection of Dr. Paul Singer

This model of a simple kitchen stove with a
bowl and a jar placed on top of it demonstrates the Chinese predilection for tomb
furniture that reproduces on a miniature
scale the paraphernalia of everyday life.
Small models of pigsties, chicken coops (see
cat. no. 59), and dog houses made their first
appearance in the funerary art of the Han
period. During the following Six Dynasties
period these pieces were often executed in the
hard-fired, grayish green glazed ware that is
typical of so-called *yüeh-yao*.

The unobtrusive typological changes in
this class of miniature models make it hazardous to establish the date of such pieces
on the basis of analogy with recently excavated specimens. At least two of the newly
discovered examples are so close to the piece
exhibited here, however, that it may safely be
assumed to date from approximately the
same time. One piece was found in a tomb
datable to A.D. 302, excavated at Pan-chiao
village near Nanking in June 1964 (fig. 64).
There is some uncertainty as to whether the
latest date found impressed on the bricks is
that of the actual construction of this tomb,
but an excavation of another grave at Mai-
kao-ch'iao near Nanking in February 1965
seems to confirm the above-mentioned date.
This last tomb was built of bricks impressed
with a date corresponding to A.D. 308. The
mortuary gifts it contained are very similar
to those found in the tomb dating from A.D.
302.

62

fig. 64

References: Commission for the Protection of
Cultural Relics of Nanking City, "Brief report on
the cleaning out of a tomb of the Chin dynasty at
Shih-chia-hu, Panchiao village near Nanking"
(text in Chinese), *Wen Wu,* 1965, no. 6, pp. 37-
44; Commission for the Protection of Cultural
Relics of Nanking City, "Cleaning out a tomb of
the Western Chin dynasty at Mai-kao-ch'iao,
Nanking" (text in Chinese), *Kaogu,* 1966, no. 4,
pp. 224-227.

63

Flask (*pien-hu*)
Gray stoneware covered with a dull olive green glaze (*Yüeh-yao*)
Chin dynasty, late 3rd-4th century A.D.; h. 22.2 cm., w. 25.3 cm.
Museum of Fine Arts, Boston, Charles B. Hoyt Collection. 50.1047

The flask has a flattened globular body and a short, straight neck. On each narrow side is attached a large loop above and a pair of smaller loops below. The body is decorated on both sides with a small *t'ao-t'ieh* mask with ring in low relief and an incised design of punch-marked ribbons forming a double volute. Similar decorative bands encircle the neck and upper loops.

Published: G. St. G. M. Gompertz, *Chinese Celadon Wares,* London: Faber and Faber, 1958, pl. 8A; Hsien-ch'i Tseng and Robert Paul Dart, *The Charles B. Hoyt Collection,* Boston, 1964, vol. 1, pl. 78.

That the unique shape of the Boston flask is due to a later accident rather than to the potter's original design became apparent only after Chinese archaeologists discovered a vase of a similar type in a brick tomb of the Six Dynasties period (fig. 65). The tomb is located on Mount Ch'ien-t'ou, to the south of Chang-chia-k'u village, a few miles outside the city of Nanking. Among the ceramics recovered from this tomb was a flask of *Yüeh* ware that bears a striking resemblance to the Boston *pien-hu*. The principal difference is that the excavated flask has a high, spreading foot ring, luted onto the piece. A closer inspection of the base of the Boston flask reveals that it has been ground down, obviously after the original foot was broken. The discovery of a complete specimen in the Ch'ien-t'ou tomb gives us an opportunity to reconstruct the base of the Boston piece.

Suspended from a strap on the shoulder, *pien-hu* of this type were probably used as water bottles. The function of the double loops on the sides of this type of flask is indicated by the piece that has preserved its original shape. Whereas it would be possible to run a strap through the loops of the Boston

63

fig. 65

fig. 66

piece and pass it along the bottom to the other side, the spreading foot of the piece from Ch'ien-t'ou makes such an arrangement impossible. The strap must therefore have been passed through one of the small loops, to go through the large loop down below, running back up through the other small loop.

The decoration of the two pieces follows basically the same pattern, but there are several minor differences. The two volutes on the body of the Ch'ien-t'ou flask are joined instead of curling back as they do on the Boston piece. That the animal masks were applied to the finished body by means of a small mold is apparent from the fact that the potter of the Ch'ien-t'ou piece inadvertently placed it upside down.

No date was found in the tomb on Mount Ch'ien-t'ou. Its excavators, pointing to analogies with other tombs in the Nanking area, attribute it to the Eastern Chin period. The tomb may even date from the last years of the preceding Western Chin period (A.D. 265-313). The decoration around the neck of the Hoyt *pien-hu* is very similar to that around the shoulder of the jar in this exhibition (cat. no. 61). Examples of this type of jar have been found in tombs dating from as early as A.D. 285. From the same tomb on Mount Ch'ien-t'ou came a covered jar decorated with a chicken's head. An almost identical piece was found in a Western Chin tomb at Chao-shih-kang near the Kuang-hua gate of Nanking.

It would seem most likely, therefore, that the *pien-hu* exhibited here dates from the years around A.D. 300. The compilers of *Selected cultural relics excavated in Kiangsu Province* (Peking, 1963) illustrate the piece from Mount Ch'ien-t'ou and state that this type has rarely been found in the tombs of this area. None of the other reports published to date illustrate another example of this type of vessel. There is, however, another *pien-hu,* excavated at Pai-kuan-chên in Shang-yü County, near Hangchow (fig. 66) that closely resembles the two pieces discussed here.

References: Chin Ch'i, "Tombs of the Six Dynasties at Kan-chia-hsiang and T'ung-chia-shan near Nanking" (text in Chinese), *Kaogu*, 1963, no. 6, pp. 305-306, pl. 3, fig. 1; The Nanking Museum et al., comp., *Kiang-su-shêng ch'u-t'u wên-wu hsüan-chi* [Selected cultural relics excavated in Kiangsu Province], Peking: Wen-Wu Press, 1963, pl. 144; Yasuhiko Mayuyama, *Chūgoku Mombutsu Kenbun,* Tokyo: Mayuyama Ryūsendō, 1973, fig. 183.

64

64
Ewer in the shape of a winged tiger
Light gray stoneware covered with a grayish
green glaze (*Yüeh-yao*)
Chin dynasty, first half of the 4th
century A.D.; h. 18 cm., l. 24.8 cm.
Museum of Fine Arts, Boston, Charles B.
Hoyt Collection. 50.1055

The vessel has the shape of a crouching tiger.
The feet, legs, shoulders, and haunches are
clearly indicated, but the head of the animal
has been reduced to a mask applied to the
top of the gaping, round orifice. The tail has
been turned into a twisted rope handle,
which is attached to the mask and to the
back. On the sides two wings are sketchily
indicated by means of incised dots and lines.

In the catalogue of the *Charles B. Hoyt
Collection, Memorial Exhibition* the piece
was erroneously attributed to the tenth century A.D., in spite of the fact that the color
and texture of the clay and glaze are typical
of early *Yüeh-yao*. The Royal Ontario Museum, Toronto, and the Tokyo National
Museum have almost identical pieces.
Published: Museum of Fine Arts, Boston, *The
Charles B. Hoyt Collection, Memorial Exhibition,* Boston, 1952, no. 212.

Vessels in the shape of a tiger, the Chinese
precursors of the mediaeval aquamanile,
seem to have first been used as mortuary gifts
in the first century A.D. Although examples
cast in bronze or carved from wood and
lacquered are among the earliest known
specimens of this type, the tiger-shaped vessel
became widely used as a mortuary gift only
during the Six Dynasties period, when the
kilns producing the green glazed *Yüeh-yao*
began to turn out pieces of this type in considerable quantities. The earliest datable tiger
vessel was found at Chao-shih-kang near
Nanking. It carries an inscription containing
a date corresponding to A.D. 251.

It has generally been taken for granted that
the tiger-shaped vessel should be identified
with the *hu-tzu* ("tiger"), which is frequently
mentioned in Han and post-Han literature as
a type of urinal. It was not long after the

fig. 67

discovery of the inscribed *hu-tzu* that a heated debate started among Chinese archaeologists as to the exact function of these pieces. One of the archaeologists who questioned the use of such pieces as urinals pointed out that a utensil of such humble use could never have been inscribed with the name of an imperial reign. But, as the strict taboos governing the use of characters occurring in the personal names of emperors do not seem to have in any way applied to their reign names (*nien-hao*), this argument is not altogether convincing.

A more compelling reason for rejecting the possibility that the *hu-tzu* was used as a urinal was the fact that at least one vessel of this type turned up in a completely undisturbed Fukien tomb, where it stood surrounded by five small cups. This naturally strengthened the case of those who argued that the vessel should be considered a ewer for pouring tea or wine. Whereas there are numerous literary references to the *hu-tzu* as a type of urinal, however, only one single Han commentary refers to the *hu-tzu* as a wine vessel.

One archaeologist has suggested that we should differentiate between vessels with an elongated, cylindrical body and those of a much more squat, round type. One of these would have been used as a urinal, the other as a pouring vessel. Even after extensive discussions of this topic during the years 1955-1957 the problem does not seem to have been definitely solved, and proponents of the two theories have taken up this problem again after each new find. In tombs in which a husband and wife have been buried, the *hu-tzu* is sometimes placed at the feet of the man. In another tomb the *hu-tzu* was found together with a sword, another indication that such vessels should be associated with men.

As to the date of the *hu-tzu* in the Hoyt Collection, a comparison with a recently excavated, almost identical piece seems to supply a reliable indication. The piece was found in a tomb at Huang-yen in the Hsiu-ling Dam region, Chêkiang Province, in December

1956 (fig. 67). The bricks in the wall of the tomb chamber were impressed with a date corresponding to A.D. 327. Apparently the only difference is that the handle imitating twisted rope makes a sharper curve than that of the Hoyt piece. A tomb dated in accordance with A.D. 308, excavated in February 1956 at Mai-kou-ch'iao near Nanking, yielded another example of the same type of *hu-tzu,* which is also practically identical in size with the Hoyt piece.

The earliest of all pieces of this type seems to be a partially broken piece (the tiger mask has disappeared), found in June 1956, at Chu-chi, Chêkiang Province. The tiles in the pair of tombs excavated there are inscribed with a date corresponding to A.D. 300. The three dated tombs in which *hu-tzu* of the same type as the Hoyt piece were found indicate that the date of these pieces should be sought in the first half, perhaps even the first quarter, of the fourth century A.D.

References: Commission for the Preservation of Ancient Monuments of Chekiang Province, "The excavation of ancient cemeteries in the Hsiu-ling Dam region, Huang-yen" (text in Chinese), *Kaogu Xuebao,* 1958, no. 1, pp. 111-129; Commission for the Protection of Cultural Relics of Nanking City, "Cleaning out a Western Chin tomb at Mai-kou-ch'iao, Nanking" (text in Chinese), *Kaogu,* 1966, no. 4, pp. 224-227; Chu Po-ch'ien, "Cleaning up two Chin tombs in the courtyard of the school for sericulture at Chu-chi" (text in Chinese), *Wen Wu,* 1956, no. 12, pp. 76-77; on the *hu-tzu* problem see *Kaogu,* 1956, no. 5, pp. 58-60; *Kaogu,* 1957, no. 2, pp. 92-93; *Kaogu,* 1957, no. 6, pp. 44-45, 52-54, 55-60.

65
Chicken-spouted vessel
Gray stoneware, covered with a greenish glaze (*Yüeh-yao*)
Eastern Chin period, 2nd half of the 4th century A.D.; h. 23.8 cm.
Ashmolean Museum, Oxford, Sir Herbert Ingram Collection

The vessel has a broad, flanging lip to which the curving handle is attached. On the shoulder are two square-cut loops. The spout is in the shape of a chicken's head. The greenish glaze has dark spots at the lip, and the rough, concave base is unglazed.

Published: Mary Tregear, "Early Chinese Green Wares in the Collection of the Ashmolean Museum, Oxford," *Oriental Art,* n.s., 13, no. 1 (spring 1967), 29-35.

Ewers with a spout in the shape of a chicken's head (*t'ien-chi-hu*) began to appear in *Yüeh* ware during the Eastern Chin period (317-414 A.D.). This may be concluded from the fact that none of the many tombs datable to the early years of the fourth century seem to have contained examples of this type of vessel. Somewhat rashly, perhaps, a Chinese archaeologist concluded as early as 1956 that chicken-spouted vessels do not occur in Chin tombs at all. Unknown to him, in May of 1955 the excavation of a tomb at Ch'ang-sha, datable by the inscription impressed in one of its bricks to A.D. 375, had already yielded an early example of the *t'ien-chi-hu* (fig. 68). The piece from the Ashmolean Museum is sufficiently close to this excavated specimen to allow us to date it to approximately the same time.

References: Cultural Commission of Hunan Province, "Brief report on the cleaning out of a Chin tomb at Lan-ni-ch'ung in the southern suburbs of Ch'ang-sha" (text in Chinese), *Wen Wu,* 1955, no. 11, pp. 19-22; The Hunan Provincial Museum, "Chin dynasty, southern dynasties and Sui dynasty tombs at Ch'ang-sha" (text in Chinese), *Kaogu Xuebao,* 1959, no. 3, pp. 75-106.

fig. 68

65

66

66
Chicken-spouted vessel
Gray stoneware, covered with a greenish
glaze (*Yüeh-yao*)
Six Dynasties period, 5th century A.D.;
h. 24 cm.
Ashmolean Museum, Oxford, Sir Herbert
Ingram Collection

Except that the spout in the shape of a chicken's head has been transformed into a merely decorative, nonfunctional addition, the vessel resembles the piece described in the preceding entry, but there is a difference in proportions and shape. The body of the vessel has become less bulbous and resembles a vase rather than a jar. The neck is longer, and its tapering shape has become more pronounced.

The gradual typological changes in the *t'ien-chi-hu* can be documented and dated with the help of several datable examples.

fig. 69

Closest in shape to the vessel exhibited here is a piece from tomb no. 49 dating from A.D. 447 at the cemetery in the Hsiu-ling Dam region at Huang-yen, Chêkiang (fig. 69). The only important difference between the latter and the Oxford piece is that its curving handle has been embellished with a dragon's head.

With the passing of time the tendency toward a more elegant, slender, and elongated shape became increasingly evident. The final development of the *t'ien-chi-hu* cannot be shown in this exhibition. We see it, for example, in the vessel excavated from the tomb of Li Ching-hsün, a young girl who died in A.D. 608 (see cat. nos. 76-82). The dragon's head has already acquired the shape it was to retain on the amphoras of the T'ang period. The neck has become even longer than before and is accentuated by rings, while the chicken's neck has acquired the jaunty curvature of that of a strutting rooster.

The early type of chicken-spouted ewer seems to have been current almost exclusively in the territory governed by the Chin dynasties. The only piece reported from Szechwan, although resembling the pieces from Canton, Nanking, and Ch'ang-sha, has a double spout. As is evident from the Sui piece from Li Ching-hsün's tomb, the later types have been found in northern areas as well.

References: Commission for the Preservation of Ancient Monuments of Chêkiang Province, "The excavation of ancient cemeteries in the Hsiu-ling Dam region, Huang-yen" (text in Chinese), *Kaogu Xuebao,* 1958, no. 1, pp. 111-129, pl. 6, fig. 2; Shih Kuang-ming et al., "Brief report on the cleaning out of rock graves at Ch'ang-shan village, Chang-ming County, Szechwan Province" (text in Chinese), *Kaogu,* 1955, no. 5, pp. 37-42, pl. 12, fig. 2.

67 a-d
A set of four mortuary ceramics
Light gray stoneware covered with a greenish glaze (*Yüeh-yao*)
Six Dynasties period, late 5th-early 6th century A.D.
Collection of Dr. Paul Singer

This group of mortuary ceramics was acquired by James Marshall Plumer at Foochow, when he was serving in the Chinese Maritime Customs some forty years ago. The set consists of the following pieces:

a. An incense burner *(po-shan-lu)* with a domed cover, pierced and fitted with appliqués in the shape of flames. The receptacle for the incense stands upon a round dish; h. 10.4 cm.

b. A vessel in the shape of a crouching tiger with gaping mouth *(hu-tzu)*; h. 12 cm., l. 16.1 cm.

c. A stand (perhaps for flowers or incense sticks?), consisting of four vertical tubes, supported by dwarflike figures in relief and placed on a round, stepped base; h. 14.6 cm.

d. In addition to these three pieces there is a fourth piece from the Plumer collection, which in all likelihood belongs to the same set. It is an object of uncertain use, perhaps a candelabra, which has the shape of a branch or lotus bud, rising like a pillar from the center of a round dish. The branch carries two flower-shaped receptacles near the base of the pillar and is provided with two rings near the pointed top; h. 13.3 cm.

Previously published as part of this set, but now no longer together with it, is a tripod with a long handle in the shape of a bird's head and neck *(chiao-tou)*. A similar piece, accompanied by a stand with five vertical tubes, is in the Museum of Asiatic Art, Amsterdam, on loan from Dr. R. Flaes. The catalogue of that museum labels both pieces as T'ang.

The stand for flowers and the candelabra do not seem to be duplicated in other collections in the West, but of this type of incense burner at least two other examples are

known. One piece, formerly in the Eumorfopoulos collection, was described by R. L. Hobson as "Late T'ang"(*The George Eumorfopoulos Collection,* London: Benn, 1925, vol. 1, no. 451). Fujio Koyama described another, very similar piece as "probably Han dynasty" ("The Yüeh-chou yao Celadon Excavated in Japan," *Artibus Asiae* 14 [1951], pp. 26-42, esp. p. 32, fig. 4). Koyama mentioned that Plumer, upon being shown this piece in Japan, identified it as a product of the so-called Nan-t'ai kiln, of which he had discovered the site on the south bank of the Min River at Foochow. In the two publications listed below the Plumer set has been correctly attributed to the Six Dynasties period, but no more precise date within this period has been suggested.

Published: Los Angeles County Museum, *Chinese Ceramics from the Prehistoric Period through Ch'ien Lung,* 1952, no. 54; The Detroit Institute of Arts, *Selections from the James Marshall Plumer Collection of Oriental Art* (exhibition catalogue), 1962, no. 22 a-d.

Recent finds in the vicinity of Foochow demonstrate that the Plumer set, once unique because of its well-established provenance, shares the same typological features with several mortuary sets found in this area. During the Six Dynasties period it seems to have been a local Fukien tradition to include among the mortuary gifts certain pieces that do not have an exact counterpart in other areas south of the Yangtze River. The *hu-tzu,* or tiger-shaped vessel (for its possible function see cat. no. 64), is as common in Fukien as it is in the Nanking area, but it is of a squat, less elegant type. However, the incense burner and the two types of candelabras, or flower stands, are of a type that seems to be found only in and around Foochow.

A set of mortuary ceramics, excavated from tomb no. 3 on the south slope of Mount Wên-lin near Foochow on November 5, 1956, consists of pieces (fig. 70) that closely resemble the four pieces of the Plumer set. As this tomb yielded a total number of twenty-six ceramics, one may assume that Plumer

67a

67b

67c

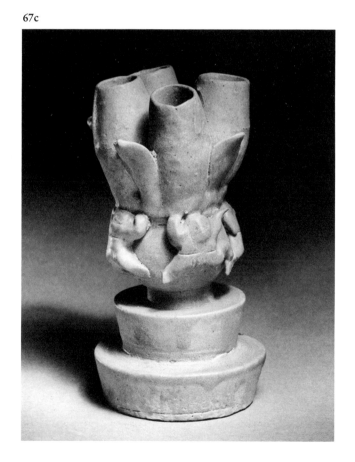

67d

fig. 70

Of special interest is an excavation at Mount Chiao-t'ou, Kuan-k'ou village, Min-hou County, in August 1958. Of the four tombs found there two could be dated by inscriptions impressed in the bricks. Tomb no. 2, datable to A.D. 497, yielded an incense burner of typical Foochow shape. Tomb no. 1, which resembles tomb no. 2 in almost every respect, and which the excavators date in the same period, contained an incense burner of the same type with a rather interesting technical refinement. Whereas the incense burner of the Plumer set has a pierced dome with flamelike appliqués, on the piece from tomb no. 1 the flames themselves are pierced to allow the incense to escape. That such pieces were not merely *ming-ch'i* (useless tomb gifts) but actually used, perhaps in the burial ceremony, is indicated by the ashes found inside this piece. Although the Plumer *po-shan-lu* appears to be a simplified version of the type found at Mount Chiao-t'ou, the dates of these two pieces do not seem to be far apart, and the Plumer set can therefore probably be dated in the late fifth or early sixth century.

References: Tsêng Fan, "Report on the cleaning out of tombs from the Six Dynasties period outside the West Gate of Foochow" (text in Chinese), *Kaogu,* 1957, no. 5, pp. 48-52; Huang Han-chieh, "Ancient tombs discovered at Mount Chiao-t'ou, Kuan-k'ou village, Min-hou County, Fukien" (text in Chinese), *Kaogu,* 1965, no. 8, pp. 425-427; see also *Wen Wu,* 1955, no. 11, p. 87, fig. 8; *Kaogu,* 1958, no. 6, pp. 18-28; ibid., 1959, no. 4, pp. 191-192.

acquired only the "most interesting" pieces of a closed find, and that the jars and dishes of a more common type somehow were excluded from the transaction. Besides the ceramics that have their counterparts in the Plumer set, the report on the Wên-lin tomb illustrates one additional piece. It is a stem cup that closely resembles a piece in the Ashmolean Museum, Oxford. According to Mary Tregear ("Early Chinese Green Wares," p. 32, fig. 14), the Oxford stem cup closely resembles a piece she saw in the Historical Museum, Peking. That piece was labeled as having come from Foochow, but it is not known whether this is the stem cup from the tomb at Mount Wên-lin.

Several other pieces resembling the Plumer set, including incense burners, candelabras, and flower stands, have been found at Ching-shan, Min-hou County, in September 1958 and at Fêng-chou, Nan-an County, in March 1957. In both cases the tombs contained many more burial gifts than the number of pieces in the Plumer set.

68

Buckle and links of a belt
Gilt bronze with reticulated decoration
Chin period, ca. A.D. 300; rectangular
pieces: l. 7 cm., hinged pieces: l. 6.5 cm.
Museum van Aziatische Kunst, Rijks-
museum, Amsterdam

The four gilt bronze pieces, described in the catalogue of the Amsterdam collection as "Late Han or later," obviously belong to a set. The rectangular pieces, one of which has a movable pin, have a pierced decoration consisting of a tigerlike animal in combat with a bird. The two other pieces consist of two parts hinged together, one rectangular with a pierced design resembling the cloud-collar motif, and one in the shape of a keyhole.

Published: Museum van Aziatische Kunst, Amsterdam, *Catalogue,* Amsterdam, n.d., no. 48.

One of the very few, and perhaps the only, datable Chin tomb excavated in the years prior to the Second World War was discovered in 1931 on Mount Ta-tao in the western suburbs of Canton. An inscription established its date as corresponding to A.D. 324. In this tomb were found a buckle, thong, and links of a gilt bronze belt that resemble in every respect the Amsterdam pieces.

Although the excavation of 1931 seems to have hardly been noticed in the Western world, the first discovery of this type made after the founding of the People's Republic of China aroused the attention of specialists in metallurgy all over the world. In March and April 1953, archaeologists of the Nanking Museum excavated the tomb of the famous general Chou Ch'u (A.D. 242-297) at I-hsing, Kiangsu Province. In addition to some of the finest and most unusual pieces of *Yüeh* ware ever found, the tomb contained sixteen buckles and links of a belt. When a small fragment of one piece was submitted to a research laboratory for spectographic analysis, the sample turned out to contain no less than 85 percent aluminum. Since it was only during the nineteenth century that Western technology mastered the technique of ex-

68

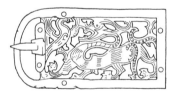

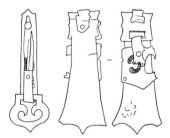

fig. 71

tracting aluminum from bauxite (which is done by an electrolytical method known as the Hall process), the occurrence of aluminum in this high degree of purity at such an early date in history caused a sensation among technicians in the field of metallurgy. When tests were repeated with other samples, however, the links of the belt turned out to be made of silver, and after years of discussion and controversy, it became clear that the piece of metal first submitted for analysis must have been merely a red herring, inadvertently left behind in the tomb by one of the robbers who had paid an illegal visit to this tomb on several occasions prior to its official excavation by archaeologists.

In addition to these two belts, another gilt bronze set was discovered in a tomb near Loyang, generally thought to date from the Western Chin period (A.D. 265-313) (fig. 71). The tomb was located in a cemetery consisting of more than fifty graves, among which were some datable between A.D. 287 and 302. That belts of this type were known far beyond the boundaries of the Chin Empire is evident from the find of a buckle and some links in a tumulus at Niiyama, Nara Prefecture, Japan. Those pieces, virtually identical with the Amsterdam set, were either imported from the Chin Empire or copied by Japanese after an imported set.

Although the tomb of Chou Ch'u had been repeatedly disturbed by grave robbers, the pieces of the belt were found near the waist of the skeleton, but, unfortunately, no reconstruction of the exact sequence and position of the different pieces could be undertaken. From literary sources, however, even the names of the different parts of a belt are known. It is evident that the buckle and links were stitched to some sort of backing or attached to it by means of small rivets. The *I-wên lei-chü*, an encyclopedic work written by Ou-yang Hsün (A.D. 557-641) refers to a silver set with reticulated decoration attached to a silk belt. It is known, however, that belts were insignia of rank and that not everybody was entitled to a silver belt, as was General Chou Ch'u. The gilt bronze

belts made for persons of lesser rank may have been attached to a leather backing, a material more in keeping with the lower status of the wearer.

The belt of Chou Ch'u has several hinged pieces, with one part in the shape of a leaf or heart. This detail resembles that of Korean silver and gold belts of the fifth and sixth centuries, of which the Museum of Fine Arts has a fine example (in silver, acc. no. 68.45). The hinged pieces of the Chin belts, all in the shape of a keyhole, may have been used to suspend insignia in the manner that was later customary in the Korean kingdom of Silla.

References: The Second Working Team of the Honan Provincial Bureau of Culture, "Excavation of tombs of the Chin dynasty at Loyang," *Kaogu Xuebao*, 1957, no. 1, pp. 169-185, esp. p. 180, fig. 11, nos. 5-6; Lo Tsung-chên, "Report on the excavation of a Chin tomb at I-hsing, Kiangsu" (text in Chinese), *Kaogu Xuebao*, 1957, no. 4, pp. 83-106; Kobayashi Yukio et al., *Sekai Kōkogaku Taikei*, vol. 3, Tokyo: Heibonsha, 1959, pl. 131 (the Niiyama set); on the controversy concerning the aluminum see *Kaogu Xuebao*, 1959, no. 4, pp. 91-97; *Kaogu*, 1962, no. 9; ibid., 1963, no. 3, pp. 165-166, and no. 12, pp. 674-678; Hsia Nai, "New determination of the metal belt excavated from the tomb of Chou Ch'u of the Chin Period" (text in Chinese), ibid., 1972, no. 4, pp. 34-39.

69
Vase
Bronze, light gray with green patina
Northern Wei period, first half of the
6th century A.D.; h. 11.7 cm.
Collection of Laurence Sickman

The ovoid body ends in a ribbed neck, which first tapers and then expands into an everted mouth.

A slightly larger, but otherwise practically identical version of this bronze vase was found in March 1964 in the village of Chia-yü-ts'un in Ch'ü-yang County, Hopei Province (fig. 72). It was the tomb of the wife of the Wei official Han Hui, *née* Kao. From the family relationships mentioned in the mortuary inscription it is evident that the Kao family belonged to the high Wei nobility, who often intermarried with the imperial house. She must have married below her class, for, whereas all of her own family is mentioned in the official annals of the Wei dynasty, her husband, even though an official of rank, was not singled out for this honor.

Although the type of tomb figurines associated with the Northern Wei period is known well enough, the number of dated Wei tombs that have been excavated under controlled conditions is quite small. The bronze vase from Chia-yü-ts'un, measuring 14.5 cm. in height, comes close to another piece of the same type found in the cemetery of the Fêng family at Ching-hsien, Hopei Province, in 1955. The finds in that cemetery range from the Northern Wei to the Sui period. From these examples it seems likely that vases of this type belonged to the tomb furniture of the Wei nobility of this area.

References: The Hopei Provincial Museum, Cultural Office, "A Northern Wei tomb discovered at Ch'ü-yang, Hopei" (text in Chinese), *Kaogu*, 1972, no. 5, pp. 33-35; Chang Chi, "Report on the investigation of the Fêng family cemetery at Ching-hsien, Hopei Province" (text in Chinese), *Kaogu*, 1957, no. 3, pp. 28-37.

fig. 72

69

70

Dancing man (shaman?)
Gray pottery, partially covered with cold
pigment
6th century A.D.; h. 22.8 cm.
William Rockhill Nelson Gallery of Art,
Kansas City, Missouri

This tomb figurine of a man is remarkable in
more than one respect. Unlike most other
figurines, it is made in two parts; the separately modeled head and neck fit into the
hollow between the shoulders. Moreover,
whereas the majority of tomb figurines strike
a motionless, standing pose, this man is
shown walking, his right foot placed in front
of the left, his body slightly bent forward.
He is clad in a long, red robe and wide, bell-
bottom trousers. His headgear is unusual,
somewhat reminiscent of the Phrygian cap;
it is undoubtedly of Central Asian origin. Its
prototype occurs already on the wall paintings in the distant sanctuary of Miran (late
third century A.D.). He wears shoes with
slightly upturned toes. Holes in both hands
suggest that they originally held objects of a
nonceramic, perishable material. Whereas
many tomb figurines exist in more than one
example, no other statuettes of this type have
yet been found.

Reference: Aurel Stein, *Serindia*, Oxford: Clarendon Press, 1921, vol. 1, figs. 136-137.

In December 1957 farmers digging a well
in the fields south of the village of Hsüeh-
chuang-ts'un, Têng-hsien County in southwest Honan, hit upon a polychromed tile. In
the flush of discovery they continued digging
and found a large tomb built of brick and
molded tiles with polychromed reliefs. The
arched entrance of the tomb was framed with
fine wall paintings of guardians standing to
attention, their hands resting upon their
swords, the same pose as that struck by the
magnificent figurines guarding the tomb of
General Chang Shêng (A.D. 502-594). Unfortunately, the energetic but inexperienced
farmers created a considerable amount of
damage before a team of the Bureau of Culture of Honan Province was able to investi-

fig. 73

gate the site. This team recovered fifty-five
tomb figurines and a considerable number of
brick reliefs, each of which measures 38 by
19 cm. and is 6 cm. thick. Altogether, there
are about sixty extant reliefs representing
thirty-four different scenes. The themes include several processions of musicians and
men bearing gifts, the Four Directional
Animals, the Paragons of Filial Piety, and
even the Four Graybeards of Mount Shang
(which is here named the Southern Mountain). Often framed by a border of simple
floral scrolls, many scenes display a natural-
ism of unusual liveliness and great charm.
The decorative effect is heightened by the use
of bright colors, a dark red, yellow, and
green, to accentuate the shapes in low relief.

One relief (fig. 73) shows, in the words of
its excavators, a "dancing scene . . . in front
an old man clad in a cinnabar red robe." The
"old man," who leads a procession of four
other men, bears a striking resemblance to
the Nelson Gallery figurine. He is dressed in
a robe of the same type and color; his headgear and shoes are also of the same type.
He is even shown in a pose that is almost the
same as that of the tomb figurine.

The "old man" on the relief illustrates the

attributes that the tomb figurine may have
held in its hand. In the left hand he holds a
so-called *chu-wei* (fly whisk), which was,
during the Six Dynasties period, the attribute
of the masters of "Pure Discussions" and,
later, of Taoist priests. Even on sixth century
Taoist stone sculpture this attribute was
often carved separately and, consequently,
later lost. In the right hand the man holds
what seems to be a shaman's wand. It is
possible, therefore, that the "dancing scene"
represents a ritual of exorcism, performed by
a shaman. However, this would not be a
shaman *(fang-hsiang)* of the classic Chinese
type, clad in bearskin and holding a spear
and shield; the costume and headgear of this
figure are of northern origin. And yet the
attributes seem to be typically Chinese. *The
Prose Poem of the Eastern Capital*, by Chang
P'ing-tzu (ca. A.D. 100), describes the great
annual purification ceremony. In it the *fang-
hsiang* held a ceremonial axe *(yüeh)*, and a
sorcerer held a bunch of reeds or rushes.
Other men involved in the ceremony held a
peachwood bow and arrow cut from the
branches of the jujube tree. Perhaps the
"wand" held in the right hand represents one
of these magic paraphernalia. The *chu-wei*,

which need not have a specifically Taoist meaning, may be interpreted here as a sign of spiritual authority.

The date of the tomb at Têng-hsien has not been firmly established. The excavators cautiously put the date in the period of Southern and Northern Dynasties. The fifth century date proposed by Akiyama seems too early. The range of possible dates can perhaps be indicated by two limits. The upper limit seems to be the end of Northern Chou and the beginning of the Sui dynasty. The figures in brick relief on the back wall of the tomb and the relief of a spirit riding a fantastic animal are related to the figures engraved on the side walls of the sarcophagus of Li Ho (died A.D. 581). On the other hand, the brick reliefs with the swiftly moving deities, men, birds, and animals are reminiscent of the scenes painted on the ceiling of Tun-huang cave 285 (Pelliot 120N), which dates from A.D. 538. A date toward the middle of the sixth century therefore seems to be the likeliest possibility.

It is of interest to note that all figurines excavated from this tomb have detachable heads. The heads and the bodies are marked to facilitate assemblage. The fact that such markings occur on the Nelson Gallery figurine indicates again its close relationship to Têng-hsien figurines. It is most likely, therefore, that this figurine at one time held the same attributes as those carried by the dancing figure on the relief.

References: Working Team of the Honan Bureau of Culture, *Têng-hsien ts'ai-sê hua-hsiang chuan-mu* [The brick tomb with painted reliefs at Teng-hsien], Peking: Wen Wu Press, 1958; The Shensi Cultural Committee, "Brief report on the cleaning out of the tomb of Li Ho of the Sui Dynasty" (text in Chinese), *Wen Wu*, 1966, no. 1, pp. 27-42; Terukazu Akiyama et al., *Arts of China, Neolithic Cultures to the T'ang Dnyasty: Recent Discoveries, Tokyo and Palo Alto:* Kodansha International Ltd., 1968, pls. 189-190, 214-216.

70

71

Pilgrim flask (*pien-hu*)
Pinkish pottery with molded decoration,
covered with a green glaze
Northern Ch'i period, third quarter of the
6th century A.D.; h. 13.4 cm.
Museum of Fine Arts, Boston, Charles B.
Hoyt Collection. 50.883

The vase has a flattened ovoid body, a short
flaring neck, and a splayed foot. On the
shoulder are two loop handles in the shape of
leaves. The unglazed bottom is of concave
shape. The molded decoration inside a frame
of double lines is the same on both sides.
It shows four musicians and one dancer, all
male. Judging from his small size, the dancer
is a young boy; he is standing on a lotus
pedestal. His head is turned back, looking
over the left shoulder; his right arm is
raised, while his left hand is placed on his
hip. The right leg is slightly raised in a posture suggestive of a dance step. Of the two
musicians on the dancer's left one is playing
a flute, while the other is clapping his hands
to the rhythm of the tune. On his right side
are a man playing the five-stringed *p'i-pa*
(an "Indian" type of lute), while the other
holds a pair of cymbals connected with a
string. All the costumes are typically Central
Asian.

Published: Hsien-ch'i Tseng and Robert Paul
Dart, *The Charles B. Hoyt Collection*, vol. 1,
Boston: Museum of Fine Arts, 1964, pl. 83.

In the Hoyt Collection catalogue this vase
has been given a T'ang date, but an excavation carried out in the spring of 1971 has
brought to light four larger vases of an almost identical type from a tomb at An-yang,
Honan Province, in which was buried Fan
Ts'ui, who lived from A.D. 549 to 575.
Although the four vases are considerably
larger (h. 20 cm.) and covered with an amber
glaze, the molded design is extremely close to
that of the *pien-hu* in the Boston Museum.
This similarity even extends to the curious
shape of the bottom of the frame, where two
volutes come together to form a base, resembling a Greek capital, for the lotus

71

fig. 74

pedestal on which the dancing boy performs. Although the loop handles of the excavated pieces have a simpler shape, the leaves are repeated in thread relief inside the frame on the sides (fig. 74).

Even though the Northern Ch'i state was denied direct access to Central Asia by its western neighbor, the Northern Chou, it developed a lively interest in Central Asian exoticism. This later became an important feature of Sui and T'ang culture. The chapter on music in the *Sui Shu* (History of the Sui Dynasty) mentions many types of music and dances from Central Asia. It is stated that since the Ho-ch'ing era (562-565) the popularity of Central Asian music in China reached its highest peak. Among the musical instruments mentioned in this text are the five-stringed *p'i-p'a* and the flute. Judging from the posture of the dancer shown on the vase, it is quite possible that he is shown performing the *hu-hsüan* dance ("nomadic whirl"), the exact geographic origin of which is somewhat uncertain. The popularity of this type of music and dance continued long into the T'ang period, as is evident from the wall painting in the tomb of Su Ssu-hsü (died A.D. 745) in the eastern suburbs of Sian. There the orchestra consists of ten musicians, including men playing a harp, a zither, and a mouth organ. The *p'i-p'a* is of the four-stringed, "Persian" type.

The *pien-hu* is traditionally called a "pilgrim's flask," although the shape probably derives from the *pien-hu* bronze vessels of the Late Eastern Chou period, long before there were pilgrims in China. An early Six Dynasties type included in this exhibition (cat. no. 63) still retains some of the features of the bronze prototypes. Small *pien-hu* similar to the piece shown here are in the Myron S. Falk Collection and in the British Museum. During the following Sui period a whole series of large *pien-hu* were made, although diminutive examples like the piece exhibited here as cat. no. 77 also occur frequently. An unusually fine example of the T'ang period (h. 28 cm.) was found in the western suburbs of T'ai-yüan, Shansi Prov-

ince. It is decorated with a molded design of a Central Asian flanked by two lions. The loops have disappeared on this vessel and have been replaced by elephant masks; the neck is more elongated and is encircled by a band of decoration.

The *pien-hu* continued to be part of the repertoire of shapes of the Chinese potter through the ages; many fine examples exist in fourteenth century blue and white. One *pien-hu* in the Palace Museum Collection, Taiwan, even shows a nomadic dance, attesting to the durability of the Chinese interest in this motif.

References: The Honan Provincial Museum, "Brief report on the excavation of the tomb of Fan Ts'ui of the Northern Ch'i period at An-yang, Honan Province" (text in Chinese), *Wen Wu*, 1972, no. 1, pp. 47-57; "Tomb of Su Ssu-hsü of the T'ang period unearthed at eastern suburb of Sian City, Shensi Province" (text in Chinese), *Kaogu*, 1960, no. 2, pl. 4, fig. 1; *Sui Shu* (Official History of the Sui Dynasty), Music Section, ch. 9/19a-b (Po-na ed., 1958 reprint); Kao Shou-t'ien, "A *pien-hu* decorated with human figure and lions unearthed at the western suburb of T'ai-yüan City, Shansi" (text in Chinese), *Kaogu*, 1963, no. 5, p. 263; National Palace Museum, Taipei, *Blue and White Ware of the Ming Dynasty*, Taipei, 1963, Book 1, pl. 11.

72
Seated Buddha
Brownish gray sandstone
Northern Wei period, ca. A.D. 475; h. 73 cm.
Museum of Fine Arts, Boston. 07.750

The Buddha is seated in cross-legged position on a rectangular pedestal against an elaborately carved nimbus with a border of stylized flames and two halos filled with representations of Transformation Buddhas. His hands are folded in the Gesture of Meditation. His monk's garb, draped over both shoulders, falls down in evenly flowing, narrowly spaced folds across the body, arms, and legs.

Chinese sculpture of this type is relatively rare, and as this was the first of these pieces to be discovered, one can hardly blame Okakura Kakuzō, who acquired it in China for the Boston Museum in 1907, for having failed to establish its correct date. His verdict of "Northern Ch'i Dynasty, Honan; somewhat degenerate Northern Wei style foreshadowing the T'ang types" was still adopted by Osvald Sirén almost twenty years later, when he assigned this type of sculpture to the same period, established its provenance as Northern Shensi and concluded "The main interest of these sculptures lies in the fact that they are quite naïve and rustic translations of foreign models which probably have come from Central or Western Asia."

Published: Osvald Sirén, *Chinese Sculpture from the Fifth to the Fourteenth Century,* London: Benn, 1925, pl. 277b.

Sirén was misled by the fact that a statue of the same class, at that time preserved in the Royal Yi Household Museum, Seoul, was thought to be inscribed with a date corresponding to A.D. 578. The Japanese scholar Matsubara Saburō added to the confusion by his questionable interpretation of the inscription on the back of the Boston statue. From the nearly effaced inscription engraved below a relief representing the Seven Buddhas of the Past, Matsubara thought to extract the information that the piece had been carved in A.D. 476 and that it represented the Buddha Amitabha. In neither instance does his conjectural reading of the inscription stand up under closer scrutiny of the original.

It is evident, however, that Matsubara's interpretation was already influenced by knowledge of the excavation of a piece closely resembling the Boston statue. The sculpture, excavated in Hsing-p'ing County, at some distance west of Sian, is now in the Shensi Provincial Museum, Sian (fig. 75). On the back is carved an inscription containing a date corresponding to A.D. 471. The main differences between the excavated piece and the Boston statue are due to the fact that they represent different figures of the Buddhist pantheon. The crossed feet and the deity supporting them as well as the gesture made by the hands are different, but except for some very minor discrepancies in details, the halos are virtually identical. One of the bands of the halo in the Hsing-p'ing sculpture is filled with scroll work, whereas it has been left blank in the Boston statue. The statues are the same in every other respect, including the curious treatment of the Transformation Buddhas, most of whom are represented in an inclined position, adapted to the curve of the halo.

Sirén was the first to realize the stylistic affinity between the rather primitive Taoist statuary from Fu-hsien, about 150 miles north of Sian, and the Boston statue, which he considered to come from the same area but to date from a century later. The relationship is real but of a different kind, for both schools of sculpture must have flourished at approximately the same time. In the Taoist sculpture from Fu-hsien and in the Buddhist sculpture from the same area, which is virtually indistinguishable from it, the reduction of the folds of the garment to thin lines seems to be a solution found by local artisans who had not yet mastered the art of rendering such essential details. The Hsing-p'ing sculpture and its mate in the Boston Museum, on the other hand, give evidence of a more sophisticated handling of the same problem. Their unusual treatment of the folds may have been due to the influence of prototypes modeled in clay.

References: Werner and Bedřich Forman, *Ancient Reliefs of China,* Peking: The People's Publishing House, 1962, pl. 185; Terukazu Akiyama et al., *Arts of China, Buddhist Cave Temples: New Researches,* Tokyo and Palo Alto: Kodansha International, Ltd., 1969, pl. 147; Matsubara Saburō, "A study of the stone Buddha images of the early Northern Wei period" (text in Japanese), *Yamato Bunka,* no. 51, 1969, pp. 4-13; Matsubara Saburō, "Three Stone Buddhist Images in the Shensi Style" (text in Japanese), *Bukkyō Geijutsu/ Ars Buddhica,* no. 90 (1973), pp. 8-17.

fig. 75 and 75a

73

Standing Kuan-yin
Gray limestone, originally covered with
polychromy
Late Northern Chou or Early Sui period,
ca. A.D. 580; h. 249 cm.
Museum of Fine Arts, Boston, Francis
Bartlett Fund. 15.254

The figure of Kuan-yin is standing on a
double lotus pedestal placed on top of a
square base, which is decorated with lions at
the four corners. In his raised left hand
Kuan-yin holds a cluster of lotus pods instead of the lotus, which is the regular attribute. The gently flowing garments are richly
adorned with different kinds of pendants and
jewelry in the manner that is typical of the
sculpture of the Late Northern Chou and Sui
periods. A long scarf falls from the shoulders
and touches the pedestal, giving additional
strength to the tall, monumental figure. A
small statue of Amitabha in the elaborate
headdress confirms the identification of this
figure as Kuan-yin (Sanskrit: Avalokiteśvara).

Osvald Sirén called this figure "one of the
best preserved and most powerful specimens
of early Chinese statuary." Perhaps closest
in style is a standing figure of Kuan-yin in the
Minneapolis Institute of Arts. An inscription
on its base refers to the dedication of an
image in A.D. 570, and this date has sometimes been offered as an argument for placing
the Boston statue in the same period. As
Marylin M. Rhie has correctly pointed out,
however, the inscription contains a second
date, corresponding to A.D. 581. Moreover,
as both parts of the inscription mention the
Historical Buddha rather than Kuan-yin,
the epigraphical evidence seems to be rather
inconclusive. Nevertheless, there can be little
doubt that the Boston statue dates from
the late years of the Northern Chou period or
the early years of the Sui dynasty.

References: John Ellerton Lodge, "Introduction
to the Collection of Chinese Sculpture," Museum
of Fine Arts, Boston, *Bulletin* 13 (1915), 60;
Osvald Sirén, *Chinese Sculpture from the Fifth
to the Fourteenth Century,* London: Benn, 1925,
pl. 274; Marylin M. Rhie, "Aspects of Sui K'ai-

huang and T'ang T'ien-pao Buddhist Images,"
East and West, n.s. 17 (1967), 96-114.

The provenance of the statue in the
Minneapolis Institute of Arts is stated to
have been Sian, the capital of the Sui and
T'ang Empires. The exact provenance of the
Boston statue, which has always been known
to have come from that same city, can be
reconstructed with the help of a letter
written by Hayasaki Kōkichi, the son of
Okakura's stepsister. In this letter, dated
April 15, 1915, Hayasaki wrote "I discovered this statue on October 6 of the 42nd
year of the Meiji era (1909) in the grounds
of the Old Monastery of the Stone Buddha
(Ku Shih-fo-ssu) outside the Northern Gate
of Sian. I tried to obtain it for myself with
the help of such friends as Li Tsung-yang,
head of the Pa-hsien-an, and Li Chên-pai of
the Hua-yang apothecary, but all my efforts
were in vain. Later, at the time of the troubles
of the revolution, I departed three times
from Tokyo to get this statue, but each time
I was detained on the way, and I had no
choice but to go back. At the time I first saw
it, its lion base was buried, so I could not tell
if there was any inscription" (translated
from the Japanese).

In his letter Hayasaki committed a strange
slip of the pen. The Old Shih-fo-ssu is not,
as he said, outside the Northern Gate, but to
the southeast of the present city of Sian,
within the old city walls of the much larger
T'ang capital Ch'ang-an. That Hayasaki
must have known this temple quite well is
confirmed by the fact that a beautiful marble
statue of a Buddha, dating from the T'ang
period, in his own collection was discovered
by him in the grounds of this dilapidated
sanctuary. Another indication that the
Boston statue comes from this temple is the
fact that Hayasaki mentioned his friend
Li Tsung-yang as an intermediary in the
negotiations with the monks of the Shih-fo-
ssu. The Pa-hsien-an (Temple of the Eight
Immortals), was just one (ancient T'ang city)
block to the north of the Shih-fo-ssu, and
its abbot, a neighbor of the priests of the

Shih-fo-ssu, would have been the right person to help him get the piece.

The reason for treating the problem of the
provenance of the Boston statue in detail
here is that the Old Shih-fo-ssu, according to
the Sian gazetteers, should be identified
with the famous Monastery of the Green
Dragon (Ch'ing-lung-ssu) of the T'ang
period. During the 1920's several Japanese
scholars visited there to pay homage to the
temple where their great patriarch Kōbō
Daishi (774-835), one of the founders of
Esoteric Buddhism in Japan, was supposed
to have resided. However, the traditional
identification of the Old Shih-fo-ssu with the
temporary residence of this venerated priest
soon gave rise to a considerable amount of
Japanese scholarly discussion.

The controversy started when a monk of
the Shingon sect visited Sian in 1924, photo-
graphed the Old Shih-fo-ssu and published
an account of his experiences. His remarks
came to the attention of the eminent scholar
Tokiwa Daijō, who questioned the identification of the few remaining buildings with
the famous Ch'ing-lung-ssu (1925). Two
years later, however, Kuwabara Jitsuzō again
defended the traditional point of view.

Although not a single map exists on which
the exact location of the Old Shih-fo-ssu
is shown, its stated proximity to the village
of Ch'i-t'ai-ts'un is difficult to reconcile with
the considerable amount of ancient literary
evidence concerning the location of the
Ch'ing-lung-ssu. The streets of Ch'ang-an
were laid out in checkerboard pattern, each
block, or ward, having its own name. All
literary sources place the Ch'ing-lung-ssu in
the Hsin-ch'ang ward, one of the blocks
immediately adjacent to the outer wall of the
eastern part of the city. Even though the
Shih-fo-ssu lies a short distance to the northeast of Ch'i-t'ai-ts'un, this location would
seem to be much too far to the west to have
been included in the Hsin-ch'ang ward.

The discussion among Japanese scholars
was doomed to remain inconclusive, as it
centered mainly around such questions as the
sources of information and the reliability of

Chinese gazetteers. Adachi Kiroku, like Hayasaki, an Old China Hand who had been invited to teach "new subjects" at Sian after the educational reforms of 1906, and who used his spare time to survey the city, never was drawn into the argument. His limited survey *(Chōan shiseki no kenkyū,* Tokyo: Tōyō Bunko, 1933) was the only source of exact information available at the time. During the last twenty years, however, Chinese archaeologists have made great progress with a detailed survey of the old T'ang city. With the help of the much more reliable maps they have prepared it is not difficult to establish that Tokiwa Daijō was quite right when he rejected the identification that devout Buddhists had accepted without questioning.

The exemplary manner with which the T'ang Capital Archaeological Team of Academia Sinica dealt with the Ch'ing-lung-ssu problem should be mentioned here, as it provides such a clear contrast with the old traditions of "armchair archaeology." After carefully reviewing the literary evidence, the archaeologists rejected the traditional view, but they then went one step further. Knowing that the Ch'ing-lung-ssu had been situated in the Hsin-ch'ang ward, that it was "pillowed on the north against a high bluff, and that the view toward the south was high and clear" (as a description dating from the T'ang period maintains), they set out in search of the real Ch'ing-lung-ssu (map, fig. 76). First they located the road that marked the southern edge of the Hsin-ch'ang ward and that led to the now ruined Yen-hsing gate in the outer walls. The oldest gazetteers specify the location as "to the East of the South Gate of Hsin-ch'ang ward." By locating inside the old Hsin-ch'ang ward an ancient north-south road crossing the road leading toward Yen-hsing gate, it was possible to establish the original site of the Ch'ing-lung-ssu. The reference to the high rise north of the temple had always been regarded as a point in favor of the Shih-fo-ssu, where such a feature does occur. The configuration to the north of the east-west road (and north of

73

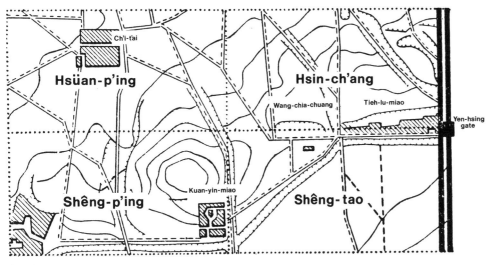

fig. 76

74
Doorway of a tomb
Dark gray limestone
T'ang period, early 8th century A.D.;
h. (total) 171 cm., w. 122 cm.
Museum of Fine Arts, Boston, William
Sturgis Bigelow Collection by exchange.
37.467

The tomb doorway consists of a semicircular tympanum, a lintel, two vertical posts, and two doors. On the tympanum is an engraved and carved representation of two confronting phoenixes with a background of stylized clouds and floral scrolls. On the lintel is a similar scene with two confronting pairs of mandarin ducks. The posts are engraved with flying birds among floral scrolls. On the left door is portrayed an official holding a *kuei* (jade tablet); on the right door is the standing figure of a woman, holding her hands in her sleeves.

When this sculpture came to the museum, it was said to have come from the area of Chin-ts'un near Lo-yang, Honan Province, where it was supposed to have been excavated from the tomb of a relative of the founder of the T'ang dynasty. It was consequently attributed to the early T'ang period.

Excavations carried out in China since the establishment of the People's Republic of China have thrown some light on the original placement and the date of this tomb doorway. Although our knowledge of this type of mortuary art has not yet reached the point of refinement where we can distinguish between the products of the two capitals of the T'ang Empire, the fact that our closest parallels are found in the area of Ch'ang-an (Sian) does little to support the dealer's provenance of this piece from Loyang. The date in the early T'ang period originally claimed for this architectural fragment is most likely to be incorrect.

The first piece of mortuary art found to resemble quite closely the gate in the Boston Museum is a huge stone sarcophagus in the shape of a house found in the tomb of Wei Chiung, the younger brother of Lady Wei,

the village Tieh-lu-miao along that road) is characterized by a flat stretch of land bordered on the north by a high rise. Although much earth has been moved, the original features of the land, as described in the literary sources, can still be recognized. Among the objects recovered during a reconnaissance of the area are a large number of T'ang tiles and an inscribed *dhāraṇī* pillar dated in accordance with A.D. 858. If one considers the close association of *dhāraṇī* pillars with Esoteric Buddhism—the type of Buddhism practiced at the Ch'ing-lung-ssu during T'ang times—this find may be considered additional evidence for the supposition that this is the original site of the Green Dragon Temple.

As to the Old Shih-fo-ssu, of which the T'ang predecessor still remains to be identified, the report of the T'ang Capital Archaeological Team mentions "It is said that in the old days there were several stone Buddhas in the temple, but they no longer exist." Through Hayasaki we now know that there were at least two such images. One is the marble Buddha now in the Eisei Bunko, Tokyo, and the other, the Kuan-yin in the

Boston Museum. Which of the two caused the name Old Stone Buddha Temple to be given to the sanctuary is uncertain. It need not necessarily be the much smaller Buddha image. In a country where the empress dowager was nicknamed "Old Buddha," because of her love of *tableaux vivants* in which she herself took the role of Kuan-yin, a temple of which the ancient name was forgotten could easily have been named Old Stone Buddha Temple after a representation of the Merciful Bodhisattva.

References: Kuwabara Jitsuzō, "On the remains of the Green Dragon Temple at Ch'ang-an" (text in Japanese), *Shirin* 12, no. 3 (1927), 47-69; The Commission for the Preservation of Ancient Monuments of Shensi Province, "Preliminary survey of the foundation of the walls of the T'ang capital Ch'ang-an" (text in Chinese), *Kaogu Xuebao*, 1958, no. 3, pp. 79-94; The T'ang Capital Archaeological Team at Sian, Institute of Archaeology, Academia Sinica, "Brief report on the reconnaissance of the site of the Ch'ing-lung-ssu" (text in Chinese), *Kaogu*, 1964, no. 7, pp. 346-348; Arthur F. Wright, "Viewpoints on a City," *Ventures, Magazine of the Yale Graduate School*, Winter 1965, pp. 15-23.

74

fig. 77

wife of the T'ang emperor Chung-tsung. Wei Chiung died in A.D. 692 at the age of sixteen (fifteen by our count). After Chung-tsung had been reinstated on the throne in A.D. 705, the younger brother of his chief consort, no doubt at her instigation, was posthumously raised in rank. His coffin was sent to the capital, and he was reburied in this tomb at Nan-li-wang-ts'un, Ch'ang-an County, Shensi Province, toward the end of A.D. 706.

The figures engraved on the panels of the stone house in his tomb (fig. 77) are very similar to those on the gate doors exhibited here. Not only is the style of the engraving related, but even the men and women wear the same type of costume, and the same type of pouch is suspended from their belts; the headgear and hair style are virtually the same. The typical early eighth century mannerism of indicating the lower contours of the sleeves by means of a wavy line, clearly visible in T'ang wall paintings in tombs of this period, has been translated here into engraved line.

These characteristics indicate that the Boston gate is a product of the building boom in tombs that occurred after the empress Wu had been deposed and the T'ang dynasty was restored to its imperial prerogatives (A.D. 705). A number of imperial victims of Empress Wu, assassinated, poisoned, or forced by her to commit suicide, were posthumously promoted in rank and reburied in order to placate the vengeful spirits of the victims and to assuage the guilt of those who had failed to intervene (see also cat. nos. 87-88).

The tombs built for these junior members of the imperial family are all of basically the same structure. Most have a sloping passageway leading into a tomb that consists of two chambers, one behind the other and connected by a corridor. The tombs of Wei Chiung, Princess Yung-t'ai (died A.D. 701, reburied 706), Crown Prince Chang Huai (died A.D. 684, reburied 711), and Prince I-tê (died A.D. 701, reburied 706) all follow this same basic architectural plan. A gateway of the type exhibited here was part of each of these tombs. It was either placed in the corridor leading from the sloping passageway into the tomb or in the corridor between the two mortuary chambers.

References: The Shensi Cultural Committee, "Report on the excavation of the tomb of Wei Chiung of the T'ang dynasty at Nan-li-wang-ts'un, Ch'ang-an County," *Wen Wu*, 1959, no. 8, pp. 8-18; for the tombs of the other junior members of the imperial family see *Wen Wu*, 1972, no. 7.

75

Seated Bodhisattva
Marble, originally polychromed and gilt
T'ang period, second quarter of the 8th
century A.D.; h. 77.5 cm.
**Museum of Fine Arts, Boston, Special
Japanese Fund. 12.63**

The Bodhisattva is seated on a richly
adorned pedestal. The robe leaves bare the
right shoulder and breast. The right arm,
originally doweled to the shoulder, has been
lost. The left hand is broken; originally, it
must have held the stem of a lotus, part of
which still clings to the left of the elaborately
dressed hair, which is held together by a
jeweled band. The Bodhisattva is seated on
a lotus throne of overlapping petals, decorated with beads. The lotus is supported by
a pedestal consisting of deeply carved,
scrolling leaves and petals in high relief. The
round base has inset panels with wavy
borders.

The statue was bought in China by Okakura Kakuzō in 1912, and the museum's records indicate Shensi as its provenance. In
several other cases where Shensi is stated to
be the provenance of a piece, it turns out that
the acquisition was made in Sian, where
Okakura and his agent Hayasaki Kōkichi,
had their best contacts (see cat. no. 73). Soon
after it came to the museum, the statue was
published by Langdon Warner, who attributed it to the end of the T'ang or to the Five
Dynasties period. Although Warner was undoubtedly correct in placing this statue at the
end rather than earlier in the development of
T'ang sculpture, he did not take into account
the steep decline in the arts in the metropolitan area, first after the uprising of An Lu-
shan in 756 and then, almost a hundred years
later, after the anti-Buddhist persecution of
the Hui-ch'ang era (A.D. 841-846). The
statue predates these tragic events and represents the last great flourishing of Buddhist
sculpture in the capital of the T'ang Empire.

Published: Langdon Warner, "A New Chinese
Marble," Museum of Fine Arts, Boston, *Bulletin*
10 (1912), 14-16; Osvald Sirén, *Chinese Sculpture from the Fifth to the Fourteenth Century,*

75

fig. 78

London: Benn, 1925, vol. 1, p. 157, vol. 4, pl. 583b.

In July 1959 men of the Department of Public Works of Sian City, working at a water conduit about five hundred yards outside the northeast corner of the walls of the present city, discovered a tunnel, about three feet in diameter and some thirty feet below the surface. In it they found ten large stone statues, eight of which were carved in white marble, and the other two in bluish limestone. The marble statues were covered with traces of gold and polychromy.

Most of the statues represent deities of the Esoteric pantheon (such as Acala, Trailokyavijaya, and Hayagrīva, seated on thrones in the shape of rocks. Representations of these figures are extremely rare in Chinese art. Of Acala, represented twice in this find, only one other Chinese statue is known; it is now in the Field Museum of Natural History, Chicago. As most of the collections in that museum were acquired by Berthold Laufer in Sian, the statue could be part of the same metropolitan religious tradition.

One sculpture (fig. 78), representing a Bodhisattva, holding a lotus in the left hand, is seated on a pedestal that resembles quite closely that of the Boston statue exhibited here. The round base with the inset panels are virtually identical, while the carving of the scrollwork supporting the lotus throne is in the same baroque manner. Matsubara has suggested that the two statues could differ somewhat in date. Even if that is correct, however, it would seem that the two statues are part of the same sculptural tradition, perhaps even the product of the same atelier.

The spot where this extremely important discovery was made belonged during T'ang times to the Ch'ang-lo ward. Historical sources agree that the great monastery An-kuo-ssu was situated in this ward. It is probable, therefore, that the statuary once belonged to this sanctuary. Although such contemporary sources as the *Li-tai-ming-hua-chi* and the *Ssu-t'a-chi* list the wall paintings of this temple and record anecdotes about its abbots, no written records of its

sculpture survive. During the K'ai-yüan era (A.D. 713-741) an Indian, or Central Asian, monk Li-shê lectured here on the *Avatam-saka-sūtra*. As the doctrine expounded in this holy text is relatively free from Tantric accretions, one may perhaps consider this group of statues as artistic creations of a religious development that took place after the death of this foreign ecclesiastic.

The An-kuo-ssu was abolished (or demolished) during the anti-Buddhist persecutions of the middle of the ninth century. Religious fear, which the *krodha* (wrathful) forms of the Buddhas have so often inspired, may have caused people to bury these statues of terrifying deities at such great depth.

References: Ch'êng Hsüeh-hua "T'ang gilt and polychrome statuary (text in Chinese), *Wen Wu,* 1961, no. 7, pp. 61-63; Matsubara Saburō, "The development of sculpture after High T'ang" (text in Japanese; abstract in English), *Bijutsu Kenkyu,* no. 257, May 1968, pp. 11-30; William R. B. Acker, *Some T'ang and pre-T'ang Texts on Chinese Painting,* Leiden: Brill, 1954, pp. 271-273; Alexander C. Soper, "A Vacation Glimpse of the T'ang Temples of Ch'ang-an," *Artibus Asiae* 23 (1960), 22-23; Yasuhiko Mayuyama, *Chūgoku Bumbutsu Kembun,* Tokyo: Mayuyama Ryūsendō, 1973, fig. 68.

The Tomb of Li Ching-hsün

Li Ching-hsün, who died June 30, A.D. 608, at the tender age of nine Chinese years (eight by our reckoning), came from a privileged family repeatedly struck by misfortune. Her paternal grandfather, Li Ch'ung, the first of the family to have his biography recorded in the official *History of the Sui Dynasty*, was a general who died in A.D. 583 on the battlefield in one of the wars against the Turkic tribes of the north. Her father, Li Min, was a prominent official in the Sui administration. Her mother's maiden name was Yü-wên; she belonged to the reigning house of the Northern Chou dynasty, which the Sui had replaced when they unified the country for the first time since the fall of the Han dynasty four centuries earlier. Li Ching-hsün was raised in the palace of her maternal grandmother, an empress of the *ancien régime*. As far as we know she was an only child. Soon after her premature death, her father became the victim of a court intrigue and was put to death at the emperor's orders. Her mother was poisoned a few months later.

At the time of the death of Li Ching-hsün, her parents were still in a position to give her a funeral in keeping with their affluent style of living. She was laid to rest in a solid, stone-built tomb in a mound just outside one of the city gates of Sian. On the outside of the outer stone coffin, as well as on the sarcophagus, which was given the shape of a small house, was engraved the imprecation "open this and you'll drop dead." The curse seems to have been effective, for when staff members of the Sian Archaeological Institute rediscovered the tomb of Li Ching-hsün in August 1957, it was found intact, not once disturbed by the grave robbers who have entered most of the tombs in this area at one time or another.

In 1929 archaeologists working on the Shang site near Anyang, Honan Province, were the first to discover a datable Sui grave. It contained the skeletal remains of Pu Jên, who died in A.D. 603. Some ceramics found in his grave were exhibited in the Chinese exhibition at Burlington House, London, 1935-36. For a long time Pu Jên's grave remained the only known datable Sui burial.

Since the establishment of the People's Republic of China, however, more than twenty such tombs have been discovered and excavated. By far the finest mortuary furniture was yielded by the tomb of the Sui general Chang Shêng (died A.D. 595). The monumental guardians of this tomb are currently shown in the traveling exhibitions from the People's Republic of China in Europe and Japan.

No collection in the West can boast of a large Sui figurine as fine as those from the tomb of Chang Shêng. The mortuary gifts from the tomb of Li Ching-hsün, on the other hand, are of interest for exactly the opposite reason. Many of the ceramics in her tomb are duplicated by pieces in Western collections, giving us an opportunity to exhibit here what may be called the archaeological equivalent of our "period rooms." The following entries (cat. nos. 76-82) describe ceramics that closely resemble the pieces in Li Ching-hsün's tomb.

As a rule clandestine excavators do not handle their booty with the same care that professional archaeologists lavish upon their discoveries. Although it is quite certain that the Sui ceramics in Western collections represent the contents of a large number of tombs, the most fragile mortuary gifts that usually accompany the pottery, such as the glassware found in Li Ching-hsün's tomb, do not seem to have counterparts in Western collections.

In other respects too, our reconstruction is far from perfect. A chicken-spouted ewer of almost the same type is known from reproductions to exist in a Japanese collection, but it has not yet been located. A jade cup of the same type as the gold-rimmed example from Li Ching-hsün's tomb may well have been preserved somewhere. If one exists in a public or private collection in the West, it is unlikely to be labeled Sui, for this period is an almost complete blank in the history of Chinese jade.

The Sui ceramics exhibited here were brought together from five different museums. To find a gold cup of almost identical shape, however, we would have to go a much greater distance. The closest of all is not a Chinese piece but its Sassanian prototype, found near Poltava (U.S.S.R.) as early as 1911 (see J. Orbeli and C. Trevor, *Orfèvrerie Sassanide*, Moscow: Academia, 1935, no. 60). Of the elegant jewelry no comparable piece has been found in Western collections. Of the mirror in Li Ching-hsün's tomb an exact counterpart was once in the Murray collection (Albert J. Koop, *Early Chinese Bronzes*, New York: Scribner's, 1924, pl. 74), but its present location is unknown.

The social distinctions that characterized life in China's highly stratified society made their influence felt even in the grave. Not only wealth but especially the status a person held during his life on earth often determined the size, quality, and number of mortuary gifts. For a nine-year-old girl, whose status derived exclusively from that of her distinguished parents and grandparents, the mortuary gifts had to be of the finest quality but modest in size. In addition to their obvious stylistic resemblance to the gifts found in Li Ching-hsün's tomb, all the pieces that have been grouped together here share this same and unusual combination of small size and high quality.

References: T'ang Chin-yü, "Brief report on the excavation of the tomb of Li Ching-hsün of the Sui dynasty in the western suburbs of Sian" (text in Chinese), *Kaogu*, 1959, no. 9, pp. 471-472, pls. 2-3; the best reproductions of pieces from this find have been published in Terukazu Akiyama et al., *Arts of China, Neolithic Cultures to the T'ang Dynasty: Recent Discoveries*, Tokyo and Palo Alto, Calif.: Kodansha International, 1968, pls. 164, 165, 360, 347-349, and in The Institute of Archaeology of Academia Sinica, ed., *Archaeology in New China*, Peking: Wen Wu Press, 1962, pls. 103-106; for the chicken ewer see Koyama Fujio et al., *Sekai Tōji Zenshū*, Tokyo: Zauhō and Kawade Shobō, 1956, vol. 9, fig. 43, p. 183.

76
Double-bodied amphora
White clay, partially covered with an olive
green and brownish glaze
Sui period, ca. A.D. 600; h. 14.9 cm.
Museum of Fine Arts, Boston, anonymous
gift in memory of Charles B. Hoyt. 54.1126

The two ovoid bodies are connected and
share the same tall neck; each body has a
handle that ends at the rim of the neck in a
stylized dragon's head. On the shoulder are
two double loops with rivetlike studs. The
olive green glaze, turning to brown in the
thick spots, flows down in irregular lines to
the base, leaving bare parts of the lower half
of the body. An amphora of a similar shape
is in the Seattle Museum.

Published: Hsien-ch'i Tseng and Robert Paul
Dart, *The Charles B. Hoyt Collection in the Museum of Fine Arts, Boston,* vol. 1, Boston, 1964,
pl. 107.

The amphora excavated from Li Ching-
hsün's tomb (fig. 79) is slightly larger (h. 18.6
cm.) than the piece exhibited here and differs
from it in two other respects. The excavated
piece is partially covered with a cream-
colored glaze; it lacks the double loops on the
shoulder and the rivetlike studs at their base.
Exactly the same type of loops appear on a
chicken-spouted ewer from the same tomb,
however, indicating how closely related
these ceramics are in spite of these small
differences.

References: Terukazu Akiyama et al., *Arts of
China,* pl. 164.

76

161

fig. 79

fig. 80

77

77

Pilgrim flask (*pien-hu*)
Light gray pottery, covered with a white glaze, molded decoration
Sui period, ca. A.D. 600; h. 9.1 cm., w. 6.6 cm.
Royal Ontario Museum, Toronto

The flattened ovoid body, splayed foot, and the two loops on the shoulder are characteristic of the so-called pilgrim flask, which until recently was considered to be a typical product of the cosmopolitan T'ang culture. Recent excavations have demonstrated that it existed already during the Northern Chou period (see cat. no. 71). The low relief decoration, produced by means of a mold, consists of an animal mask surrounded by a band of pearls.

The only difference between this piece and the small *pien-hu* from Li Ching-hsün's tomb (fig. 80) appears to be one produced by accident rather than by design. A repair of the neck slightly changed the appearance of the Toronto piece, adding a few millimeters to its height. In the Sian piece the molded design is somewhat less sharply impressed, but there can be little doubt that the two miniature flasks were produced from the same mold.

Reference: The Institute of Archaeology of Academia Sinica, ed., *Archaeology in New China,* Peking: Wen Wu Press, 1962, pl. 104, fig. 1.

78
Jar
Grayish clay, covered with a white slip under a gray green glaze
Northern Chou or Sui period, late 6th century-early 7th century; h. 18 cm.
Yale University Art Gallery

The upper body is decorated with an incised design of petals. Around the neck are eight handles in alternating horizontal and vertical positions. The gray green glaze covers only two-thirds of the body.

Published: George J. Lee, *Selected Far Eastern Art in the Yale University Art Gallery,* New Haven: Yale University Press, 1970, no. 408.

This jar lacks the expanding base that is typical of its counterpart from Li Ching-hsün's tomb (fig. 81) as well as of another jar excavated from a Sui tomb dated in accordance with A.D. 610. The eight alternating horizontal and vertical loop handles attached to the vessel around the rim are identical with those of the Sian piece, however, and are quite typical of the ceramics of that period.

References: *Kaogu,* 1959, no. 9, pl. 2, no. 16; The Kuang-tung Cultural Committee, "Brief report on the cleaning up of tombs of the Six Dynasties, Sui, and T'ang periods at Shao-kuan City, Kuang-tung" (text in Chinese), *Kaogu,* 1965, no. 5, pp. 230-235.

fig. 81

78

79
Small jar
Cream-colored clay, covered with a gray green glaze
Sui period, ca. A.D. 600; h. 5.4 cm., diam. 7.5 cm.
The Brooklyn Museum, gift of Francis M. Sedgwick

The globular body is encircled by two decorative bands of pinched clay. The pale gray green glaze stops short of the splayed foot.

Although not entirely identical in shape with the Brooklyn piece, the small jar found in the tomb of Li Ching-hsün (fig. 82) is very similar. The piece shown here must once have been provided with a similar cover with knob.

Reference: *Kaogu,* 1959, no. 9, pl. 3, fig. 3.

fig. 82

79

80
Jar
Whitish clay, covered with a gray green glaze
Sui period, ca. A.D. 600; h. 16.8 cm.
Yale University Art Gallery

The jar has a flat foot, four loop handles around the beveled rim, and a horizontal line encircling the middle of the globular body. Only the upper part of the body is covered with glaze. Although originally thought to date from the T'ang period, the shape was recognized to be typical of the preceding Sui dynasty after the excavation, in 1929, of the tomb of Pu Jên (died A.D. 603) in the vicinity of An-yang, the famous Shang site. Several examples of the same type found in Pu Jên's tomb were excavated with their covers.

Published: George J. Lee, *Selected Far Eastern Art in the Yale University Art Gallery*, New Haven: Yale University Press, 1970, no. 277; *Illustrated Catalogue of Chinese Government Exhibits for the International Exhibition of Chinese Art in London*, Shanghai: Commercial Press, 1936, vol. 4, p. 149.

Like the Yale jar, the piece excavated from the tomb of Li Ching-hsün (fig. 83) has no cover. Judging from the illustrations it seems to be partially covered with a glaze that is much darker than the gray green of the Yale piece. The An-yang region seems to be rich in tombs dating from the Sui period. Another

fig. 83

80

dated Sui tomb, of which the date in the mortuary inscription is illegible in illustration (and remains unmentioned in the report of the find), contains several jars of the same type as those from the Pu Jên find. The tomb was located at Ch'i-ts'un, 18 *li* to the southwest of An-yang.

Reference: *Kaogu,* 1956, no. 6, pp. 71-72.

81
Amphora-shaped vase
Gray stoneware, partially covered with a
green and yellowish glaze
Sui period, ca. A.D. 600; h. 15.6 cm.,
diam. 10 cm.
Buffalo Museum of Science, Buffalo, N.Y.

The ovoid body ends in a slender, tapering neck with a cup-shaped mouth. On the shoulder, between two horizontal lines encircling the body, have been attached two loop handles. The glaze stops at three-quarters of the height of the body, leaving bare the lower part and base.

Published: Walter Hochstadter, "Ceramics of the Six Dynasties, Sui, and T'ang Periods," *Hobbies* (Buffalo) 26, no. 4 (April 1946), fig. 27.

Although somewhat squat in comparison to the more elongated shape of the vase from Li Ching-hsün's tomb (fig. 84) the two vases are of a similar type. Additional documentation for its Sui date is provided by a vase excavated from a tomb datable to A.D. 615 at Pai-lu-yüan near Sian. The vases from Li Ching-hsün's tomb and the piece exhibited here have only two loop handles, whereas the example from Pai-lu-yüan has four.

All three pieces have grooves around the neck and shoulder. The glaze covers only part of the vessels. A small lump of clay stuck to the surface of the Buffalo amphora is covered by the glaze.

References: *Kaogu,* 1959, no. 9, pl. 32, fig. 14; Yu Wei-chao, "Report on the excavation of tombs at Pai-lu-yüan, Sian" (text in Chinese), *Kaogu Xuebao,* 1956, no. 3, pp. 33-76, esp. pl. 3, fig. 6.

81

82
Standing ox (tomb figurine)
Dark gray pottery, covered with a slip,
partially painted
Late 6th century - early 7th century A.D.;
h. 19.2 cm., l. 25.4 cm.
Yale University Art Gallery

The piece has been cast in a two-piece mold, covered with a white slip and painted in red.

Published: George J. Lee, *Selected Far Eastern Art in the Yale University Art Gallery,* New Haven: Yale University Press, 1970, no. 408.

Standing straight and erect, the head slightly lifted, the ox is closely related to the piece from Li Ching-hsün's tomb (fig. 85), even though the latter strikes a more lively pose. Oxen of this breed became part of the standard repertoire of the modelers of tomb figurines during the Northern Wei period; they remained in fashion to the middle of the eighth century.

Reference: *Kaogu,* 1959, no. 9, pl. 2, no. 14; Terukazu Akiyama et al., *Arts of China,* fig. 360.

fig. 84

fig. 85

83a, b

83 a, b
A pair of fantastic animals (tomb figurines)
Light pink clay covered with a greenish
white glaze, traces of black and red cold
pigment
T'ang period, ca. A.D. 625; h. 28.2 cm.
Museum of Fine Arts, Boston, Charles B.
Hoyt Collection. 50.1771-2

The legendary animal, obviously a composite
of several specimens of real fauna, has the
head of a lion and bovine hooves. Its function
was to guard the entrance of tombs. Because
of the single curved horn protruding from the
top of the head, this animal has sometimes
been confounded with the *kylin,* the unicorn
generated spontaneously during the rule of a
virtuous emperor as a result of an excess of
male *yang* energy in the universe. The two
identical pieces were cast from the same mold
and were placed at the entrance of a tomb to
ward off evil spirits, supernatural as well as
human.

Published: Museum of Fine Arts, Boston, *The
Charles B. Hoyt Collection, Memorial Exhibition,* Boston, 1952, no. 127.

84
Standing warrior in armor (tomb figurine)
White clay with cold pigment painted over a
cream glaze, traces of gold leaf
T'ang period, ca. A.D. 625; h. 36 cm.
Museum of Fine Arts, Boston, anonymous
gift in memory of Ruth Harland Duff. 37.205

The standing warrior is clad in armor and a
mail skirt. Details of armor, mail, and facial
features have been painted in cold pigments
and gold over the glaze. Jane Gaston Mahler,
who mentions the province of Honan as the
possible provenance of this piece, has determined the ethnic extraction of the warrior as
"Tocharian with Altaic mixture."

Published: Jane Gaston Mahler, *The Westerners
among the Figurines of the T'ang Dynasty in
China,* Rome: Is.M.E.O., 1959, pl. 37c.

85
Standing woman (tomb figurine)
White clay covered with a thin yellowish
glaze
Sui or early T'ang period, first quarter of the
7th century; h. 20.4 cm.
Museum of Fine Arts, Boston. 10.478

The standing woman has her hands clasped
in front of her. The dress, resembling our
Empire fashion, has narrow, tight sleeves and
a full, long skirt. A scarf is draped from the
shoulders. Figurines of this type were produced by molds and belong to the most common mortuary gifts of the Sui and early
T'ang periods. Many collections contain examples of this type.

86
Standing man (tomb figurine)
White clay covered with a yellowish, green-
tinted glaze, traces of cold pigments
Sui or early T'ang period, first quarter of the
7th century; h. 21.8 cm.
Museum of Fine Arts, Boston. 10.514

The standing man holds his hands clasped
together in front of him, the wide, long
sleeves falling down. On his head he wears
an official's hat.

The piece exhibited here from our own
collection has been damaged and has lost its
legs, but numerous complete examples of
this mold-produced tomb figurine are known
to exist in Western collections.

The five figurines described above have
several things in common. All are made of a
soft, white or light pink clay and are covered
with a yellowish glaze. On all of these pieces
details were painted in cold pigments over
the glaze; sometimes gold was added. Although pieces of this type were for a long
time considered to date from the T'ang
period, several more recent Western publications have classified them as Sui or early
T'ang.

An excavation in 1953 of an early T'ang
tomb at the famous Shang dynasty excavation site of Ta-ssu-k'ung-ts'un near An-yang,
Honan Province, has brought to light a group

84

fig. 86

fig. 87

of tomb figurines (figs. 86-87) of the same type as those exhibited here; four of these match exactly with the Boston pieces. The An-yang tomb did not contain a mortuary inscription, and the find cannot therefore be dated exactly. Inside the undisturbed tomb, however, was found a coin of the so-called *K'ai-yüan t'ung-pao* type, first minted in A.D. 621, three years after the founding of the T'ang dynasty .Although the figurines are of a type now often associated with the Sui period, there can be no doubt that these particular examples of their type must date from the first years of the T'ang at the earliest.

The excavators, for no apparent reason, attribute the tomb to the first half of the eighth century, but it would be hard to explain the presence of so many Sui types of tomb figurines in a tomb dating from a century or more after the fall of that dynasty. A combination of archaeological data with literary evidence can give us a clue to the approximate date of this find.

One of the most conspicuous differences between tomb figurines representing women dating from the Sui and the T'ang period is in the hairstyle. Although women of the Sui period wore their hair on top of the head, it was dressed and combed flat. Later, it became fashionable to wear the hair much higher, and it was combed up in chignons and tufts on top of the head. In tomb figurines, which faithfully followed fashions, the "new look" in hairstyle begins to make its appearance toward the middle of the seventh century. Unfortunately, even with the many dated tombs that have become known in recent years, those dating from the first half of the seventh century are still only small in number. The earliest datable tomb with figurines in the new hairstyle dates from A.D. 642. It is quite possible, however, that the "new look" was already current in tomb figurines well before that time.

A literary source, the biography of Ling-ku Tê-fên in the *Old history of the T'ang period,* records a conversation that took place in A.D. 622 when the emperor expressed surprise at seeing court ladies wearing the new, tall hairstyle. Ling-ku Tê-fên gave a typical sycophant's explanation of this novelty. If the new fashion caused astonishment at court in A.D. 622, it must have been a brand new phenomenon at that time. The figurines of women in the tomb at Ta-ssu-k'ung-ts'un, datable after A.D. 621, still show the old hairstyle. We may assume, therefore, that the tomb dates from only a few years later.

The tomb at Ta-ssu-k'ung-ts'un also helps in solving another problem. The two so-called *kylins* from the Hoyt Collection are identical pieces. Although they are cast from the same mold as the damaged specimen from the tomb illustrated with the excavation report, there can be little doubt that they did not originally belong together. The Ta-ssu-k'ung-ts'un report states that the other piece of the pair of guarding animals had a face resembling that of a man. From several other tombs dating from the Sui period and later we know that two monsters, one with a lion's face and one with a human face, guarded the entrance to the tomb chamber in the company of two guardian figures.

There may be a simple explanation for the fact that we have two identical pieces rather than two with different faces. The bootleg excavators who dug up the Boston pieces probably found the tombs of two members of the same family next to one another. (From excavation reports we know that this is quite often the case.) The contents of the two tombs were perhaps mixed up, however, and when the mortuary gifts were sorted out for sale and dispersal, the two pairs of guarding animals were divided by keeping the identical pieces together as "pairs."

References: Ma Tê-chih, "A T'ang tomb at Ta-ssu-k'ung-ts'un, An-yang" (text in Chinese), *Kaogu*, 1955, no. 4, pp. 54-56; Wang Ch'ü-fei, "The Four Spirits, caps and dressed hair" (text in Chinese), *Kaogu*, 1956, no. 5, pp. 50-54.

85

86

87 a, b
Two standing men (pair of tomb figurines)
Soft red pottery, traces of white slip
T'ang period, early 8th century; h. 22.3 cm.
Museum of Fine Arts, Boston. 10.476-7

The men are wearing long-sleeved coats with wide lapels and caps that cover the head and neck. A long robe covers the lower legs and feet. The left arm hangs down along the body, the hand covered by the long sleeve. The right hand is held up in front of the breast.

The two pieces came to the Museum of Fine Arts on September 29, 1910, as part of a large shipment of pieces purchased in China by Okakura Kakuzō through the intermediary of Hayasaki Kōkichi. Hayasaki was a longtime resident of Sian, who collected most of his Chinese art objects there (see cat. no. 73). It is most likely, therefore, that these pieces came from the Sian area.

Whereas some of the larger tomb figurines were individually modeled and are therefore unique, the majority of T'ang tomb figurines were mass-produced by means of molds. These molds remained in use for a few years, to be replaced by new ones, made in order to keep up with the latest changes in fashion. The male statuettes exhibited here are typical examples of the tomb figurines that were produced in great numbers.

The approximate date of their production can be established because pieces obviously cast from the same mold have been found in datable tombs. A pair of these figures was discovered in a tomb at Kuo-chia-t'an near Sian in July 1954 (fig. 88). The tomb is that of a Mrs. Jên, who died in A.D. 707. The other tomb in which the same figurines make their appearance is that of the unfortunate princess Yung-t'ai, younger sister of the crown prince I-tê. One of the victims of the empress Wu, the princess lost her life in A.D. 701. That this type of figure was really mass-produced is evident from the inventory of Yung-t'ai's tomb. Of two slightly different types of tomb figurines representing standing men Yung-t'ai's tomb contained no less than 264 examples.

87a, b

fig. 88

References: The Shensi Cultural Committee, "Brief report on the excavation of the tomb of Princess Yung-t'ai of T'ang" (text in Chinese), *Wen Wu,* 1964, no. 1, pp. 7-33; The Shensi Cultural Committee, "Brief report on the cleaning out of a T'ang tomb at Kuo-chia-t'an, Sian" (text in Chinese), *Kaogu,* 1956, no. 6, pp. 51-53.

88

Horse (tomb figurine)

White pottery with a yellowish glaze, green and amber splashes

T'ang period, early 8th century; h. 59.2 cm., l. 76 cm.

Museum of Fine Arts, Boston. 27.2

The horse's head arches down toward the slightly bent left foreleg. A fur robe partially covers the saddle; on the left side it is folded back, revealing the saddle and one of the stirrups underneath. The richly ornamented bridle and body straps are hung with pendants. The tail is docked, and three angular tufts (one broken) stick out of the clipped mane. This tomb figurine has undergone numerous repairs, although they are hardly visible to the naked eye.

The same characteristic pose, which is found rarely among figurines of the T'ang period, is struck by a horse excavated from a tomb whose occupant died in A.D. 703, in the vicinity of Sian, Shensi Province. Sian, under the name of Ch'ang-an, was once the great capital of the T'ang Empire. Another conspicuous distinguishing feature is the crenelated mane. This motif has been the subject of detailed studies by Otto Maenchen-Helfen and Harada Yoshihito, who have traced its origins back to the fifth century B.C., and who have assembled examples of this type of embellishment of horses from areas as widely apart as southern Russia, Iran, Central Asia, and China. In China the crenelated mane disappeared after the Han period, to return during T'ang times. During its many peregrinations all over Asia the mane with crenels "remained what it had been from its first appearance: a sign of distinction, either of the horse, or its rider, or both" (Maenchen-Helfen).

There is ample literary evidence of the association of the crenelated mane with horses belonging to persons of exalted rank. In recent years excavations have confirmed this association. According to the *New history of the T'ang period,* horses of the Office of Imperial Carriages were branded with marks reading "Three Flowers" and "Flying Phoenix." The expression "Three Flowers" is the name by which the crenelated mane of the horses was known in T'ang times. In the Royal Ontario Museum, Toronto, is a tomb figurine of a horse inscribed with the words "Flying Phoenix." The inscription is obviously an imitation of the mark branded into a horse of the imperial stable.

Although the crenelated mane may thus have served for some time as an imperial emblem, the custom of clipping the mane with three, sometimes even five "flowers" seems to have enjoyed a popularity that extended beyond the Forbidden City. In the *Ming-hua yao-lu* (Summary record of famous paintings), a contemporary record, it is mentioned that the use of "three flowers" was very popular during the K'ai-yüan and T'ien-pao eras (A.D. 713-742). As tomb sculpture often reflected the vogue of the times, T'ang figurines of horses dating from the first half of the eighth century sometimes display this popular feature. Whereas the crenels on the mane of the famous horse on the stone relief from the mausoleum of the T'ang emperor T'ai-tsung (died A.D. 636) have a bent, pointed shape resembling the tip of a sabre, the angular, straight shape first appears on horse figurines of a slightly later date.

Most clearly related to the horse in the Boston Museum is a figurine (fig. 89) from the tomb of the T'ang general Hsien-yü T'ing-hui, who died at the T'ang capital in A.D. 723. Although the two pieces differ in that the horse from the general's tomb is represented in the more common straight, upright pose, the modeling and the details of decoration of the two figurines are very similar. Even the amber glaze used to color one of the pendants has dripped down each horse's leg in exactly the same fashion. On the mane of the general's horse are three crenels, closely spaced together.

Several other finds of figurines representing horses with crenelated manes tend to confirm the idea that these should be associated with persons of exalted, imperial rank. In the imperial cemetery Ch'ien-ling, near Sian, horses of this type were found in the tombs of two of the imperial victims of the notorious empress Wu. One was found in the tomb of the crown prince Li Hsien (Chang Huai), who was forced to take his own life in A.D. 684. The lavish funerary gifts date from the time of his official reburial in A.D. 711. Yet another horse with three crenels came from the tomb of Crown Prince Li Ch'ung-jun (I-tê, 682-701), another victim of Empress Wu.

The posture and modeling, as well as the size and the ornaments of the horse, suggest that the Boston figurine displayed here must have come from a tomb of a Chinese high official or prince who died during the first quarter of the eighth century.

References: Otto Maenchen-Helfen, "Crenelated mane and scabbard slide" *Central Asiatic Journal* 3, no. 2, pp. 85-138; Harada Yoshihito, *Tō-a ko-bunka ron-kō*. Tokyo: Yoshikawa Kobunkan, 1963, pp. 266-275; Ma Tê-chih and Chang Chêng-ling, "Brief report on the excavation of three T'ang tombs in the suburbs of Sian" (text in Chinese), *Kaogu*, 1958, no. 1, pp. 42-52; T'ang tombs excavation team, the Shensi Provincial Museum, "Brief report on the excavation of the tomb of Crown Prince Chang Huai of the T'ang" (text in Chinese), *Wen Wu,* 1972, no. 7, pp. 13-25; idem, "Brief Report on the excavation of the tomb of Crown Prince I-tê of the T'ang" (text in Chinese), ibid., pp. 26-31; *Hsin T'ang-shu* (Pona ed.), vol. 8, *po-kuan-chih,* ch. 37, p. 7b.

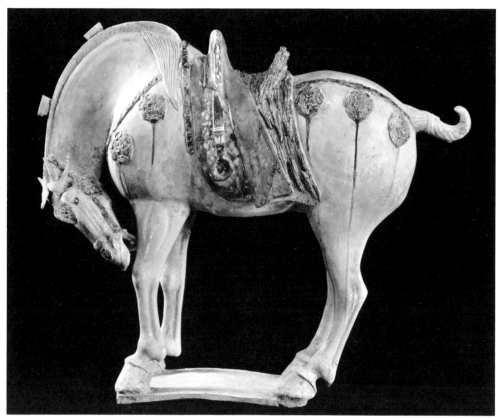

88

fig. 89

89

89

Standing lady (tomb figurine)
Buff clay, partially covered with white slip
T'ang period, ca. middle of the 8th century;
h. 46 cm.
Museum of Fine Arts, Boston, gift of Mr. and
Mrs. Eugene Bernat. 47.1550

The lady is standing in a graceful pose; she is
clad in a dress with long sleeves, one of which
covers the raised left hand. The right hand,
which originally held a bird or an object, has
lost most of its fingers. She has a round,
plump face, framed by a heavy wiglike headdress with a knot of hair aslant on top. The
folds of the garment are indicated by incised
lines with shallow cuttings.

Before archaeological information on
tomb figurines had become available, mortuary sculpture was often dated by the color
of its clay and glazes. This method could
have been successfully applied to the white
and yellowish glazed figurines that we now
know to date from the Sui and early T'ang
period (see cat. nos. 83-86). Other types,
however, seem to have been manufactured
over a much longer period of time, and dating by ceramic type alone therefore only led
to confusion.

A typical case is that of the figurines in buff
or dark ochre-colored clay, covered with a
white slip. For a long time these were thought
to date from before the T'ang period. For
example, Alfred Salmony, on the advice of
the collector Richard Goldschmidt, who in
turn claimed to have adopted the dating from
Chinese scholars, dated all pieces of this type
in the Sui period. Salmony observed "This
group breaks with the stylistic tradition of
the preceding art . . . For the first time it is the
modeling tools of the clay artist which deter-
mines the form."

Recent discoveries have given an adequate
explanation for the "break in stylistic tradition" that Salmony thought to observe. The
figurines of this type do not precede the
flourishing art of mortuary sculpture of the
seventh century and the first half of the
eighth century. On the contrary, they date
from the very end of this continuous tradi-

fig. 90

tion. A comparison of the figurine exhibited here with examples excavated from datable tombs reveals a close similarity to the figurines excavated in 1954 from tomb no. 50 in a cemetery at Kuo-chia-t'an, a few miles to the northwest of Sian (fig. 90). The tombstone states that the person buried in this tomb died in A.D. 744. The treatment of the folds in the garment and of the sleeves is virtually identical, leaving no doubt as to the approximate date of our piece.

The plump, round-faced woman depicted by this tomb figurine has often been associated with the famous imperial concubine Yang Kuei-fei, the *femme fatale* whom traditional history blames for the disasters attendant upon the end of the reign of Emperor Hsüan-tsung (reigned 713-756). Although there can be no doubt that the ideals of feminine beauty of those days are reflected in mortuary sculpture, a direct connection with Yang Kuei-fei is rather unlikely. Figurines representing this type were found in the tomb of General Hsien-yü T'ing-hui, who died in A.D. 723, well before the concubine's spectacular rise to power.

Such figurines continued to be made until the middle of the eighth century. The latest datable find with statuettes of this type dates from A.D. 748. Soon afterward the economic decline caused by the uprising of An Lu-shan and the civil war following it led to a drastic reduction in the number and size as well as deterioration of the quality of tomb figurines. This difference is especially noticeable in the area surrounding the T'ang capital, which was most immediatedly affected by the political turmoil and the economic recession it brought about.

References: Shensi Archaeological Reconnaissance Team, Institute of Archaeology, "Brief report on excavations at Pao-chi and in the vicinity of Sian" (text in Chinese), *Kaogu,* 1955, no. 2, pp. 33-40; The Shensi Cultural Committee, comp., *Shensi-shêng ch'u-t'u T'ang-yung hsüanchi* [Selected tomb figurines excavated in Shensi Province], Peking: Wen Wu Press, 1958, pls. 66-70; Friends of Far Eastern Art, *Exhibition of Chinese Tomb Statuettes,* San Francisco, 1937, catalogue by Alfred Salmony, p. 23.

The Hoard of Ho-chia-ts'un

The area of the ancient metropolitan centers Sian and Loyang, once the twin capitals of the T'ang Empire, are the likeliest places for finding hoards of gold and silver. The pyramidal structure of Chinese government and society concentrated the wealth of the empire in its capital cities. When the violence of civil war began to affect the metropolitan centers in the middle of the eighth century, the rich followed the example of their Son of Heaven, whose flight to faraway Szechwan is recorded in literature and painting. Before fleeing, many must have carefully buried their costliest worldly possessions in the ground. In the tragic days of the An Lu-shan rebellion only a few returned to claim their treasures.

Among the few recorded finds of T'ang silver in the pre-war period, the largest is that of Pei-huang-shan near Sian. It consists of fifteen pieces, one of which is datable to A.D. 877. The entire hoard was sold to the British Museum in 1925. As late as 1957 Bo Gyllensvärd, the leading authority on T'ang silver in the Western world, wrote after a visit to China: "In Hsi-an the finds from the last excavation by Academia Sinica are still wanting in gold and silver objects, as the archaeologists have not had an opportunity of investigating the old palace area or a large number of T'ang tombs containing such objects." That same year already the first major discoveries of T'ang gold and silver occurred. In May 1957 seven silver cup stands, one inscribed with a date corresponding to A.D. 860, were found in the northeast corner of the ancient P'ing-k'ang ward of Ch'ang-an. A fine plate decorated with a lion, accompanied by inscribed plaques dating from between A.D. 743 and 751, was discovered in the grounds of the former Ta-ming-kung Palace, and a hoard of fifteen pieces, including four spherical censers, was found at Sha-p'o-ts'un, a southeastern suburb of Sian.

All of these discoveries, as well as those made elsewhere in the country, were completely eclipsed by the enormous hoard that was excavated in the village of Ho-chia-ts'un in October 1970. Hidden in two large pottery jars was a treasure consisting of more than 270 objects in gold and silver, as well as more than 700 other objects, medicinal and mineral samples, Chinese and foreign coins. The gold and silver vessels represent a cross-section of the repertoire of the familiar shapes, decorative motifs, and techniques. In addition there are many shapes and motifs that had never been seen before. The gilt silver wine ewer with a dancing horse clenching a cup in its teeth and the tureen with a design of parrots among flowers are masterpieces of the T'ang silversmith that surpass in quality anything previously discovered.

It is obvious that such a hoard could have belonged only to a person of the highest rank in T'ang society. Owing to the increased knowledge of the geography of the T'ang capital Ch'ang-an, the excavators were able to come up with a plausible attribution of the former ownership of this cache. The *Liang-ching hsin-chi* ("New record of the two capitals") mentions that the Hsing-hua ward, which included the area in which the hoard was excavated, comprised the residence of Li Shou-li, Prince of Pin and a cousin of Emperor Hsüan Tsung. After Li's death in A.D. 741 his son inherited the title and continued to live here until he joined the flight of the imperial entourage to Szechwan in A.D. 756. It is thought that the treasure was buried before the prince fled.

It will be obvious that an exhibition of this type could not possibly do justice to the quality and variety of the objects in the Ho-chia-ts'un hoard. However, two superb examples of T'ang silverware as well as a number of other comparable pieces can give the visitor to the exhibition at least an inkling of some of the precious and highly interesting types of material that were preserved there.

References: Hsia Nai, "Treasures of Hochiatsun, Sian," *New Archaeological Finds in China,* Peking: Foreign Languages Press, 1972, pp. 3-5; *Wên-hua ta-ko-ming ch'i-chien ch'u-t'u wên-wu* [Cultural relics discovered during the period of the Great Cultural Revolution], Peking: Wen Wu Press, 1972, pls. 44-70; Shensi Provincial Museum, "A cache of cultural relics of the T'ang period discovered in Ho-chia-ts'un in the south ern suburbs of Sian" (text in Chinese), *Wen Wu,* 1972, no. 1, pp. 30-38; Shensi Provincial Museum," Brief report on the reconnaissance of the foundation remains in Hsing-hua ward in the T'ang city of Ch'ang-an" (text in Chinese), ibid., pp. 43-46.

90
Lotus-shaped bowl
Beaten silver, embossed and engraved, partially gilt
T'ang period, 7th or first half of the 8th century A.D.; h. 6.1 cm., diam. 16.3 cm.
William Rockhill Nelson Gallery of Art, Kansas City, Missouri

The exterior of the bowl is decorated with an embossed design of large lotus petals that frame the entire piece and reach almost up to the flaring rim. The petals are decorated with chased and gilt floral sprays, running animals, and flying birds against an overall punched background. On the inside of the base is a repoussé gilt design of dragon heads, fishes, catfish, and birds on a chased design of stylized waves. The bottom has a finely chased and gilt rosettelike floral ornament.

Of the few bowls of this type and quality in collections outside China the piece closest to the bowl exhibited here is the example in the Hakutsuru Museum, Kobe. Both bowls represent the art of the T'ang gold and silversmiths at its apogee, when the strong Sassanian influence was gradually being absorbed and transcended, and a new, refined style, as cosmopolitan in character as T'ang culture itself, was beginning to emerge.

Published: Los Angeles County Museum, *The Arts of the T'ang Dynasty,* 1957, no. 332 (frontispiece); Kano Jihei, *Hakutsuru-cho,* vol. 1, Kobe: Hakutsuru Sanso, 1931, pl. 44.

None of the large number of vessels and bowls in the Ho-chia-ts'un hoard matches exactly the style and shape of the Kansas City bowl. A pair of gold cups with a repoussé design of lotus petals, though slightly smaller (diam. 13.5 cm.), comes closest to it in shape and in type of decoration (fig. 91). A shallow silver bowl (fig. 92) has a repoussé design of two juxtaposed lions with floral scrolls that is similar in style to the aquatic scene on the inside of the base of the Kansas City bowl. The fact that all of the principal features of this bowl occur on different pieces in this find indicates that all date from approximately the same period.

References: *Wên-hua ta-ko-ming ch'i-chien ch'u-t'u wên-wu* ("Cultural relics discovered during the period of the Great Cultural Revolution"), Peking: Wen Wu Press, 1972, pls. 44, 55.

90

fig. 91

fig. 92

90

177

91

91
Censer
Beaten silver with reticulated decoration
T'ang period, 7th-8th century A.D.;
diam. 4.5 cm.
William Rockhill Nelson Gallery of Art,
Kansas City, Missouri

The censer is made up of two hemispheres joined together by a hinge on one and a bolt on the other side. It is suspended from a short chain. The reticulated decoration consists of birds among floral scrolls. Inside, a cup for incense is suspended from gimbals like a ship's compass, allowing the piece to swing without spilling the contents of the receptacle. According to the *Miscellaneous Records of the Western Capital* the "Cardan" method of suspension was already in use during the Western Han period (see Joseph Needham, *Science and Civilization in China*, vol. 4, part 2, Cambridge: University Press, 1965, pp. 228-236).

Several examples of this type of censer are found in Western collections, including the British Museum, London, the Hakutsuru Museum, Kobe, and the Kempe Collection, Ekolsund, Sweden.

Published: Bo Gyllensvärd, *Chinese Gold and Silver in the Carl Kempe Collection*, Ekolsund, 1953, no. 96.

Judging from the number of spherical hanging censers in Western collections, these objects may have been fairly common in T'ang times. A hoard of fifteen pieces of silver, excavated at Sha-p'o-ts'un near Sian, contained no less than four censers, but the hoard of Ho-chia-ts'un, surprisingly, contained only a single example of this type (fig. 93). All of these excavated examples are basically of the same construction, and although the openwork design varies at times, the pieces probably all date from approximately the same time.

References: The Cultural Committee of Sian City, "A group of silver pieces discovered at Sha-p'o-ts'un in the southeast suburbs of Sian," (text in Chinese), *Wen Wu*, 1964, no. 6, pp. 30-32; *Wên-hua ta-ko-ming ch'i-chien ch'u-t'u wên-wu*

("Cultural relics discovered during the periods of the Great Cultural Revolution"), Peking: Wen Wu Press, 1972, pl. 60.

fig. 93

92

fig. 94

92
Padlock
Bronze
T'ang period, 7th-8th century A.D.;
l. 20.3 cm.
Collection of Dr. Paul Singer

That clasplike padlocks of the type exhibited here were used in T'ang times to lock chests and boxes is indicated by the occasional use of miniature examples on models of chests found in tombs. The padlocks were made of bronze or silver. In addition to this bronze piece there are gilt bronze padlocks in the collection of Laurence Sickman and in the Sackler Collections. The Hakutsuru Museum, Kobe, has a group of five very similar pieces, all cast in silver. These are said to have been excavated at Mu-tan-shan ("Peony Hill") near Lo-yang, Honan Province.

References: Bo Gyllensvärd, "T'ang Gold and Silver," Museum of Far Eastern Antiquities, Stockholm, *Bulletin* no. 29 (1957), 51; Kano Jihei, *Hakutsuru- chō,* vol. 1, Kobe: Hakutsuru Sansō, 1931, pl. 60; for the art of the Chinese locksmith see Joseph Needham, *Science and Civilization in China,* vol. 4, part 2, Cambridge: University Press: 1965, pp. 236-246.

The gold and silver hoard of Ho-chia-ts'un contained a large number of padlocks of exactly the same shape and construction (fig. 94) as the piece exhibited here. Seventeen of these were in silver and gilt, six in silver. The gilt pieces are all covered with a minutely chased decoration. Like the fine floral decoration on the bottom of the bowl (cat. no. 90), this detail illustrates the meticulous care for detail that characterizes the art of the T'ang silversmith during its heyday.

References: *Wên-hua ta-ko-ming ch'i-chien ch'u-t'u wên-wu* [Cultural relics discovered during the period of the Great Cultural Revolution], Peking: Wen Wu Press, 1972, pl. 60; *Asahi Graph,* June 20, 1973, p. 95.

93
Stem cup
Gilt bronze with chased decoration
T'ang dynasty, 7th-8th century A.D.;
h. 6.3 cm., diam. 5.1 cm.
Center for Asian Art and Culture, the Avery
Brundage Collection, San Franicsco

Small goblets with an oval body, a stem with
a thick nodule, a spreading foot and a slightly
everted mouth rim were quite common during the T'ang period; examples exist in
pottery, gilt bronze, glass, silver, and gold.
On several of the pieces in gilt bronze and
silver appear, as on the piece exhibited here,
the revived version of the classic hunting
scene, in which galloping hunters practice
their skill in the "Parthian shot" (shooting
backward on horseback) at a variety of lifelike or imaginary animals. The swiftly moving scene is set against a summarily indicated
landscape and an overall punched background. Stylized clouds decorate the band
around the rim.

Published: René-Yvon Lefebvre-d'Argencé,
*Ancient Chinese Bronzes in the Avery Brundage
Collection,* San Francisco: M. H. De Young
Museum Society, 1966, p. 128, pl. 59a.

Among the pieces in the hoard of Ho-chia-
ts'un are two gilt silver stem cups decorated
with the same design, but slightly smaller in
size (h. 7 cm., diam. 5.9 cm.; fig. 95). The
band around the rim, marked off by a raised
line, is decorated with floral scrolls. A goblet
closely resembling this stem cup is found in
the British Museum (formerly in the collection of Mrs. Walter Sedgwick).

References: *Wên-hua ta-ko-ming ch'i-chien ch'u-
t'u wên-wu* [Cultural relics discovered during the
period of the Great Cultural Revolution], Peking:
Wen Wu Press, 1972, pl. 51; Bo Gyllensvärd,
"T'ang Gold and Silver," Museum of Far Eastern
Antiquities, Stockholm, *Bulletin* no. 29, 1957, pl.
17a.

93

fig. 95

94

Rhyton in the shape of a bull's head
Dark brown jade
T'ang period, 7th-8th century A.D.;
h. 8.7 cm.
Center for Asian Art and Culture, the Avery
Brundage Collection, San Francisco

The libation cup, or rhyton, reached the Far East through Central Asia. It is, in all probability, part of the artistic heritage that the Sassanian silversmiths brought to China, for it is in silverware of the Sassanian period that the closest parallels are to be found with the rhytons in pottery, gilt bronze, and jade that are known in Chinese art. That the Chinese were aware of the way foreigners used the rhyton is evident from a relief in the Museum of Fine Arts, Boston, which shows a Central Asian chieftain raising his rhyton while surrounded by a retinue of subjects. This relief dates from the Northern Ch'i period (A.D. 550-577), when the taste for exotic foreign things reached its first peak (see cat. no. 71).

With the exception of those made in glazed pottery (as, for example, the piece in the British Museum, which probably dates from the late sixth or early seventh century), the Chinese rhytons that have been preserved are often difficult to date. The gilt bronze example in the Seligman Collection is attributed, for no apparent reason, it would seem, to the Ming period. The jade rhyton exhibited here is one of several pieces of this type in the Avery Brundage Collection. It closely resembles another jade rhyton that is reproduced in the ancient catalogue *Ku-yü t'u-p'u* by Chu Tê-jun, first published in A.D. 1341. Its somewhat dull luster may be due to treatment of the surface, designed to make it resemble natural horn, which the Chinese liked to use for drinking vessels because of its alleged poison-detecting property. Although the date of this piece is as uncertain as that of the other cups of this genre, it could well date from the time when Sassanian art exerted its strongest influence on Chinese culture.

Published: René-Yvon Lefebvre d'Argencé, *Chinese Jades in the Avery Brundage Collection,* San Francisco: Center for Asian Art and Culture, 1972, pl. 34, p. 82; Gustina Scaglia, "Central Asians on a Northern Ch'i Gate Shrine," *Artibus Asiae* 21 (1958), pp. 9-28; S. Howard Hansford, *The Seligman Collection of Oriental Art,* vol. 1, London: Lund Humphries, 1957, p. 90, A. 90.

That Chinese rhytons may not always have been made after prototypes in Sassanian silver, as is usually taken for granted, but may have imitated pieces in other materials as well, emerged suddenly as a possibility when the hoard at Ho-chia-ts'un yielded a superb example of a rhyton, carved in onyx (fig. 96). The rhyton, in all probability one of the greatest rarities in this precious collection of objects, measures only 15.5 cm. in length; its mouth has a diameter of 5.9 cm. The origin of this masterpiece of hard stone carving must probably be sought in Central Asia, but no other pieces of this type have come to light that could give us an indication of its exact provenance.

As the size of the onyx piece is similar to that of the jade rhyton shown here and smaller than the rhyton on the Northern Ch'i relief, the Chinese jade carver could well have used a similar piece as a prototype, rather than a larger piece in silver. The Chinese piece has pierced nostrils, presumably serving as a suspension hole. One wonders, however, if these holes could not have been drilled in order to secure a gold nose of the type attached to the onyx piece.

References: *Wên-hua ta-ko-ming ch'i-chien ch'u-t'u wên-wu* [Cultural relics discovered during the period of the Great Cultural Revolution], Peking: Wen Wu Press, 1972, pl. 70.

fig. 96

94

95

fig. 97

95
Sassanian coin, known as a "mithqal"
Silver
Reign of Khusrau II (A.D. 590-628);
diam. 2.6 cm.
Museum of Fine Arts, Boston, gift of
William O. Comstock. 15.303

On the obverse of this silver coin, one of millions minted during his reign, the bust of Khusrau II is represented in profile facing right. The head of the king is shown with a mustache, a beard, and flowing curls. The king is wearing an earring and a necklace, and his crown is surmounted by two wings enclosing a crescent and a star. During the Sassanian period each king was distinguished on his coinage by a different crown, which was more or less the trademark of the reign. To the right and left of Khusrau's head are inscriptions in Pahlavi. A double grenetis, or border, circumscribes the bust, and in the margin are three crescents with stars. On the reverse a portable fire altar is represented, ringed by a triple grenetis. The fire altar, a central symbol of Zoroastrianism, is guarded by two "mobeds," or magi, the priests of the Zoroastrian faith. Three crescents with stars and the fragment of a fourth appear in the margin of the reverse. An inscription and the mint mark in Pahlavi appear to the left and the right of the magi respectively.

To the right of Khusrau's head on the obverse the inscription reads "Khusrui" and to his left, "afzu" or "afzutu," with an undeciphered monogram. While the precise meaning of the word "afzu" is conjectural, it probably signifies "long live the king" or a similar expression of royalist sentiment. On the reverse the inscription on the left reads "hasht-vist," translated as twenty-eight, which indicates that the coin was minted in the twenty-eighth year of the reign of Khusrau II, or 617 A.D. The two Pahlavi letters that are inscribed to the right on the reverse represent the mint monogram translated either as MB or MR. Since approximately 120 mints were in operation during the reign of Khusrau II, the interpretation of mint

monograms from this period has been the source of much debate among Sassanian numismatologists. Some scholars believe that the two or three letters of a monogram might refer to local princes as well as to names of sites. To confuse the issue, the Arabs, who conquered Persia in 641, changed the names of many of the towns and ordered all Pahlavi books destroyed. Nevertheless, the Arabs did continue for a while to print their own currency at Sassanian mint sites. Thus, while the mark on the coin might signify MB, an abbreviation for Maibud in the southern province of Kirman, it probably is MR, standing for Merv, a major city in northern Persia.

References: John Walker, *A Catalogue of the Arab-Sassanian Coins,* London: British Museum, 1941, pp. ci-cvii, cxxii-cxxiii; J. de Morgan, "Contribution à l'étude des ateliers monétaires sous la dynastie des rois sassanides de Perse," *Revue numismatique,* 4th ser., 17 (1913), 15-41; Furdonjee D. J. Paruck, *Sasanian Coins,* Bombay: Times Press, 1924, pp. 21-27, 67-68, 114-115, 125-129, 132, 161, 267-269, 284-285, 386-390, 407-409.

Sassanian coins, of which about a hundred examples have been found in China's western territories, Sinkiang and Chinghai, have turned up occasionally in tombs in China proper. The easternmost find of Sassanian coins occurred in 1956 at Shan-hsien, Honan Province, which is where the Han watchtower in the exhibition (cat. no. 48) came from. The two coins, datable to 555 and 575, were found in the tomb of Liu Wei and his wife, who were brought to Shan-hsien from Ch'ang-an and who were interred together in A.D. 584. At Sian, the capital of the T'ang Empire, two coins were found in two separate graves. The Ho-chia-ts'un hoard, which contained a coin similar to the type exhibited here, has brought the total number of Sassanian coins found in China proper up to five (fig. 97).

The general description of the Sassanian coin found at Ho-chia-ts'un matches that of the coin shown here. The inscriptions, however, do differ, and their dissimilarities are evident in the photograph of the coin from

183

Ho-chia-ts'un. On the obverse the words on either side of Khusrau II's head appear to be the same as on the Boston coin. In addition to these, the word "afid" appears in the margin of the obverse. "Afid" is translated as "praise" and is printed on some of the coins of Khusrau II from the eleventh year of his reign (600 A.D.) onward. The inscriptions on the reverse of the Ho-chia-ts'un coin are distinctly different from those on the Boston coin. To the right of the fire altar and figures are the letters AHM, standing for Hamadan, the mint site and a very important town throughout Sassanian and Islamic Persian history. The date mark on the left of the fire altar group reads "sij-sih," translated as thirty-three and corresponding to the thirty-third year of Khusrau II's reign, or 622 A.D.

The mint date of the Khusrau II coin found at Ho-chia-ts'un coincides with the year in which Heraclius, Emperor of Byzantium (see cat. no. 96), launched the first of his campaigns to regain territory in the Middle East lost to Persia. The war lasted for six years until the death of Khusrau II and the signing of a peace treaty with his son in 628.

References: Hsia Nai, "Sasanian Persian coins recently discovered in China" (text in Chinese), *Kaogu Xuebao*, 1957, no. 2, pp. 49-60; idem, "Sasanian coins newly discovered at Hsi-ning" (text in Chinese), *Kaogu Xuebao*, 1958, no. 1, pp. 105-110; *Wên-hua ta-ko-ming ch'i-chien ch'u-t'u wen-wu* [Cultural relics discovered during the period of the Great Cultural Revolution], Peking: Wen Wu Press, 1972, pl. 69; Shensi Provincial Museum, "A cache of cultural relics of the T'ang period discovered at Ho-chia-ts'un in the southern suburbs of Sian" (text in Chinese), *Wen Wu*, 1972, no. 1, pp. 36-37.

96
Byzantine coin, known as a "solidus"
Gold
Reign of Heraclius (A.D. 610-641);
diam. 2.1 cm.
Museum of Fine Arts, Boston, anonymous gift in memory of Zoe Wilbour. 35.363

On the obverse of this gold coin, Heraclius is represented with his son Heraclius Constantine, who was born in 612 and crowned Augustus in 613. Both are depicted in bust form and are wearing crowns with a globus crucinger, an imperial cloak, and a cuirass. A cross appears between the two heads to the right of Heraclius' crown. On the reverse we see a cross potent on three steps, a motif restored to the coinage of Heraclius to replace the figure of Victory seen on the coins of the preceding emperor, Phocas. The appearance of Heraclius' son on the coin marks an innovation of the reign—the depiction of family members in conjunction with the emperor on his coins.

Inscriptions are printed on both the obverse and the reverse of the coin. Encircling the two heads, the obverse inscription reads "ddnnheracliusetheraconstppau"; "ddnn," the plural of "dn," is an abbreviation for Domini Nostri and is written in the plural when Heraclius is shown with his son. The last four letters "ppau," following the names of the emperor and his son, stand for Perpetuus Augustus. On the reverse, on either side of the cross, are written the words "Victoria" and "Avgu," short for Augustorum. The word "Conob" is printed below the steps. "Con" is an abbreviation for Constantinople, the mint location of this coin, and "ob" is a latinized form of the Greek word "obryzum," meaning "refined gold." Although twelve mints were in operation during the reign of Heraclius, Constantinople, the capital of the empire, was by far the most important of them. Moreover, gold coins were minted only at Constantinople, Ravenna, and Carthage during the reign of Heraclius. The other mints produced bronze and silver coins. While the word "Conob" appears on all gold coins of the reign, regard-

96

less of their mint site, the lettering and engraving are usually reliable indications of the origin of specific coins.

Published: *Byzantine Coins, Gallery Book,* Boston: Museum of Fine Arts, 1936, p. 8, no. 3.

The Byzantine coin found in the Ho-chiats'un hoard at Sian, like the one exhibited here, is printed with Heraclius and his son on the obverse and a cross potent on the reverse. While the face of Heraclius appears from the photograph to be more elongated than that on the Boston coin, the two coins almost definitely date from the same period, between 613 and 630 or slightly later. Unfortunately, the rather unclear photographs of the coin from Ho-chia-ts'un do not permit serious comment on the differences in inscriptions. Although the single grenetis appears to be more clearly imprinted on both the obverse and the reverse of the Ho-chiats'un coin than on the Boston coin, the writ-

fig. 98

ing on the first coin is illegible in the photograph. One must therefore assume that the word "Conob" appears below the cross potent on the reverse, as it did on all gold coins of the period. Beyond that the inscription is probably quite similar to that of the Boston coin with variations limited to single letters. Since such small details as the impressions of single letters are the only reliable indications of the mint site, the mint site of the Ho-chia-ts'un coin remains uncertain.

It is tempting to speculate that the coins of Heraclius found their way to Persia during the campaigns and that they traveled from there to China with Persian traders. However, Byzantine merchants themselves did trade with the Chinese in the seventh century, so that the coins might have come to Sian independently of Persian tradesmen. Clarification of the way in which these coins arrived in China of course awaits further documentation.

References: John B. Stearns and Vernon Hall, Jr., *Byzantine Gold Coins from the Dartmouth College Collection,* Hanover, N.H.: Dartmouth College Library, 1953, pp. 3-5, 9, 18, pl. 9; Hugh Goodacre, *A Handbook of the Coinage of the Byzantine Emipre,* London: Spink, 1960, pp. 93-101; Warwick Wroth, *Catalogue of the Imperial Byzantine Coins in the British Museum,* London: British Museum, 1908, vol. 1, pp. xxiii-xxvii, lxxxviii-lxxxix, xcix-cxi, 186; *Wen-hua ta-ko-ming ch'i-chien ch'u-t'u wên-wu* [Cultural relics discovered during the period of the Great Cultural Revolution], Peking: Wen Wu Press, 1972, pl. 69; Shensi Provincial Museum, "A cache of cultural relics of the T'ang period discovered at Ho-chia-ts'un in the southern suburbs of Sian" (text in Chinese), *Wen Wu,* 1972, no. 1, pp. 36-37.

97
Headgear for an official envoy
Gilt silver with repoussé decoration
Northern Sung-Liao period, late 10th or 11th century A.D.;
h. 206 cm., circumference 62 cm.
Museum of Fine Arts, Boston, William Sturgis Bigelow Collection by exchange. 40.749

This fine example of the art of the silversmith is unique, not only in this exhibition but probably also in the entire Western world, as the only object that has been restored to its original shape on the basis of archaeological evidence supplied by a recent excavation in China. When it entered the collection of the Boston Museum in 1940 it was a repoussé plaque (fig. 99). Although the motif of its decoration, two dragons chasing a flaming jewel, is typically Chinese, the workmanship and shape of the piece were considered unusual and indications of a non-Chinese origin. The piece was thought to be part of the decoration of a box made by a Korean silversmith during the Koryŏ period (A.D. 918-1392).

Published: Kojiro Tomita, "Korean Silverwork of the Koryŏ Period," Museum of Fine Arts, Boston, *Bulletin,* vol. 39, no. 231 (1941), pp. 2-5.

The attribution of the Boston plaque to the Koryŏ period remained unchallenged until an excavation carried out in 1956 at the village of Chang-chia-ying-tzu in Chien-p'ing County, Liao-ning Province yielded another gilt silver piece (fig. 100) closely resembling this plaque. However, the excavated specimen was not a plaque but a similar piece bent into circular shape. Its placement in the tomb at the head of the funerary couch clearly indicated that it was the headgear of the deceased. The other funerary objects leave no doubt as to the fact that the person buried in this tomb was a Khitan tribesman.

That the Boston plaque must have had the same shape as the excavated piece is indicated by two vertical slits at each end. These slits suggest that a ribbon or broad band was used to join the two ends together, thus allowing for adjustments in accordance with

the size of the head of the wearer. We may assume that the Boston piece came out of a tomb in a battered and warped condition, after which an overzealous restorer flattened it into a plaque. The available archaeological evidence warranted the decision to restore the plaque to its original shape, a task carried out successfully by William J. Young of the museum's research laboratory. Although the dragons strike a different pose and reveal slight discrepancies in appearance, and although the borders of stylized clouds framing each piece are somewhat different, there can be no doubt that the two pieces are of approximately the same period, from the same area, and that they were made for the same purpose.

Just as it is often hazardous to draw clear lines of distinction between Liao and Northern Sung ceramics (see cat. no. 98), it is difficult to establish the ethnic and artistic background of the artist who created this masterpiece of silverwork. On the one hand it does seem doubtful that we may attribute a piece of such great artistic refinement to a Khitan artisan. On the other hand, even though the combination of what would seem to be a non-Chinese shape with artistic skill equaling that of Chinese masters made the original attribution to Korea a plausible one, there is nothing in the arts of that country to lend support to this attribution.

The only pieces that show dragons of exactly the same type against a background of identical waves are repoussé silver saddle parts, excavated in Liao-ning and Inner Mongolia (fig. 101). Such bow-shaped pieces are found as two pairs, two for a man's saddle, decorated with dragons, and two for a woman's saddle, decorated with phoenixes. Such finds are invariably associated with Liao funerary objects. In addition to this archaeological evidence, which clearly points to a Khitan origin for such pieces, there is contemporary documentary evidence, which seems to supply a clear answer to the question.

After forty-five years of almost continuous warfare on China's northern frontier, in A.D.

1005 the Khitans and the Chinese concluded a peace treaty, whereby the Khitans ceded some territory recently taken from the Chinese in exchange for full diplomatic recognition and an annual payment of three hundred thousand taels. This treaty, which satisfied the needs of both parties, effectively guaranteed peace in the area for more than a hundred years.

In historical sources a considerable amount of information has been preserved concerning one of the most important rituals in the regular diplomatic contacts between the two peoples, i.e., the exchange of gifts between Khitan and Sung envoys. The Khitans usually brought gifts typical of their own nomadic life style: iron swords, horses, and trained falcons. Although the *chef de mission,* sent on New Year's Day, the emperor's birthday, or on other important occasions, usually was a Khitan, his aides often were Chinese from the occupied northern regions. The Sung court always made a distinction between the gifts for these Chinese, who received traditional Chinese gifts, and the Khitan envoys, to whom they made gifts most likely to please barbarians of nomadic taste.

In the *Sung-hui-yao kao,* a collection of miscellaneous Sung documents, the gifts made by the Chinese are listed and described. It is remarkable to see how often the inventories of Sung gifts include items with which we are familiar through excavations in Liao territory. Iron stirrups, often found in Liao tombs, are repeatedly mentioned in the lists. The above-mentioned gilt silver saddle parts, decorated with dragons and phoenixes, also appear on the inventory of diplomatic gifts. A protocol attached to the treaty of A.D. 1005 even went so far as to specify to which gifts ambassadors of the Khitans would be entitled when they visited the Chinese court. Wittfogel and Fêng translated the first item on this list as "one hat decorated with gold and silver," but the original reads *chin-t'u-yin-kuan,* i.e., "gilt silver headgear."

This literary evidence explains the problem of the shape, style, and workmanship of the Boston Liao crown and its recently excavated

fig. 99

counterpart. Made on order for the Chinese court to be presented to a Khitan envoy of full ambassadorial rank, the piece represents an early type of Chinese export ware, made with all the skill of the Chinese court artist but reflecting what the Chinese considered to be Khitan taste. The fact that such presents accompanied the recipient into his grave underlines the extraordinary importance the Khitans attached to such gifts. This attitude is fully confirmed by the documents, which bear testimony of the Khitan's concern for these seemingly less important details during their negotiations with the Sung.

References: Robert T. Paine, "A Crown of the Liao Dynasty," *Boston Museum Bulletin* 62, no. 328 (1964), 44-47; Fêng Yung-ch'ien, "Three Liao dynasty Tombs in Hsin-min and Chien-p'ing County, Liao-ning Province" (text in Chinese), *Kaogu,* 1960, no. 2, pp. 15-19; *Hsin Chung-kuoti k'ao-ku shou-huo* [Archaeology in New China], Peking: Wen Wu Press, 1962, pl. 125, figs. 1-2; Hsü Sung, *Sung-hui-yao kao,* Peking: Ta-tung shu-chü, 1936, vol. 196, p. 36b; Karl A. Wittfogel and Fêng Chia-shêng, *History of Chinese Society, Liao,* New York: Macmillan, 1949, p. 358, no. 60.

fig. 100

fig. 100

fig. 101

98
Buddhist water vessel (*kundikā*)
**Buff stoneware, covered with an amber glaze
with splashes of green, both turning dark in
thick places**
**Northern Sung-Liao period, 10th century
A.D.; h. 11.5 cm.**
Collection of Dr. Paul Singer

The tall-necked bottle with an ovoid body
has been provided with two spouts; one
tapering tubular spout is attached to the
flaring lip at the top, the other protrudes
from the shoulder of the vessel. Under the
glaze is an incised design of combed wavy
lines. A band of stylized flowers encircles
the shoulder.

This type of vessel, which is a Chinese
adaptation of the Indian *kundikā*, or two-
spouted vessel, seems to have been little
known in China until the T'ang period. The
famous pilgrim I-ching (late seventh century
A.D.) gave the first description of its use
among Buddhist monks in the diary of his
pilgrimage to India. From this description it
appears that the spout on the top is used for
pouring and the curved funnel on the
shoulder is for filling the water vessel.

The amber glaze and the incised wavy lines
place this vessel in a group of ceramics formerly thought to date from the T'ang period
but now usually associated with the Liao
dynasty. The recent exhibition "Ceramics
in the Liao Dynasty" included several pieces
with a similar incised design and covered
with the same type of glaze. In the catalogue
of the exhibition Mino Yutaka points out
how difficult it is at the present state of our
knowledge to attribute ceramics, especially
those of the Ting and Tz'u-chou types, to
the Khitans or to the Northern Sung Chinese.

References: For the form and function of the
kundikā see Ananda K. Coomaraswamy and
Francis Stewart Kershaw, "A Chinese Buddhist
Water Vessel and Its Indian Prototype," *Artibus
Asiae,* 1928, no. 1, pp. 122-141; Mino Yutaka,
*Ceramics in the Liao Dynasty North and South
of the Great Wall,* New York: China Institute in
America, 1973, nos. 55, 59, and 60.

98

fig. 102

fig. 103

In May 1969, a team of archaeologists from the local museum discovered the relic chambers of two Northern Sung pagodas in the city of Ting-hsien (Hopei Province). Both pagodas have disappeared long ago, but the underground chambers had remained completely intact. The relic chamber of the *śarīra*-pagoda of the monastery Ching-chih-ssu, to which the excavators assigned the number 5, is an underground chamber, accessible only through a square manhole in the ceiling. The access was blocked by a heavy stone slab in the shape of a roof. The chamber contained more than seven hundred objects in gold, silver, jade, iron, wood, and ceramic ware, as well as twenty-seven thousand coins, ranging in date from the Warring States period up to the Northern Sung period. Many objects had been deposited in four stone caskets, datable by their inscriptions to A.D. 453, 606, 858, and 889. Inscriptions in the chamber indicate that the pagoda was destroyed on several occasions. The hoard found in the relic chamber represents the accumulated wealth of several successive sacral deposits, made when the pagoda was built or reconstructed. The last rebuilding took place in A.D. 976-977, and the majority of the objects found in the chamber date from about that time.

Almost all of the more than a hundred ceramics found in the chamber are white glazed Ting pieces, obviously of local manufacture (fig. 103). Only three pieces are of a different type. One is a bowl covered with a bluish glaze, decorated with a carved design of lotus petals. The two other pieces are an amber glazed vessel in the shape of a parrot (h. 15.6 cm.) and the other a green glazed *kundikā* (fig. 102) of a shape and with a decoration very similar to that of the piece exhibited here. Except for a slight discrepancy in the shape of the spout protruding from the shoulder and the difference in the color of the glaze, the two pieces are practically identical.

No other example of this type of *kundikā* has been found, but of the vessel in the shape of a parrot a second example is known. It was found in a tomb at the ruined city of T'u-ch'êng-tzu, near Holinkoêrh, just north of the Yellow River bend in Inner Mongolia. The four tombs excavated there in January 1960 yielded a rich assortment of funerary objects of a type usually associated with the Liao period. The parrot vessel found there is slightly larger than the Ting-chou piece. It is covered with a green glaze with amber splashes on the foot, the breast, and the beak of the bird. Judging from a color reproduction its glaze would seem to resemble that of the Singer *kundikā*, except that green is the dominant color.

The tombs at Holinkoêrh have a round floor plan and a domed ceiling, resembling the yurt of the nomads. This type of tomb is thought to date from a relatively early period in the ascendancy of the Liao tribes, when the Chinese had not yet exerted the full impact of their influence upon Liao culture. The excavators date these tombs in the late T'ang or early Liao period (late ninth to early tenth century A.D.). In the light of this find and the discovery at Ting-chou the *kundikā* may therefore be dated in the tenth century.

Although the date does not seem to pose a problem, the question of the provenance of this type of glazed stoneware remains unresolved. From the fact that only two pieces of this type occur among the large number of white ceramics in the Ting-chou relic chamber, it would seem safe to assume that the parrot vessel and the *kundikā* were not made at any of the Ting-chou kilns. They could well have been offered to the monastery by some monk or other visitor from the northern regions. The presence of such pieces in Manchurian and Inner Mongolian tombs seems to argue in favor of the supposition that they were manufactured in one of the northern kilns.

References: Ting-hsien County Museum, "Two pagoda foundations of the Sung period discovered at Ting-hsien in Hopei" (text in Chinese), *Wen Wu*, 1972, no. 8, pp. 39-48; *Nei-mêng-ku ch'u-t'u wên-wu hsüan-chi* [Selected cultural relics excavated in Inner Mongolia], Peking: Wen-Wu Press, 1963, pl. 107; The Cultural Team of

the Inner Mongolian Autonomous Region, "Brief introduction to the ancient tombs excavated at T'u-ch'êng-tzu, Holinkoêrh" (text in Chinese), *Wen Wu*, 1961, no. 9, pp. 30-33.

99
Whistle with three holes
Buff pottery, covered with white slip and a three-colored glaze
Liao-Chin periods, 12th-13th century A.D.; h. 3.8 cm.
Museum of Fine Arts, Boston, Charles B. Hoyt Collection. 50.1370

The whistle has the shape of a human head with a grim facial expression, the corners of the mouth turned downward. The hair is combed back in thin parallel lines. The hollow head is made up of two halves joined together. The top of the head and both cheeks are perforated with a small round hole. Whistles of this type produce a sound when blown with the mouth from behind the cranial aperture, the first finger of each hand covering the holes in the cheeks. By opening and closing of the apertures four different tones can be produced.

Four almost identical whistles are in the Royal Ontario Museum, Toronto; another example is in the C. G. Seligman Collection, London. Its late owner labeled it as T'ang (as was originally the piece in the Hoyt Collection) and considered the face a representation of an American Indian.

Published: John Ayers, *The Seligman Collection of Oriental Art*, vol. 2, London: Lund Humphries, 1964, no. D52, 43; C. G. Seligman, "An Amerind Type in China in T'ang Times," *Man*, vol. 24, no. 84 (August 1924), pl. H, figs. 2-3.

100
Whistle with three holes
Buff pottery, unglazed and slip painted
Liao-Chin periods, 12th-13th century A.D.; h. 4 cm.
Collection of Dr. Paul Singer

Basically of the same construction as the preceding piece, this whistle shows the face of an owl. It was left unglazed, a fact that suggests that the piece may have been found in a kiln site rather than in a tomb.

99

100

fig. 104

fig. 105

Whistles of slightly different types are known to have been made in China during the T'ang period. In the collection of Chêng Tê-k'un and L. E. R. Picken in Cambridge, England, are several specimens found at the well-known kiln site at Hsiung-lai, Szechwan Province. The typological differences make it quite clear, however, that the whistles exhibited here belong to a different category. This supposition is confirmed by recent archaeological excavations.

In 1962 the Chilin Provincial Museum dispatched a team of archaeologists to the ruins of P'ien-lien City, about 22 km. to the north-west of Ssu-p'ing, Li-shu district, in Chilin Province. Inside the city walls surveyed by the team, a number of objects were found which, according to the archaeologists, are very similar to those found at the ancient city of Pa-li-ch'êng, Chao-tung district, in the adjacent Heilungkiang Province in 1958.

Both finds included a whistle of the type exhibited here. The whistle found at P'ien-lien (fig. 104) is practically identical with the piece in the Singer collection, except that its upper half is covered with a brownish glaze. In size the two pieces are identical. The whistle found at Pa-li-ch'êng represents an interesting variation. Although similar in construction to the other pieces, it has been modeled into the shape of a pig's head (fig. 105).

As both pieces were surface finds, dispersed within the walls of ancient cities, they are not directly related to other objects found within the same area. Among the objects found in these sites there are some that are quite similar to pieces associated with the Khitans of the Liao dynasty, who reigned here until they were defeated by their neighbors, the Jurčen or Chin, in the early twelfth century. The tiles with an impressed design of an animal mask found at Pa-li-ch'êng are very similar to those found in the Royal Liao tombs in East Mongolia (cf. Ch'ing-ling, Kyoto University, 1952, vol. 2, pls. 111 and 116). On the other hand, the quadrangular layout of these cities, as well as the preponderance of Chin coins among the money found in them, seems to argue in favor of a date in the Chin period.

So far none of the Manchurian kiln sites that have been investigated by Japanese before and by Chinese after the Second World War seems to have yielded any whistles of the type shown here. However, in the course of a series of excavations at the Yao-chou kiln sites at T'ung-ch'uan, Shensi Province, in 1959, several similar pieces were found. Judging from their report, the excavators do not seem to have realized the function of these pieces, probably because some of them were found unsuitable for the purpose for which they were intended. The report (pl. 8, fig. 7) illustrates what is called a "black glazed human head." The cranial aperture is not visible, but it is evident that the holes in the cheeks have been filled with glaze, thereby rendering the piece useless. Another piece with a yellowish green glaze shows two apertures in the eyes (pl. 21, fig. 5). The first piece was found in a stratum that the excavators date in the T'ang period. The woman's head with the perforated eyes was found in the stratum dating from the Chin or Yüan period.

A booklet on miniature pottery figurines published by the Honan Provincial Museum contains another example of a human head with perforations in the cheek. Here again the cranial aperture is not visible, and the museum labels it as a head of a demon dating possibly from the T'ang period. The piece was excavated at Sian.

References: Chao-tung County Museum, "Brief report on cleaning up Pa-li-ch'êng, Chao-tung District, Heilunkiang Province" (text in Chinese), Kaogu, 1960, no. 2, pp. 36-41; Chilin Provincial Cultural Administrative Committee, "Report on the reinvestigation of the Old City of P'ien-lien in the district of Li-shu in Chilin Province" (text in Chinese), Kaogu, 1963, pp. 612-615; Shensi Institute of Archaeology, Shensi T'ung-ch'uan Yao-chou-yao [Excavations of Yaochou kiln sites at T'ung Ch'uan, Shensi], Peking: Science Press, 1965 (text in Chinese, English abstract); Li Shun, "The Neolithic and Shang Potter Hsün" (text in Chinese), Kaogu Xuebao, 1964, no. 1, pp. 51-54; Honan Provincial Museum, Chung-kuo ku-tai t'ao-tz'u i-shu hsiao-p'in [Ancient Chinese miniature pieces of pottery and porcelain], Peking, 1958, fig. 36.

101

Death mask

Silver-coated bronze

**Liao period (A.D. 907-1125), h. 22.5 cm.,
w. 14.3 cm.**

The University Museum, Philadelphia

The mask has a flat, oval shape, in which
only the barest minimum of facial features
have been indicated in repoussé. The eyes
and mouth are slit open, the eyebrows are
indicated by striations. It is said to have been
excavated at P'ing-ting (Shansi Province), to
the east of T'ai-yüan.

Although a considerable number of masks
of this type, hammered in thin sheets of silver, silver-coated bronze or gilt bronze, have
entered Western collections, the provenance
and cultural origin of these pieces remained
obscure for many years. R. R. Tatlock, probably the first to publish one of them in 1923,
failed to establish its function and date; he
considered the possibility that it was Chinese,
although he thought he also saw elements
pointing to a possible Korean provenance.
Henri d'Ardenne de Tizac a few years later
identified a fragmentarily preserved example
of the same type as a death mask. He correctly surmised that it must have come from
the Sino-Mongolian border region, but attributed it to the Han period. The same date
was suggested for yet another piece of this
type by the distinguished Japanese archaeologist Hamada Kōsaku.

It was only after the Japanese occupation
of Manchuria, when Japanese archaeologists
began to extend their activities into this area,
that these masks came to be identified as the
products of the mortuary culture of the
Khitan herdsmen, the founders of the Liao dynasty (A.D. 907-1125). This connection was
first suggested by the fact that the area in
which these pieces were found, near Ch'ih-
fêng and Chien-p'ing in the present Autonomous Region of Inner Mongolia, once
formed the heartland of the Khitan territory.
Although solid archaeological evidence remained scarce, the fact that at least one of
these masks was found together with a typical example of Liao pottery provided the

final proof. Moreover, Masao Shimada as
well as Wittfogel and Fêng produced literary
evidence from a contemporary Chinese
source, which, in spite of its obvious *dédain*
for the customs of the Khitan, provides a
graphic description of the burial customs of
these northern herdsmen. In this source, the
Lu-t'ing Shih-shih by the Sung author Wên
Wei-chien, the burial customs of the north
are described as follows: "The mourning and
burial customs of the northerners vary [ac-
cording to their ethnic background]. The Han
people preserve the body and then bury it;
their ritual for mourning is exactly the same
as that of the inhabitants of the Central Plain
[of northern China]. The Jurčen, on the other
hand, put their dead in a wooden trough and
bury them in the hills and woods without
sealing the trough with a lid. Only the
Khitans, however, have the following very
strange custom. When a man from a rich or
noble family dies, they cut open the abdomen
and remove the intestines and the stomach.
After washing it they stuff the body with
fragrant herbs, salt, and alum. Afterward
they sew it up again with five-colored thread.
They then prick into the skin sharply pointed
reeds in order to drain off the fluid and blood
until it is all gone. They use gold and silver to
make masks and they wind copper wire
around the hands and feet. When Yeh-lü Tê-
kuang [i.e., the Liao Emperor T'ai-tsung]
died, this method [of embalming] was used.
The [Chinese] people of that time saw it as
'Imperial dried meat,' and those are the true
facts."

Published: S. H. Minkenhof, "Date and provenance of death masks of the Far East," *Artibus
Asiae* 14 (1951), 62-71; R. R. Tatlock, "An Unidentified Chinese Mask," *Burlington Magazine*
47 (October 1925), 163; Henri d'Ardenne de
Tizac, "La Chine féodale et l'art chinois," *Artibus Asiae,* 1926, no. 3, 165-175; Masao Shimada, "A Death-Mask of the Liao Period," *Artibus
Asiae* 13 (1950), 250-253; Wên Wei-chien, *Lu-
t'ing Shih-shih, Shuo-fu,* Han-fên-lou ed., Shanghai: Commercial Press, ch. 8, p. 49a; Karl A.
Wittfogel and Fêng Chia-shêng, *History of
Chinese Society, Liao,* New York: Macmillan,
1949, p. 280; Hamada Kōsaku, "A study of an

fig. 106

ancient silver-plated bronze mask" (text in Japanese), *Tōa Kōkogaku Kenkyū,* Tokyo: Oka
Shoin, 1930, pp. 229-245.

Considering the fact that such a large
number of Liao death masks had been discovered and dispersed during the pre-war
years, it is surprising that only a few of the
many Liao tombs that have been excavated
in recent years seem to have contained such
masks. A possible explanation is that the
method of embalming described by Wên
Wei-chien may not have been common and
may well have been restricted to imperial
clansmen (see cat. no. 103). Among the several dozen Liao tombs—eighteen of which
could be dated exactly—the Chinese excavators found only six that contained masks,
and of these six four may be assumed to contain the skeletal remains of four members of
one family.

In spite of this small number of finds, these
controlled excavations yielded information
that the clandestine excavations of the past
had failed to produce. In 1956 farm laborers
discovered a tomb in a mound near the village of Pa-t'u-ying-tzu, Hsin-min County,

101

Liao-ning Province. Inside the yurt-shaped brick tomb, among a rich collection of mortuary gifts, the excavators found two fragmentarily preserved gilt bronze masks. The faces of both masks had been gilded, and fragments of silk, possibly of a shroud, were still attached to them. Although this is somewhat less evident from the only published illustration, the excavators claim that one mask shows undeniably the features of a man, whereas the other clearly represents a woman's face. From this it is evident that the death mask was not a male prerogative. Next to the masks were found remnants of copper wire, made into a sort of net, which was bound around the hands and feet, as described in the passage from the *Lu-t'ing Shih-shih* quoted above.

An excavation near the village of Hsiao-liu chang-tzu, in the vicinity of Ning-ch'êng (Tsaghan Suburghan), south of Ch'ih-fêng in the Autonomous Region of Inner Mongolia, yielded no less than four masks, excavated from a group of five tombs. These tombs vary considerably in shape and structure: one has a rectangular floor plan, two are hexagonal, and one is octagonal. Some are built of brick, whereas two other tombs are constructed of irregularly shaped stone slabs. In spite of these differences in structure, however, the fine ceramics from these tombs indicate that they must date from approximately the same period.

The masks, which were found in tombs nos. 1-4, were all executed in bronze, the surface of which had been gilded (fig. 106). The mask from tomb no. 1 had been attached to the skull with bronze wire, but no trace of bronze wire to bind around the hand and feet was found in any of these tombs. As at Pa-t'u-ying-tzu, there were remnants of silk shrouds attached to the inside of the mask. The piece of tomb no. 3 had the ears riveted to the masks, exactly as we can see in a mask in the Carl Kempe Collection, Ekolsund, Sweden. Whereas the masks of tombs no. 1 and 3 reveal unmistakable male features, the mask from tomb no. 4 show a round woman's face. Only in this mask have the

eyes and the mouth been slit open. The nature of the mortuary gifts in tomb no. 4 supports the view that the person interred there was a woman.

The existing masks reveal a wide range of differences, and there can be no doubt that these reflect individual facial features. That the two man's masks of tombs nos. 1 and 3 bear a close resemblance to one another need not be explained as the result of an artist's perfunctory execution of his commission. As the excavators of these tombs point out, tombs no. 1-4 are grouped together in such a way as to suggest that they may belong to a family cemetery. If this is correct, family likeness rather than unskillful portraiture could explain the striking similarity of these two masks.

References: Fêng Yung-ch'ien, "Three Liao dynasty tombs in Hsin-min and Chien-p'ing County, Liao-ning Province" (text in Chinese), *Kaogu*, 1960, no. 2, pp. 15-19; The Cultural Working Team of the Inner Mongolian Autonomous Region, "Brief report on the excavation of Liao tombs at Hsiao-liu chang-tzu, Ning-ch'êng County, Chao-wu-ta League" (text in Chinese), *Wen Wu*, 1961, no. 9, pp. 44-49.

102
Bottle-shaped vase
Red pottery covered with a green glaze
Chin period, ca. 12th century A.D.;
h. 22.3 cm.
British Museum, London, from the George Eumorfopoulos Collection

The vase has a pear-shaped body and a long, slender neck. It has a molded decoration of an archaizing type derived from bronze vessels and is covered with white slip and an iridescent green glaze. The spreading lip has been restored.

R. L. Hobson, who first published this vase, dated it T'ang or earlier; Basil Gray attributed it to the Han or Six Dynasties period.

Published: R. L. Hobson, *The George Eumorfopoulos Collection, Catalogue of the Chinese, Corean, and Persian Pottery and Porcelain*, vol. 1, London: Ernest Benn, 1925, no. 168, pl. 25; Basil Gray, *Early Chinese Pottery and Porcelain*, London: Faber and Faber, 1953, p. 4 and pl. 4.

103
Tripod censer
Gray earthenware with traces of white slip, adhesions of red earth
Chin period, ca. 12th century, A.D.;
h. 10.2 cm., diam. 11.5 cm.
Royal Ontario Museum, Toronto, George Crofts Collection

Standing on three legs decorated with animal masks, the body of the incense burner is divided into two registers. The lower part is bordered by bands of pearls and is covered with a design of rectangular meanders. The upper register contains an archaizing decor of two birds flanking a *t'ao-t'ieh* mask. The vessel has a heavy rim with a rectangular profile. Although unglazed and made of a different clay, the piece is closely related to the preceding number because of its archaizing decor, which imitates that of ancient Chinese bronzes.

In July 1958 the Cultural Bureau of the Autonomous Region of Inner Mongolia excavated three tombs at the village of Lin-

fig. 107

tung, Barin Left Banner. The village is located in the immediate vicinity of the ruins of Lin-huang-fu, the Supreme Capital of the Liao dynasty (A.D. 907-1125) between the upper course of the Shira Muren River and the Khinghan Mountains. In tomb no. 1, a vaulted brick tomb with masonry imitating columns and brackets, two pieces of pottery with a molded design were discovered. One of these (fig. 107) is a slightly larger (h. 25.5 cm.) but otherwise practically identical version of the vase in the British Museum. The other is a three-legged incense-burner (fig. 108); it is not as close to the Toronto piece exhibited here as the vase from the British Museum is to its Mongolian counterpart, but the points of similarity are numerous. The censer from the Mongolian tomb lacks the pearl bands and the plain vertical bands above the animal masks. The Mongolian censer is covered with the same type of green glaze as the bottles.

The three tombs contain no dated inscription, and it is therefore not possible to give a precise date for them. However, Li I-yu, who first reported this find, adduced several arguments in favor of a date in the Chin dynasty (A.D. 1115-1234). First of all he points out that the burial of ashes after cremation in small wooden coffins, which is the method of disposal of the human remains used in all three tombs, was practiced widely by the Khitans who inhabited this area during the Liao and Chin periods. He also argues that pieces with an archaizing decoration derived from bronze vessels are not likely to date from the Liao period. The adoption of an archaizing bronze decor was the result of the lively Chinese archaeological interest in ancient bronzes that started during the Northern Sung period. We may expect this trend in Chinese culture to have penetrated into the northern periphery of China with some delay. During the Japanese occupation and later several kiln sites were excavated in this area, but among the shards that have been published no examples of a ware resembling this pottery seem to occur. Consequently it remains uncertain whether this type of pottery was locally produced.

References: Li I-yu, "Chin Tombs in the Village of Lin-tung, Barin Left Banner," *Wen Wu*, 1959, no. 7, pp. 63-64, cover pl. 3; *Nei-mêng-ku ch'u-t'u wên-wu hsüan-chi* [Selected cultural relics excavated in Inner Mongolia], Peking: Wen Wu Press, 1963, p. 108, pl. 149.

103

fig. 108

104
Spouted basin
Silver
Yüan period, 14th century A.D.; h. 6.3 cm.,
diam. 24.1 cm.
William Rockhill Nelson Gallery of Art,
Kansas City, Missouri

The plain silver vessel is provided with a loop handle underneath the long spout. Similar shapes occur in ceramics, occasionally in celadon, but mostly in blue and white or underglaze red porcelain. It is thought that basins of this spouted type may have served as finger bowls. Laurence Sickman has suggested a possible explanation for the handle being placed under the spout rather than on the opposite side. If the basins of this type were filled with water to serve as finger bowls, there would be less likelihood of the water being spilled in passing the vessels about if they were held by the spouted side.

The basin is part of a group of eleven pieces of Chinese silver acquired by the Nelson Gallery in 1935. Because of the fact that the shape of some of these pieces resembled Southern Sung ceramic types, and the engraved designs are related to those on *ch'ing-pai* porcelain, the hoard was initially assigned to the Southern Sung period. As nothing is known about the circumstances of this find, it is difficult to establish with certainty whether all eleven pieces date from the same period. In the particular case of this basin, however, the ceramic parallels strongly suggest a date in the fourteenth century rather than any earlier time.

Published: James Cahill, *The Arts of Southern Sung China*, New York: Asia Society, 1962, no. 38; Sherman E. Lee and Wai-kam Ho, *Chinese Art under the Mongols*, Cleveland Museum of Art, 1968, no. 33c.

104

fig. 109

105
Bottle with cover
Silver
Yüan period, 14th century A.D.; h. 34.9 cm.
William Rockhill Nelson Gallery of Art,
Kansas City, Missouri

The plain silver vase has a bulbous body and a long, tapering neck. The lid, provided with a knob in the shape of a jewel or lotus bud, is attached to the vase by means of a chain. The bottom of the piece bears an engraved character, *Li,* the well-known Chinese family name. The bottle is part of the same group of silver vessels in the Nelson Gallery to which the preceding and following pieces belong.

Published: Sherman E. Lee and Wai-kam Ho, *Chinese Art under the Mongols,* Cleveland Museum of Art, 1968, no. 33d.

106
Box with cover
Silver with engraved decoration
Yüan period, 14th century A.D.; h. 5.2 cm.,
diam. 8.5 cm.
William Rockhill Nelson Gallery of Art,
Kansas City, Missouri

The box has a sixteen-lobed shape resembling a melon. On the flat cover is a crowded engraved design of aquatic plants consisting of lotus flowers and leaves as well as arrow heads. The box is part of the same hoard as the two preceding numbers.

Published: Sherman E. Lee and Wai-kam Ho, *Chinese Art under the Mongols,* Cleveland Museum of Art, 1968, no. 33f.

On October 10, 1955, workmen of the Department of Public Works of the city of Ho-fei, Anhwei Province, digging about the roots of a large locust tree standing outside one of the southern city gates of Ho-fei City, discovered a large ceramic jar, the mouth of which was covered with a bronze dish, hidden between the roots. Although the jar (h. 90 cm., largest diam. 80 cm.) was broken, a large hoard of gold and silver vessels packed inside were recovered intact and deposited in the Anhwei Provincial Museum.

105

fig. 110

106

fig. 111

107

The hoard consisted of six gold plates, four gold cups, nine silver plates, six silver cups, a large engraved silver cake box, nine silver flasks, four of which had their original covers, one long-handled silver ladle, and fifty-five pairs of silver chopsticks (fig. 109).

Eleven pieces are marked as the work of the goldsmith Chang Chung-ying and one piece is inscribed with the ancient name for Ho-fei, which suggests that the pieces of the hoard may have been made locally. Most important of all, however, is an inscription on one of the covered flasks that consists of a date corresponding to A.D. 1333.

The Ho-fei hoard, the largest find of this type ever made, contains four flasks of the same type as the piece from the Nelson Gallery exhibited here. The four flasks range in height from 43 to 51.5 cm. (fig. 110), and all four are therefore considerably bigger than the Kansas City piece. One of these four is inscribed with the date. The close resemblance of the Kansas City flask to these four pieces enables us to date it in the same period.

There are six spouted bowls, all of which differ from the Nelson Gallery piece in that the loop handles end in a tight spiral at the outer end of the handles. In this respect the Ho-fei bowls are closer to the blue and white porcelain pieces, which often display this same feature.

The large (diam. 35 cm.) cake box, ten-petaled in shape and provided with an interior tray, resembles in shape the much smaller Nelson Gallery box. Its engraved scroll borders represent a simple, early version of the scrolls in thin blue line often found on fourteenth century blue and white porcelains (fig. 111).

The well-preserved Ho-fei hoard with its dated and inscribed pieces constitutes an important group of material for the study of the art of the Chinese gold- and silversmith during the Mongol period. Although some pieces in the Nelson Gallery group do not have their counterpart in the newly discovered collection, and in spite of the fact that even the comparable specimens are not

entirely alike, their undeniable similarity suggests that the Kansas City group, the provenance of which is unknown, dates from approximately the same time as the Ho-fei treasure.

References: Laurence Sickman, "Chinese Silver of the Yüan Dynasty," *Archives of the Chinese Art Society of America* 9 (1957), 80-82; Wu Hsing-han, "Introductory comments on the gold and silver vessels and utensils of the Yüan period discovered at Ho-fei, Anhwei Province" (text in Chinese), *Wen Wu,* 1957, no. 2, pp. 51-58.

107
Plaque for a belt
Gilt bronze
Yüan period, early 14th century;
6.8 x 6.1 cm., h. 1.5 cm.
Museum of Fine Arts, Boston, Charles B. Hoyt Collection. 50.1401

Five stylized grapes and leafy tendrils in repoussé and cast relief are arranged on a rectangular plaque with thin vertical sides. The bronze is covered with a thin layer of gilt.

When this piece came to the Museum of Fine Arts in 1950, it was labeled "Korean, Koryŏ period." There was every reason to accept this attribution, especially since pieces of a similar type were known to have been kept in the Royal Yi Household Museum, Seoul, where they were attributed to the Koryŏ period. The main difference between the complete set of plaques in Seoul and the Boston piece is that the central grape in the latter has been replaced by a parrot in the plaques of the Korean collection.

Published: Museum of Fine Arts, Boston, *The Charles B. Hoyt Collection, Memorial Exhibition,* 1952, no. 707; *Chōsen Koseki Zufu,* Tokyo: Government-General of Chōsen, vol. 9, 1929, fig. 4176.

A tomb of the Yüan period, found near the famous Tiger Hill at Soochow, Kiangsu Province, brought to light seven pieces of a belt, the decoration of which is virtually identical with that of the plaque exhibited here (fig. 112). The pieces are slightly larger (8.5 x 7.8 cm.; h. 1.2 cm.) and are cast in

fig. 112

gold instead of bronze. The tomb served as the burial place for a couple. The man, a certain Lü Shih-mêng, died in A.D. 1304. His wife died eleven years later. The mortuary gifts cannot therefore, date from after A.D. 1315.

During the rule of the Mongols a China-based government extended its political and cultural influence over the Korean peninsula. However, objects found in Korea and dating from this period need not necessarily be of local manufacture. Especially during the Mongol period, when communications across Asia greatly improved, small and precious objects could easily travel to outposts of the Mongol Empire. It was only because of lack of information on finds in China that objects of which examples had been found in Korea were sometimes erroneously attributed to that country.

References: Kiangsu Cultural Committee, "Brief report on cleaning out a Yüan tomb in Wu County, Kiangsu" (text in Chinese), *Wen Wu,* 1959, no. 11, pp. 19-24; *Kiangsu-shêng ch'u-t'u wên-wu hsüan-chi* [Selected cultural relics discovered in Kiangsu Province], Peking: Wen Wu Press, 1963, pl. 197.

108

108
Vase
White porcelain with greenish blue glaze
Yüan period, ca. A.D. 1300; h. 28.5 cm.
Collections Baur, Geneva

The ovoid body has a cylindrical neck that first tapers and then spreads into a flower-shaped foliate rim. The incised decoration consists of a spiral scroll motif on the body of the vase and a band of stiff leaves around the neck.

This fine piece of porcelain was dated by John Ayers in the twelfth or thirteenth century. Jan Wirgin dates the design in the Southern Sung or Yüan period. The same date is given to a vase of a similar shape, but decorated with floral scrolls against a combed background on the body, in the Royal Ontario Museum, Toronto.

Published: John Ayers, *The Baur Collection, Geneva, Chinese Ceramics,* vol. 1, 1968, no. A123; Jan Wirgin, "Sung Ceramic Designs," Museum of Far Eastern Antiquities, Stockholm, *Bulletin,* 42, (1970), 58-59, pl. 22g; *Chinese Art in the Royal Ontario Museum,* Toronto, 1972, p. 62, no. 39.

When the railroad from Ch'êng-tu (Szechwan Province) to Pao-chi (Shensi Province) was repaired and extended in 1953, a team of archaeologists dispatched by the Preparatory Office of the Southwestern Museum worked in close cooperation with the railroad crews to excavate and preserve the archaeological finds that the groundwork brought to light. Of the more than two hundred tombs discovered in the course of this work, the majority dated from the Han and Six Dynasties periods. A relative rarity in the area was the discovery of a pair of datable Yüan tombs, located at Hung-shui-ning near Kuang-han, Szechwan Province. The tombs, built in a combination of brick and stone, had a recessed niche in the back wall, in which were placed a few porcelains. The excavators describe the type of porcelain as Szechwan *ying-ch'ing* of the finest quality. The date of the tomb, corresponding to A.D. 1306, was written in cinnabar on the walls.

fig. 113

One of the porcelains illustrated in the report is a vase (fig. 113) of the same type as the example from Geneva exhibited here. The only major difference between the two pieces is the design covering the body. The spiral scroll motif of the vase from Geneva has dissolved into a repetitive pattern of individual spirals resembling stylized clouds. The close similarity between the two vases would seem to warrant the conclusion that both date from approximately the same period and are possibly even from the same region.

References: The Preparatory Office of the Southwestern Museum, "Brief introduction to the cultural relics discovered in the course of repairs and construction work on the Pao-ch'êng railroad" (text in Chinese), *Wen Wu,* 1954, no. 3, pp. 10-34; *Ch'üan-kuo chi-pên chien-shê kung-ch'êng-chung ch'u-t'u wên-wu chan-lan t'u-lu,* Peking: Historical Museum, 1956, pl. 253.

109
Stem cup
White porcelain with molded and underglaze blue decoration
Late Yüan-Early Ming period, ca. A.D. 1370;
h. 9.8 cm., diam. 11.1 cm.
Collection of Mr. and Mrs. Myron S. Falk, Jr.

The stem cup (Chinese: *kao-tsu-wan*) is decorated on the outside with a design of three-clawed dragons chasing a flaming pearl. The inside shows a conch and two streamers; around the inside of the flaring rim is a band of scrollwork. In addition to this painted decor in underglaze cobalt blue there are traces of a molded decoration on the inside of the cup. The tall stem has several horizontal grooves.

Stem cups of this shape and type of decoration, of which at least half a dozen exist in Western collections, are known to date from the fourteenth century, but are generally attributed to the Yüan period, which covers almost three quarters of that century. In the catalogue of the commemorative exhibition of the Oriental Ceramic Society a similar piece in the collection of Mrs. Otto Harriman is dated in the first half of the fourteenth century.

Published: Philadelphia Museum of Art, *Exhibition of Blue-Decorated Porcelains of the Ming Dynasty,* 1949, no. 7; Sherman E. Lee and Wai-kam Ho, *Chinese Art under the Mongols,* Cleveland Museum of Art, 1968, no. 132; *The Ceramic Art of China,* London: Victoria and Albert Museum, 1971, no. 136.

The excavation, in October 1970, of the tomb of Wang Hsing-tsu (1338-1371), one of the great generals of Chu Yüan-chang, the founder of the Ming dynasty, has narrowed down the date for this type of stem cup (fig. 114). The piece, which was buried in Wang Hsing-tsu's tomb near Nanking in A.D. 1371, is not exactly identical with the stem cup exhibited here, but the similarity between the two pieces is very close. Measuring 11.1 cm. in height and 12.9 cm. in diameter, the excavated stem cup is slightly larger than the piece from the Falk collection. As the design on the inside of the bottom consists of a chrysanthemum spray framed in a circle, it would seem to come closest to an example in the Stephen Junkunc III Collection, Chicago (Philadelphia exhibition, no. 4), which is only a fraction smaller than the excavated piece.

As the production of stem cups of this type must have stretched out over a period of years, we may assume this period of production to have straddled the final years of the Yüan dynasty and the early years of the Ming restoration. Even if that piece were slightly earlier, there does not seem to be any indication that the stem cup in the Harriman collection should be dated in the first half of the century.

Reference: The Nanking Museum, "Brief report on the cleaning out of the tomb of Wang Hsing-tsu at Nanking" (text in Chinese), *Kaogu*, 1972, no. 4, pp. 31-33 and 23; Yasuhiko Mayuyama, *Chūgoku Mombutsu Kembun,* Tokyo: Mayuyama Ryūsendō, 1973, fig. 120.

109

fig. 114

110
Bowl
White porcelain, decorated in underglaze blue
Early Ming period, early 15th century;
h. 13 cm., diam. 28.6 cm.
Collection of Mr. and Mrs. Myron S. Falk, Jr.

A double horizontal line divides the exterior of the bowl in two registers. In the upper register is a floral scroll; the lower register is taken up by petal-shaped panels. The inside of the bowl has a design of lotuses and water plants in the middle and a floral scroll around the rim.

This fine piece of early blue and white ware was acquired by its present owners in Cairo. It may well have reached Egypt shortly after it was made. Between 1405 and 1433 seven large maritime expeditions, five of which were under the command of the eunuch Chêng Ho, reached the harbors of the Persian Gulf and the east coast of the African continent, adding to the amounts of Chinese porcelain, which had already entered these countries for several centuries.

Published: Sherman E. Lee and Wai-kam Ho, *Chinese Art under the Mongols,* Cleveland Museum of Art, 1968, no. 145.

In February 1960 a group of six tombs was discovered on the slope of Mount Lang-chê outside the Chung-hua gate of Nanking City. The large tomb, which was designated by the excavators as no. 6, was built for Lady Yeh, wife of Sung Shêng, who lived from 1356 to 1418. The tomb was found to contain a large number of fine white porcelains as well as several pieces of celadon and one single large porcelain bowl decorated in underglaze blue of the type exhibited here. The bowl (fig. 115) measures 13 cm. in height and 30 cm. in diameter and is, therefore, slightly larger than the piece from the Falk collection. There are two other differences between the two pieces. The excavated bowl has a plain horizontal band around the middle of the exterior, separated from the lower register by a single line. A bowl in the Percival David Foundation, London, has

exactly the same feature. The inside bottom of the excavated piece has an aquatic scene similar to the Falk bowl, but here two ducks have been added to complete the more common version of this motif as it occurs on plates and bowls of the period.

Even if we assume that the Nanking bowl was made a few years before it was committed to the tomb (A.D. 1418), the date would seem to be on the late side for a type of bowl that has usually been thought to date from the fourteenth century. Moreover, this is not the only example of its kind. A blue and white *mei-p'ing* vase in the collection of Sir Harry and Lady Garner is dated by the organizers of the commemorative exhibition of the Oriental Ceramic Society in the third quarter of the fourteenth century. An almost identical vase has turned up in the tomb of a certain Mu Shêng at Ying-t'ang-ts'un, Chiang-ning County, Kiangsu Province. As Mu Shêng is known to have died in 1439, only two possibilities would seem to remain. One is that the type of pieces always associated with the reign of the Mongols should be updated by at least a few decades. Or we must assume that the Chinese adopted the custom of placing in the tomb porcelain of an earlier vintage. The only firmly established example of such a case is the presence in the tomb of the emperor Wan-li (1573-1620) of a pair of blue and white *mei-p'ing* with covers bearing the mark of the Chia-ching period (1522-1566).

References: The Nanking Cultural Committee, "Brief report of the cleaning out of Ming tombs outside the Chung-hua gate of Nanking" (text in Chinese), *Kaogu,* 1962, no. 9, pp. 470-478; "China's Beauty of 2000 years, exhibition of ceramics and rubbings in the Sian Museum" (text in Japanese), Tokyo: Mainichi Shimbun, 1965, no. 32; *The Ceramic Art of China,* London: Oriental Ceramic Society, 1971, no. 139; The Nanking Museum, *Kiangsu-shêng ch'u-t'u wên-wu hsüan-chi* [Selected cultural relics discovered in Kiangsu Province], Peking: Wen Wu Press, 1963, pls. 210, 212.

fig. 115

110

110

111
Incense burner
White porcelain with molded, underglaze
blue and enameled decoration
Ming dynasty, Wan-li (1573-1620) mark and
period; h. 17.6 cm.
Fogg Art Museum, Harvard University,
bequest of Samuel C. Davis

The round incense burner has large semi-circular handles decorated with a pierced floral design. It has three legs in the shape of dragons standing upside down to support the vessel with their jaws and front claws. The body of the dragons, their hind legs, and their bifurcated tails are indicated in relief on the vessel itself. The shapes are accentuated by contrasting colors: the dragons are colored in underglaze blue with brown touches, the vessel is covered with a bright yellow enamel. On the bottom is a six-character mark of the Wan-li period.

Published: Suzanne B. Valenstein, *Ming Porcelains, a Retrospective,* New York: China Institute in America, 1970, no. 56.

From the tomb of Emperor Wan-li, excavated in 1956, came a tripod incense burner (fig. 116) of the same shape as the piece exhibited here. Together with two vases of the type exhibited here as no. 112, the incense burner was placed in the main burial chamber of the tomb between the coffin of the emperor and that of Empress Hsiao-tuan. Because of the collapse of the coffin of the empress the piece was slightly damaged. Inside it was placed a bronze holder for incense sticks.

Although the shape of the two censers is similar, the decoration is of a different color. The excavated piece is decorated in enamels, aubergine for the dragons, with patches of green and yellow for the body of the vessel. The latter is remarkable for its size (h. 25.3 cm.), which suggests that the traditional connection between the status in life of the deceased and the size of the mortuary gifts accompanying him into the grave was still valid in Ming times, although it may not have been as rigidly maintained as it was in earlier periods (see cat. no. 112).

Reference: *China Reconstructs,* Peking: China Welfare Institute, vol. 7, no. 3 (March 1959), color pl. 20.

fig. 116

fig. 117

111

112
Vase in the shape of an archaic bronze
White porcelain, covered with aubergine and yellow enamel
Wan-li (1573-1620) mark and period;
h. 26.6 cm.
Fogg Art Museum, Harvard University, bequest of Samuel C. Davis

The vase has a shape resembling that of the classic *ku* or *tsun* with a bulging waist and flanges. It is decorated with figure scenes around the waist, flowers, rocks, and butterflies on the flaring upper section, and floral sprays on the spreading lower section. The decoration is applied in yellow and aubergine enamels with brown enamel used for details and contours. On the base is a six-character mark of Wan-li.

Published: Suzanne B. Valenstein, *Ming Porcelains, a Retrospective,* New York: China Institute in America, 1970, no. 57.

Right next to the incense burner mentioned in the previous entry, a pair of vases closely resembling the piece shown here was placed between the coffin of Emperor Wan-li and that of the empress Hsiao-tuan (fig. 117). Judging from the traces of decomposed vegetable matter found inside the vases, it is possible that they contained flowers at the time when the emperor was laid to rest in his underground palace. Surprisingly, the pair of vases measures 25 cm. in height and is thus slightly smaller than the piece exhibited here, which seems to be the largest of several pieces of the same shape and decoration.

Reference: The Archaeological Team, Commission for the Excavation of Ch'ang-ling, "Excavation of Ting-ling, the Royal Tomb of Emperor Wan Li" (text in Chinese), *Kaogu,* 1959, no. 7, p. 367.

112

113
Preface to the Gathering at the Orchid Pavilion (Lan-t'ing-chi hsü)
Calligraphy and text attributed to Wang Hsi-chih (303-ca. 379) of the Eastern Chin period
Seven pages of ink rubbings based upon a Sung stone engraving from Ting-wu, ink on paper, each 23.9 x 9.3 cm.
Collection of Wango H. C. Weng

The rubbings are done in black ink on paper; each leaf carries four lines of writing in running script (*hsing-shu*). The Ting-wu version of this Lan-t'ing calligraphy has long been considered the best among several versions of the same masterpiece of calligraphy. Since the early T'ang period, calligraphers in China, Korea, and Japan have practiced calligraphy using this preface as their model. Of the Ting-wu rubbings more than a dozen copies exist. The finest examples are in the Palace Museums of Peking and Taipei and in the Tokyo National Museum. The rubbings exhibited here were not taken directly from the Ting-wu stone but from a re-engraved copy that was based on a Ting-wu rubbing. Although some of the sensitivity and strength of the original were lost during this process of copying and recopying, we can nevertheless still obtain an impression of the original. The rubbings were remounted by Hsiang Yüan-pien (1525-1590) in 1577 and combined with other famous works of calligraphy into one album. The seals of this well-known collector can still be found along the edges of the first and last leaf. The earliest colophon was added by K'o Chiu-ssu (1312-1365), the celebrated connoisseur of calligraphy and painting in the Yüan period.

Published: Tseng Yu-ho Ecke, *Chinese Calligraphy,* Philadelphia: Philadelphia Museum of Art, 1971, no. 10.

113

113

113

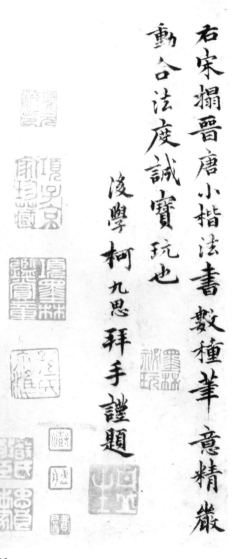

右宋搨晉唐小楷法書數種筆意精嚴

動合法度誠寶玩也

後學 柯九思 拜手謹題

113

嘗故男子琅耶臨沂都鄉南仁

里至闉之字冶民故尚書左僕

射特進衛將軍林之故尚書左僕

之之元子年廿八祖平二年三

月九日平蒔于隴墓在穎令墨

fig. 118

209

114
First half of the "Hsing-jang" letter
Traced ink copy after original writing by
Wang Hsi-chih (303-ca. 379) Eastern Chin
period
Letter mounted as a hand scroll, ink on
paper, 24.3 cm. x 9 cm., probably early
T'ang period (618-903)
Princeton University Museum

This Wang-Hsi-chih from Princeton is the only one outside of China and Japan. In terms of art history, this copy is of the greatest importance, although some calligraphers have sometimes questioned its artistic quality. The letter derives its name from the third and fourth characters of the fragment, which consists of thirteen characters written in two lines. They are written in a style that combines elements of the running (*hsing-shu*) and the cursive (*ts'ao-shu*) type of writing. The second, left half of the letter has been lost, but its appearance is said to have been preserved in rubbings (see Nakata, pp. 39-40 and fig. 29). The piece has a long pedigree of ownership, traceable all the way back to the T'ang period. Today this fragment still bears the seals of the Sung emperor Hui-tsung (see cat. no. 119). This famous collector and painter added a blank page of old brocade, probably in the hope that the missing half of the letter would replace it one day. The eighteenth century emperor Ch'ienlung without hesitation nevertheless filled the empty space with a colophon of his own.

This rare example of a traced copy after the great calligrapher Wang Hsi-chih may be compared with the preceding piece, the lineage of which leads back much less directly to the oeuvre of the celebrated calligrapher. Although a copy, the fragmentary letter still echoes certain characteristics of the period style of the fourth century A.D. and reveals occasionally certain reminiscences of the chancery script (*li-shu*). In several respects it resembles the *Li-po wên-shu* (see cat. no. 113) and other writings of the Western and Eastern Chin periods. Several good colophons are mounted after the main section.

This copied letter was formerly in the Manchu palace collection.
Published: *Hsüan-ho Shu-p'u* (text in Chinese), Taipei: Shih chieh, 1962, p. 347; *Shodō Zenshū*, Tokyo: Heibon-sha, 1968, vol. 4 (Eastern Chin period), pl. 37, pp.168-169; Nakata Yūjirō, *Ō Gishi o chūshin to suru hōjō no kenkyū*, Tokyo: Nigensha, 1960, pp. 39-40.

Recent archaeological discoveries have stirred a lively debate among Chinese scholars concerning the date and authenticity of the Lan-t'ing manuscript, the most famous work of Chinese calligraphy in all history. In order to understand the ramifications of this problem, it is necessary to sketch briefly the events that inspired the creation of the original masterpiece. The "Gathering at the Orchid Pavilion" took place on the third day of the third moon in A.D. 353 at a place now known as Shao-hsing, Chekiang Province. Altogether forty-one persons from high social circles, including the calligrapher Wang Hsi-chih (303-ca. 379), attended this gathering. Poems were composed and wine was drunk. Wang Hsi-chih, semi-inebriated and in excellent spirits, composed a preface and wrote it out instantly on a piece of "silk paper." Reportedly Wang's brushwork was so extraordinarily spontaneous and refined that when he later intended to write the same text again he never was able to recapture the spontaneity of the first, wine-inspired effort.

Not until the time of the T'ang emperor T'ai-tsung (reigned 626-649) did this calligraphy become famous. The emperor acquired it for the imperial collection from a Buddhist priest. Since that time many imitations have been made by the best calligraphers of the court. One of the T'ang copies is said to have been written by Ouyang Hsün (557-641). It was later engraved on a stone stele that was rediscovered at Ting-wu (Ting-chou), Hopei Province, during the Sung period (see cat. no. 113). According to a T'ang novel the original version by Wang Hsi-chih was buried with the emperor T'ai-tsung in his tomb (see also cat. no. 122). Because of its superb quality and the romantic pedigree attached to it, the Lan-

t'ing manuscript, in all of its versions, has always been highly respected and appreciated by Chinese and Japanese connoisseurs, including the greatest calligraphers of all successive dynasties.

However, in the era of new Chinese archaeology, even the Lan-t'ing manuscript could not escape critical reexamination in the light of recent archaeological discoveries. Since 1965 a number of scholars in China, led by the senior scholar and president of the Academy of Science, Kuo Mo-jo, have raised doubts concerning the authenticity of the Lan-t'ing manuscript as it has been handed down to the present day. Their doubts were inspired by the discovery between 1965 and 1970 of seven tombs at Hsiang-shan in the vicinity of Nanking in which were buried close relatives and other contemporaries of Wang Hsi-chih.

The earliest of these tombs, datable to A.D. 323, is that of Hsieh k'un, the latest are those of Wang Min-chih, datable to A.D. 358, and Wang Tan-hu, datable to A.D. 359 (both were cousins of Wang Hsi-chih). The remarkable fact, for which as yet no completely satisfactory explanation has been given, is that none of the tombstones in these graves has been inscribed in script that bears even a remote resemblance to the writing of the Lan-t'ing manuscript. Most of the scholars who have interpreted this as evidence against the authenticity of the Lan-t'ing manuscript are archaeologists, and few of them are established calligraphers.

Understandably this criticism of a famous masterpiece did not go unchallenged. Most of the opposing views are held by persons who either have an ardent admiration for Wang Hsi-chih or by those who personally had an axe to grind with Kuo-Mo-jo. Still others have warned against premature conclusions, as the evidence needed is not complete. The most factual study written in defense of the Lan-t'ing manuscript was published by a Chinese scholar, Kao Erh-shih.

After looking at the excavated tombstones one cannot avoid the feeling that there is a certain inconsistency between the calligraph-

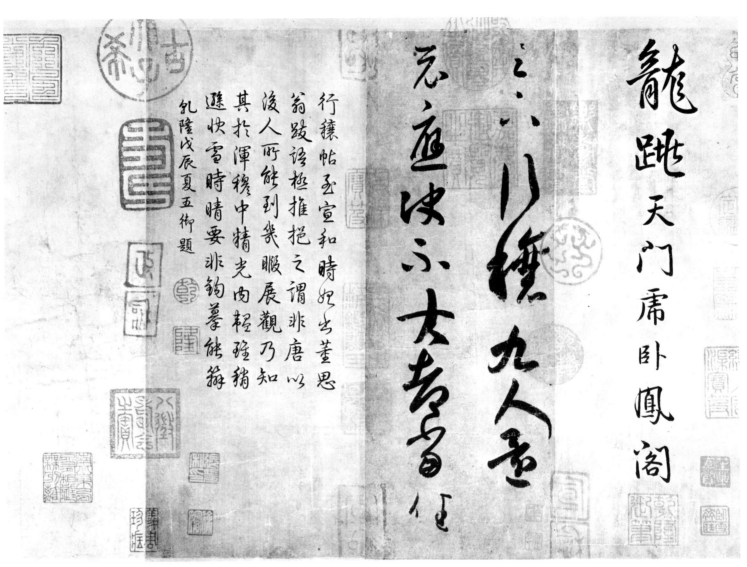

龍跳天門虎臥鳳閣

行禳帖丞宣和時妃出董思
翁跋語極推挹之謂非唐以
後人所能到幾暇展觀乃知
其於渾穆中精光內輕雖稍
遜快雪時晴要非鈎摹能辨
乾隆戊辰夏五御題

ical style of the copies of the Lan-t'ing manuscript and the inscriptions of the tombstones, which represent unalterable evidence of the calligraphical style during Wang Hsi-chih's lifetime. It comes as a surprise that even the tombstones of Wang's close relatives reveal little or no affinity with the style of the famous preface (fig. 118). However, some points need careful consideration. In the writing of tombstones, for obvious "hieratical" reasons, the calligrapher, no matter how skilled, had to observe definite restrictions of which Wang Hsi-chih, in a happy and inebriated mood, could remain totally oblivious. Moreover, the chancery script was particularly favored for tombstones even long after the fourth century A.D. in China. It is difficult to argue that because the calligraphical style of the tombstones differs from the Lan-t'ing preface that the latter is suspect. A tomb datable to A.D. 398, for example, was unearthed in 1972 at Chên-chiang, Kiangsu Province. In the tomb, two kinds of calligraphical style were found side by side. The character that is written in ink (Chên-chiang, p. 58, fig. 19) shows almost no chancery style, whereas the characters engraved on the bricks (p. 56, fig. 6) still carry on the tradition of the earlier period. All this had happened less than a quarter of a century after the death of Wang Hsi-chih, and only about seventy kilometers from the Nanking area where those tombstones were excavated.

Kuo Mo-jo and his colleagues argued that the total disappearance of the characteristics of the chancery script (li-shu) from the copies of the Lan-t'ing manuscript could be considered an anachronism, as this development took place later in the history of Chinese calligraphy. To strengthen their argument these scholars also adduced linguistic and philosophical evidence. Kuo Mo-jo and his colleagues stated the opinion that the ideas expressed in the Lan-t'ing manuscript are quite inconsistent with Wang Hsi-chih's life style and with those of the poems that follow the preface. The problem is further complicated by the fact that there is another version of the text of the preface, first mentioned by

Liu Hsiao-piao in the *Shih-shuo hsin-yü,* which is called *Ling-ho-hsü.* The ideas expressed in this preface do seem more concordant with the views voiced in the poems.

The famous seventeenth century eccentric painter and calligrapher Chu Ta (Pa-ta-shan-jên) claimed to have modeled his calligraphical style of writing upon that of the Chin period. Among the documents from the Eastern Chin period brought back from Turfan by the Ōtani mission is one known as the *Li Po wên-shu* (first half of the fourth century A.D.). It tends to confirm Chu Ta's claims and actually has many characteristics in common with the eccentric's version of the *Ling-ho-hsü.* All of these pieces, dating from or inspired by writings dating from the Chin period, reveal a fairly strong residue of influence by the chancery script (li-shu).

Among the very few scholars who challenged the authenticity of the Lan-t'ing manuscript before the recent archaeological discoveries is the nineteenth century Cantonese scholar Li Wên-t'ien. Among scholars in Taiwan only the late professor Ting Nien-hsien has expressed doubts, a view all the more valuable because it is that of a man who himself was a calligrapher of outstanding talents. In an issue of the *Hsin-i-lin Monthly* that is entirely devoted to the connoisseurship of the Lan-t'ing manuscript, he maintained his appreciation of the *Lan-t'ing-hsü* as a work of art in spite of the uncertainty as to its correct date and authorship.

The spirited discussion of this question has to be judged on its scholarly merits. At the same time we should not overlook the importance of the fact that archaeological evidence gathered in recent years in China challenges the veracity of the transmission of one of the eternal monuments of ancient Chinese art and culture. The debate is, therefore, bound to continue for many years to come and much more evidence will be needed to reach a final verdict. It is the first time in history since the discovery of the *Bamboo Annals* (see Introduction, p. 13) that an archaeological discovery has stirred up so much scholarly controversy.

References: Kuo Mo-jo, "The authenticity of the Lan T'ing Hsü in the light of the epitaphs of Wang Hsing-chih and Hsieh K'un" (text in Chinese), *Wen Wu,* 1965, no. 6, pp. 1-25; Kao Erh-shih, "Disagreement about the questioning of Lan T'ing Hsü's authenticity" (text in Chinese), *Wen Wu,* 1965, no. 7 (appendix), pp. 1-14; Ch'ên Chiao-t'ung, "Problems of the authenticity of the Lan T'ing calligraphy" (text in Chinese), *Ming Pao* (Hong Kong), no. 89, 1973, pp. 22-25; Yoshikawa Tadao, *Ō Gishi,* Tokyo, 1972, pp. 51-61; Sanada Tajima, *Chūkoku shodō shi,* Tokyo, 1967, vol. 2, pp. 61-63; Ting Nien-hsien, "About the history of the Lan T'ing" (text in Chinese), *Hsin I Lin* (Taipei), March 1969, pp. 33-39; *Hachidai-sanjin Rin Ka Jo,* Tokyo: Nigensha, 1963; Chên-chiang City Museum, "Report on the excavation of an Eastern Chin dynasty tomb built with decorated bricks" (text in Chinese), *Wen Wu,* 1973, no. 4, pp. 53, 58, fig. 19; Kuo Mo-jo, "Lan T'ing Hsü and the philosophy of Lao-tzu and Chuang-tzu (text in Chinese), *Wen Wu,* 1965, no. 9, pp. 9-11; Ch'i Kung, "About the two T'ang copies of the Lan T'ing Hsü" (text in Chinese), *Wen Wu Ching Hua,* 1964, no. 3, pp. 15-25, 35-38; Imai Ryōsetsu, "Notes on Kuo Mo-jo's opinion regarding the authenticity of the Lan T'ing Hsü" (text in Japanese), *Shodō Geijutsu,* 1971, vol. 1 (supplement), pp. 1-4; Yen Pei-min, "The authenticity of the Lan-t'ing manuscript on the basis of the calligraphical development of the Eastern Chin period" (text in Chinese), *Hsüeh Shu Yüeh-k'an,* 1965, no. 8; Wang Po-ch'in, "Re-evaluation of the Lan-t'ing calligraphy attributed to Wang Hsi-chih" (text in Chinese), *I-shih Kuan-kuei,* Taipei: Commercial Press, 1970, pp. 58-96; Hsü Fu-kuan, "On the controversy of the Lan-t'ing calligraphy" (text in Chinese), *Ming Pao* (Hong Kong), nos. 92-93, 1973.

115
Calligraphy in Running Script
Attributed to Emperor Kao-tsung (reigned 1127-1162, died 1187), Southern Sung period
Round fan mounted as an album leaf, ink on silk, h. 23.9 cm., w. 25.1 cm.
Museum of Fine Arts, Boston, Chinese and Japanese Special Fund. 12.893

The two seven-character lines of a quatrain are taken from a poem by Su Shih (1036-1101) entitled "On Meeting with Ch'in T'ai-hsü and [the monk] Shên-liao at Sung River. When Kuan Yen-chang and Hsü An-chung happened to arrive, I composed two poems rhyming with the word *Fêng* [wind]":
> "Sleeping our lives away,
>   floating down the river in the rain,
> All day long the boat sails on the breeze,
>   which beats the shores."

Most characters are written in running script (*hsing-shu*), interspersed with a few graphs in regular script (*k'ai-shu*). The two lines have been written rather far apart in order to leave open sufficient space for the shaft of the handle of the fan for which the leaf was originally intended. The silk is of the type frequently used during the twelfth century; it is tightly woven and has a delicate texture. It is well preserved except for some bronze-colored stains caused by water when the calligraphy, at that time part of a larger album, was accidentally dropped into the Yangtze River, but fortunately retrieved.

At first sight the two lines would seem to be rather evenly written, and there is an even relationship between the individual characters. Upon closer examination, however, one feels the forceful strength of character and the maturity of the personality, fully expressed in a spontaneous way. It is quite obvious that the calligrapher wanted to create variety by combining different tonalities of ink and by contrasting dark and light or wet and dry strokes. The brushwork too presents a rich variety, as if the artist brushed the sentences on the silk without any conscious effort. Under magnification it can be seen that the ink of each stroke has deeply

penetrated into the silk; even those strokes that have been lightly drawn in the "flying white" technique, as, for example, the fourth character of the right line, have the same strength.

There are altogether five seals impressed on the leaf. The gourd-shaped seal on the left is drawn with a brush, not impressed. Under the red lines there are vague traces in gray. These probably are part of a preliminary drawing executed in charcoal. The seal reads *Yü-shu*, i.e., "imperial writing." This seal was originally associated with the last Northern Sung emperor Hui-tsung (see cat. no. 119). Here, however, it would seem to have been carefully redrawn in commemoration of the imperial artist who first used it.

The large square seal at the right reads "May the sons and grandsons of the Prince Ch'ien-ning treasure it eternally." The seal belonged to a prince of Ch'ien-ning who lived during the middle of the fifteenth century. The third seal is that of Wang-yen Ching-hsien, a nineteenth century collector. To the left, mounted on the same background, is a colophon on paper written in ink by Juan Yüan (1764-1849), the original owner of the album mentioned above.

Published: Kojiro Tomita, *Portfolio of Chinese Paintings in the Museum (Han to Sung Periods),* Boston, 1933, p. 13, pl. 86; Tseng Yu-ho Ecke, *Chinese Calligraphy,* Philadelphia: Philadelphia Museum of Art, 1971, no. 24; *Kokka,* no. 225, 1911, pp. 43, 49-50.

In the tomb of Chu T'an, the tenth son of the first Ming emperor (see cat. no. 122), an album leaf of the same shape as the piece exhibited here was found (fig. 119). Inscribed with four lines of a "truncated" verse (*chüeh-chü*), written in gold on silk, it is a work by the Sung emperor Kao-tsung. It bears one damaged seal of the artist and two colophons by Fêng Tzu-chên and Chao Yen (see cat. no. 122), who confirm the attribution to this emperor, considering it a work made after the emperor abdicated in 1162 at the age of 57 to live for another twenty-five years in retirement in the Tê-shou Kung, or Palace of Virtuous Longevity.

The attribution of this calligraphy to Kao-tsung as a work written by him after his abdication is of considerable interest because of its connection with the Boston fan. Kao-tsung was a calligrapher of great creativity, and his style of writing underwent many changes. Little attention has been paid to the last phase of his creative life. Although he may have produced many specimens of calligraphy, only those that bear the seal or the sign of the Palace of Virtuous Longevity can be ascribed with certainty to the period after his retirement from official duties.

The writing on the excavated fan is of the cursive variety (*ts'ao-shu*), and the use of gold instead of ink creates an additional problem in comparing the two pieces. However, the expressive, effortless manner was first identified as that of Kao-tsung by its former owner, the Ch'ing collector Juan Yüan, who was a calligrapher in his own right. Unfortunately, he did not clearly explain his attribution. Kojiro Tomita, perhaps influenced by a brief article in the *Kokka,* rejected the attribution to Kao-tsung and attributed the calligraphy to his son and follower Hsiao-tsung, without stating his reasons for doing so.

However, the recent discovery of Kao-tsung's leaf in the tomb of Chu T'an has stimulated interest in the style of this artist during the period of his residence in the Tê-shou Palace. A comparison can be made with an album leaf in the Palace Museum collection, Taipei, the writing of which bears a striking resemblance to the Boston leaf. The leaf in the Palace Museum has a clearly impressed seal in the *ku-wên* style reading *Shou-huang shu-pao,* i.e., "written treasure of the emperor of the Tê-shou Palace." The seal on the fan from Chu T'an's tomb is damaged, although not beyond hope for definite identification. In all probability it is the same seal as that found on the Palace Museum leaf.

The Boston and Palace Museum leaves have many features in common. The calligraphical style is very similar. The closeness in spirit between the two works is further illustrated by the fact that the lines of the

平生睡足連江雨

盡日舟行摩岸風

士卿書乃宗高宗筆詩則蘇文忠公
舊句也漁隱叢話載文忠此詩作平生
睡足連江雨盡日舟橫拍岸風今蘇詩
刻本亦作舟橫壁岸風今此幅舉為行
舟設景自是南宗和本作行舟摩岸也

115

214

fig. 119

Boston fan seem to echo the painted representation on the Palace Museum leaf, which shows a man waking up in a boat after a long, deep, and dreamless sleep. If the Boston piece is indeed another example of Kao-tsung's work during his residence in the Tê-shou Palace, these two leaves reveal the imperial artist's philosophy of retirement and illustrate the way in which he combined the arts of life and calligraphy.

References: National Palace Museum, *Signatures and Seals on Painting and Calligraphy,* Hong Kong, 1964, vol. 1, p. 78, vol. 2, pp. 140-141; National Palace Museum, *Masterpieces of Chinese Album Painting in the National Palace Museum,* Tokyo, 1971, fig. 16; Shantung Provincial Museum, "Report on the excavation of the tomb of Chu T'an" (text in Chinese), *Wen Wu,* 1972, no. 5, pp. 29-30; Liao-ning Provincial Museum, *Sung Kao-tsung Chao Kou ts'ao-shu Lo-shên-fu,* Peking: Wen Wu Press, 1961.

116
The Thirteen Emperors
Attributed to Yen Li-pên (died A.D. 673)
Hand scroll, ink and colors on silk,
51 x 551 cm.
Museum of Fine Arts, Boston, Denman Waldo Ross Collection. 31.643

The hand scroll consists of a series of portraits of thirteen emperors and their attendants. It is not clear what criteria were applied for the selection of these imperial personages, for some could hardly have been chosen for their historical importance, as the painting includes several rather obscure emperors. The earliest emperor, according to titles written on each section of the scroll, is one of the former Han dynasty (206 B.C.-A.D. 23). The latest is the last emperor of the Sui dynasty, which was overthrown by the T'ang in A.D. 618, when Yen Li-pên was probably already born. The first six portraits of the scroll are obviously not of the same period as the seven of the following section. This is evident when the silk and color pigments of the two sections are compared by laboratory tests. The silk of the part of the scroll showing the group of seven emperors is not as finely and strongly woven as that of the first six. The cinnabar pigment applied to the robes of the emperors shows a difference in crystals between the two sections of the scroll. A comparison of the brushwork of the two sections reveals even more obvious evidences that the first six emperors are not from the same hand as the later seven portraits. The quality of the brushwork and the coloring technique in the first six portraits cannot match that of the later seven. The laboriously drawn lines are hesitant and restrained—characteristics of most copied paintings.

There is another explanation for the choice of emperors and the lack of chronological order in which they appear on the scroll. The date of the identifying labels, written above each emperor, seems to be later than the painting; they may very well be speculative.

The six portraits at the beginning of the scroll, although obviously inferior in execution, are painted in a manner that is fairly consistent with the following older section as far as iconography, colors, and proportions are concerned. The first section actually imitates exactly the details of dress and headgear of the second part. The close similarity between the two sections of different dates suggests that the copyist may actually have used the original section of the portraits of six emperors to produce his copy. One suspects that this was done in order to make one masterpiece into two, rather than because of the need to replace the supposedly worn-out original, as has previously been suggested. This suspicion is strengthened by the impression that the first part of the attached colophons written on silk may be a copy of colophons originally attached to the older section. The colophons, although purporting to be written by different hands at various times, are often characterized by a curious uniformity of brushwork and ink tones, especially if we compare them with those genuine ones written in the paper colophon section, immediately following those written on silk.

One interesting Southern Sung official seal reading "Chung-shu-shêng-yin" is repeatedly impressed on the scroll on the sections showing four of the copied emperors, as well as on all of the earlier emperors, and all through the two colophon sections. The reliability and identity of this official seal is beyond question. The seal ink as well as the style of carving unquestionably confirm a Southern Sung date, ca. early thirteenth century.

Of the "Chung-shu-shêng" seal impressed on the upper edge of the section representing the emperor Hsüan-ti of the Ch'ên dynasty only the left side remains. The rest of the seal was lost together with the silk of the missing original part. How many emperors originally were portrayed is difficult to know. Thirteen certainly was not the total number when the Boston scroll was painted.

This masterpiece of early Chinese painting was kept in collections in Fukien for some time. The last of these was that of Liang Hung-chih, who in 1929 through the intermediary of a Japanese dealer named Nakane

116

fig. 120

fig. 121

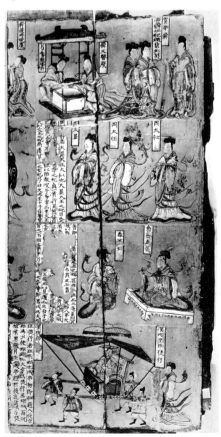

Kunsai sold it to the Yamanaka Company in Tokyo. That year the painting was exhibited in Tokyo; two years later it was acquired for the Boston Museum by its generous benefactor Dr. Denman Waldo Ross.

Published: Kojiro Tomita, "Portraits of the Emperors," Museum of Fine Arts, Boston, *Bulletin,* 30, no. 117 (1932), 2-8; Wang Yün, *Shu-hua Mu-lu* [Records of paintings and calligraphies in the Yüan Court], author's preface dated in A.D. 1277, Taipei: Shih-chieh Book Co., 1962 reprint, Mei-shu-ts'ung-shu ed., vol. 4, no. 6, pp. 32-33; *Tō Sō Gen Min Meiga Taikan,* Tokyo: Ōtsuka Kōgeisha, 1929, pl. 1.

This renowned treasure is currently under detailed study by the museum's staff. For the immediate interest of this exhibition, we merely wish to apply here the knowledge we have gained from Chinese archaeological excavations to the study of this ancient masterpiece of Chinese painting, as we have demonstrated in other entries in the catalogue.

Archaeological information coming out of China during the last twenty-five years has helped to clarify the many period styles of figure painting of the T'ang dynasty (A.D. 618-906). For instance, only now can we be confident in distinguishing between figure paintings of the seventh and the eighth century (that is, during and after the lifetime of Yen Li-pên). T'ang figures decorating tombs of the seventh century usually show stylistic affinity with those of the earlier centuries. The handling of movement, space, the relationship between figures, the systematic arrangement of draperies, and such details as facial expressions, are clearly a continuation of styles and fashions developed in the sixth century. On the other hand, in later T'ang tombs, one sees the emergence of a new figure style. Ever since the end of the seventh century, T'ang tombs with excellent wall paintings, especially those royal tombs of the princess Yung-t'ai (fig. 120) and the princess Chang-huai and I-tê, all dating from the early eighth century, display such previously unknown characteristics like thick eyebrows, wavy outlines at the lower part of the sleeves

(see fig. 77), more detailed draperies, quieter postures for individuals and groups, etc. In general, there is a noticeable tendency toward idealism and elegance in the eighth century, replacing the grandeur and solidity of the seventh century. These differences also hold true when we compare the figure paintings of the two centuries in the Buddhist caves at Tun-huang. The portraiture of a Vimalakīrti and attendants in cave 220 and its eighth century replica in cave 103 are two good examples.

Judging from the evidence mentioned above we believe both the figure style and the execution of the older section of the Boston emperors are typical of the seventh century, although at this moment there is no direct proof to confirm the traditional attribution of the emperors' scroll to Yen Li-pên.

The section showing eight bearers carrying an emperor who sits on a litter in the shape of a four-legged dais in the emperors' scroll is said to be the emperor Hsüan-ti of the Ch'ên dynasty. Chou Pi-ta (A.D. 1126-1204), a leading art critic of his time, was so much impressed by this Hsüan-ti group that he actually took this section as the sole original work from the hand of Yen Li-pên; all the rest of the scroll was judged to be a later copy. This of course is far from accurate, but Chou Pi-ta's extraordinary admiration of the Hsüan-ti section can easily be understood and be shared by other viewers of the work.

Recently the discovery of a set of lacquer-painted screens by Chinese archaeologists in a Northern Wei tomb has evoked new thoughts about this Hsüan-ti section of the emperors' scroll. The lacquer-painted screens were excavated from the tomb of a high official named Ssu-ma Chin-lung (died in A.D. 484) at Ta-t'ung, Shansi Province. The style of figures on the screen is close to the carved stone figures in the Buddhist cave-temples around the Ta-t'ung area (fig. 121). Of the many narrative figure paintings on the screen, one deals with the story of "Lady Pan's refusal to ride in the same litter with the emperor Ch'êng-ti." This illustration can be compared with the same story illustrated

217

in the well-known scroll *Admonitions of the Instructress* attributed to Ku Kai-chih (ca. 344-ca. 406) in the British Museum. The way of showing the litter-bearers in these two paintings is strikingly different. The airy, moving, and fantastically arranged litter-bearers in the *Admonitions* scroll do not find any echo at all in those of the lacquer screen found in the north. It is not clear whether this is just a matter of difference in time or is because the screen was made in northern China whereas the *Admonitions* scroll is associated with an artist from the south (today's Nanking). At any rate the litter-bearers of the Hsüan-ti section in the emperors' scroll look more or less like their predecessors in the *Admonitions*. The movement and sensitivity of the eight bearers are suggested by the complicated placement of the legs and feet and by the intelligent grouping of those slightly frowning faces. To some extent, the female carriers in the hand scroll *Pu-nien t'u* (Carriers of the imperial carriage) in the collection of the Peking Palace Museum also show this "southern" tradition, despite the fact that it is a stiff, late copy after a good seventh century painting also said to be by Yen Li-pên.

This "southern tradition" can again be recognized in the section, supposed to represent the emperor Wên-ti of the Ch'ên dynasty in the emperors' scroll. This scholarly-looking emperor, gracefully dressed in a fine fur coat, reminds us of the eight portraits of the Sages of the Bamboo Grove on impressed bricks in a mid-fifth century tomb. The tomb was excavated in 1960 in the Nanking area (at Hsi-shan-ch'iao), where the southern artist Ku Kai-chih had once lived (see also cat. no. 117).

This analysis does not, of course, mean that the Boston emperors merely reflected the taste of the southerners. Actually, the fierce, heavy, powerful portraiture of Emperor Wu-ti of the Later Chou dynasty stands out as convincingly close to those Northern Wei emperors carved in relief in the Buddhist cave-temples at Lung-mên or Kung-hsien in the north. The two male attendants flanking

the emperor Wu-ti look almost exactly like pottery figurines unearthed from Northern Wei tombs. Chih-kung in his recent article "Notes on the lacquer-painted screen of the Northern Wei period" rightly points out the relationship between the emperors painted on the screen and on the Boston scroll. Naturally the emperors from the two works are not identical, but the similarities in style and costume between the fifth century screen and the seventh century scroll are readily apparent. The effort to unify a divided China, which was started with the victory of the Sui dynasty (A.D. 581-617) over the Northern Chou in A.D. 580 and the southern state of Ch'ên in A.D. 589, had been accomplished by the middle of the seventh century by the able emperor T'ai-tsung of the newly established T'ang dynasty. The artist's happy combination of different figure styles that had previously flourished in the north and south should also be viewed against the background of these historical developments.

References: Shensi Provincial Museum, "Report on the excavation of the tomb of Chêng Jên-t'ai [died in A.D. 663]" (text in Chinese), *Wen Wu*, 1972, no. 7, pp. 33-34, pl. 11; Chu Chang-ch'ao, *T'ang Yung-t'ai-kung-chu Mu Pi-hua Chi*, [Wall paintings from the tomb of Princess Yung-t'ai of the T'ang], Peking, 1963; Wu Po-lun, "Wall paintings and pottery figurines unearthed from the tomb of the Princess Yung-t'ai" (text in Chinese), *Wên-wu ching-hua*, Peking, 1964, no. 3; Shensi Provincial Museum, "Report on the excavation of the tomb of Prince I-tê [died in A.D. 706]" (text in Chinese), *Wen Wu*, 1972, no. 7, pp. 26-31, pl. 3; Shensi Provincial Museum, "Report on the excavation of the Prince Chang-huai's tomb of the T'ang dynasty" (text in Chinese), *Wen Wu*, 1972, no. 7, pp. 13-25, pl. 2; Naghiro Toshio, *The Representational Art of the Six Dynasty*, Tokyo: Bijutsu Press, 1969, pls. 1-8; Chih-kung, "Notes on the lacquer-painted screen of the Northern Wei period" (text in Chinese), *Wen Wu*, 1972, no. 8, pp. 55-60; Tang Yen Li-pen pu-nien t'u (portfolio), Peking: Wen Wu Press, 1959, pl. 1; Tun-huang Institute, *Tun-huang pi-hua*, Peking: Wen Wu Press, 1959, pp. 5-6, pls. 116-117, 141.

117

117
Scholars of the Northern Ch'i Dynasty Collating the Classics
Anonymous, traditionally attributed to Yen Li-pên (died A.D. 673), but probably Northern Sung period, second half of 11th century
Hand scroll, ink and colors on silk, h. 27.6 cm.; l. 114 cm.
Museum of Fine Arts, Boston, Denman Waldo Ross Collection. 31.123

Except for the first section, this extremely important document in the history of Chinese figure painting has been remarkably well preserved. The tonality of the ink and the colors may have somewhat deteriorated, but the overall condition is still close to what it must have been at the time the picture was painted.

The theme of the painting, *Scholars of the Northern Ch'i Dynasty Collating the Classics*, refers to an event that took place in A.D. 556, when the emperor Wên-hsüan-ti of the Northern Ch'i dynasty ordered the scholar Fan Hsün and eleven associates to collate the texts of the classics for use of the heir apparent. This event, a milestone in the history of

fig. 122

Chinese bibliography, became a favorite subject for pictorial representation.

The present painting does not represent the entire original work, for it shows only five of the twelve scholars. These five, together with their servants and attendants, form a large assemblage, which the painter has divided up into three groups concerned with different activities. Each group in turn is divided into parties of three, so that the composition is made up of a regularly arranged sequence of triangular groupings.

The center of the first group is the scholar Fan Hsün, who is seated on a folding stool (*hu-ch'uang*) surrounded by six servants arranged in two groups of three. The central part of the entire assemblage is formed by a group of four scholars seated on a dais and surrounded by five servants. Two scholars hold a brush in their hands, and one of them is actually writing, while the other seems to concentrate his thoughts. His piercing eyes are focused on the paper he holds up with his left hand. He may also be watching the scene in the foreground, where two of the scholars are engaged in the preliminaries of taking

leave from each other. One is assisted by his boy servant *(shu-t'ung)* in putting on his boots, while the other interrupts his playing on the lute in an effort to detain him. As he tries to hold onto the other's clothes he overturns a *tazza*, spilling the food placed upon it over the dais. Behind the dais stands a maid who is cleaning a wine cup, while another servant prepares a sheet of paper for her master to write on. Separated from this group to the left stand six servants, three women holding various utensils and three men leading two horses. The entire assemblage is shown against an empty background. Another version of the central group, attributed to the tenth century artist Ch'iu Wên-po (Palace Museum, Taipei), is placed against a garden background.

The entire painting is colored mainly in red, white, and black in tones ranging from pitch black to light gray. The white and red parts have been carefully distributed over the entire composition. The way the white paint has been applied to the forehead, the nose, and the chin of the women is highly unusual; it gives the faces an almost sculptural quality.

The two styles of hairdo of the women show the hair tied in two tufts with pearls attached to the tops, or rolled up in a rather flat chignon on top of the head. The wavy hairline of the ladies is not shown on any other Chinese figure painting.

On both edges of the hand scroll are placed more than a dozen collector's seals, ranging in date from the Southern Sung to the Ch'ing dynasty. Attached to the painting is a long section of colophons, the first of which is written by the well-known Southern Sung scholar Fan Ch'êng-ta (1126-1193). He is the first to associate the style of painting with Yen Li-pên (died A.D. 673), but a later erasure of two characters reading "in the manner of" has made his attribution firmer than originally intended. Among the last owners were the late nineteenth century collector Wang-yen Ching-hsien and Chin Ch'êng.

The first extensive study of this painting was published by Kojiro Tomita in the *Bulletin* of the Museum of Fine Arts. His detailed analysis of the painting and the origins of the theme represented in it led him to the conclusion that the painting, far from being a work by Yen Li-pên, probably dates from the Northern Sung period, but that the theme itself may be traced directly to the painter Yang Tzu-hua of the Northern Ch'i period. He concluded that the scroll may therefore furnish valuable material for the study of the costumes and culture of those days.

Published: Kojiro Tomita, "Scholars of the Northern Ch'i Dynasty Collating Classic Texts," Museum of Fine Arts, Boston, *Bulletin*, vol. 29, no. 174 (1931), 58-63; Osvald Sirén, *Chinese Painting,* London and Bradford, 1956, vol. 3, pls. 76-78; Laurence Sickman and Alexander Soper, *Art and Architecture of China,* Baltimore: Penguin Books, 1956, pl. 93; Jan Fontein and Pratapaditya Pal, *Museum of Fine Arts, Boston: Oriental Art,* Tokyo: Kodansha, 1968, pl. 74, p. 171; Wu Tung, "Notes on the Scroll Scholars of the Northern Ch'i Dynasty Collating the Classics" (text in Japanese), *Bukkyō Geijutsu/ Ars Buddhica,* no. 90 (1973), pp. 77-86, pl. 11.

The abundance of archaeological data that can be obtained from excavations carried out during the last twenty-five years gives us new clues to the date of the painting and its possible prototypes by comparing the many utensils and other objects shown in this painting with excavated, datable pieces.

The dais on which the scholars are seated closely resembles the stands in the Shōsōin collection and may well be considered typical of the T'ang period, as distinguished from the type of the Northern Ch'i and Sui types, exemplified in the stand of the Tuan Fang altar (A.D. 593) in the Boston Museum.

Together with the "Seven Sages of the Bamboo Grove" the hermit Jung Ch'i-ch'i, a contemporary of Confucius, is represented on stamped bricks in a tomb of the Eastern Chin period (317-419), discovered at Hsi-shan-ch'iao near Nanking in 1960 (fig. 122). The hermit is shown with a lute *(chin)* of the same type with a straight, tapering shoulder as the T'ang instrument carrying an inscription datable to A.D. 724. It would seem, therefore, that the shape of the *chin* did not undergo any really drastic changes during the Six Dynasties and T'ang periods. In later times, however, the straight lines of the tapering shoulder were given a curved shape, and the small indentations on the sides were enlarged. The *chin,* with an inscription datable to A.D. 1164, which was found in the tomb of Chu T'an (see cat. no. 122) is perhaps the earliest datable example of this later type, which is exactly the same as that shown in the hand scroll.

The inkstone represented in the painting is of a well-known ceramic type. Its circular body rests upon a large number of curved feet. This kind of inkstone was highly popular among the calligraphers of the Sung period. Mi Fu (1052-1107) called it a "hoof inkstone." Pieces of the same type have been found in the Korean kingdom of Paekche and in Japan. Sometimes the inkstone is supplied with a flat ring that connects the feet, a type fashionable at least into the tenth century (fig. 123). So far no pieces of this type have been found in tombs antedating the seventh century. Next to the inkstone are two wine cups standing on cup-stands *(t'o-tzu).* They are practically identical in shape with a

fig. 123

fig. 124

cup and cup-stand shown in a wall painting in a T'ang tomb at T'ai-yüan, Shansi Province, dating from the late seventh to early eighth century.

Of all the objects shown in the hand scroll perhaps the *tazza* comes closest in date to the Northern Ch'i period. Although this type, which was made in bronze and glass as well as ceramic ware, occurs throughout the T'ang period; it antedates the founding of this dynasty. In the tomb of Pu Jên, who died in A.D. 603 and was buried near An-yang (see cat. no. 80), a *tazza* of the same shape was found. The examples in the Shōsōin collection suggest that the type did not undergo drastic changes during the T'ang period. The arrow vase *(t'ou-hu)* is painted over a repair in the hand scroll and should therefore not be taken into consideration for the present purpose of determining the chronological origin of the painting.

The type of armrest *(p'ing-chi),* one carried by the maid and another placed under the elbow of one of the scholars, has an almost exact counterpart in a lacquered piece excavated from a tomb in Huai-an County, Kiangsu Province, in 1959 and datable to the middle of the eleventh century (fig. 124). This type of armrest is quite different from its pre-T'ang predecessor, which usually had a curved shape.

The brushes with a rather thick, short shaft that we see in the hand scroll are quite similar to examples in the Shōsōin collection. Two pottery brushes excavated from an early T'ang tomb near Ch'ang-sha are of the same type.

In 1955 a tomb was discovered near T'ai-yüan, Shansi Province, in which was buried a certain Chang Su, who died in A.D. 559. This tomb, one of the few that are firmly datable in the Northern Ch'i period, contained a large number of tomb figurines. The dress of the women still closely resembles that of the Northern Wei period. On the other hand, the dresses of the women in the scroll, all of whom are shown with a large scarf tied around the shoulders, have little in common with those of the Northern Ch'i tomb figurines.

Finally, the stirrups in the painting are quite different from the actual examples excavated from tombs datable to A.D. 664 and A.D. 693. On the other hand, a stirrup from a Liao tomb datable to A.D. 959 has the same thin, broad, and slightly curved part for receiving the foot of the rider as the stirrups shown in the hand scroll (see cat. nos. 88, 97).

Summing up the results of these comparisons it would seem that exactly datable archaeological evidence fails to confirm the hypothesis that the original design of the painting derives directly from a Northern Ch'i prototype. Although some of the objects shown in this painting represent types current during the early T'ang period—the time when Yen Li-pên was active—none can be traced with certainty to the Northern Ch'i period. The mixture of T'ang and Sung elements makes it most likely that the painting dates from the Northern Sung period, but that it is based on a T'ang model.

References: *Pei Ch'i Shu* (Po-na ed.), Peking, 1958 reprint, ch. 37/18a-19a; Tokyo National Museum, *Illustrated Catalogue of Treasures Originally from the Hōryū-ji*, Tokyo, 1959, pls. 275-277; Shantung Provincial Museum, "Report on the excavation of the tomb of Chu T'an" (text in Chinese), *Wen Wu*, 1972, no. 5, pp. 28, 36, figs. 27-28; National Palace Museum, *Three Hundred Masterpieces of Chinese Painting in the Palace Museum*, Taichung, 1959, vol. 2, pl. 56; Shansi Provincial Museum, *T'ai-yüan K'uang-p'o Pei Ch'i Chang Su mu wên-wu t'u-lu*, Peking, 1958, pls. 16-17; "Report of a tomb of the T'ang dynasty unearthed at Niu-chiao-t'ang, Changsha City, Hunan province" (text in Chinese), *Kaogu*, 1964, no. 12, p. 634, fig. 1; "Report on two tombs of the T'ang dynasty unearthed at Chin-shêng-ts'un, T'ai-yüan" (text in Chinese), *Kaogu*, 1959, no. 9, pl. 4, fig. 1; "Report on tombs of Northern Sung excavated at Hui-an, Kiangsu Province" (text in Chinese), *Wen Wu*, 1960, nos. 8-9, pp. 43-51; "Report on the tomb of Wei Chiung of T'ang dynasty unearthed in Sian, Shensi Province" (text in Chinese), *Wen Wu*, 1959, no. 8, p. 17, fig. 29; see also "Report on the excavation of the tomb of Chêng Jên-t'ai of the T'ang dynasty" (text in Chinese), *Wen Wu*, 1972, no. 7, p. 39, pl. 12, fig. 4; *Wu-shêng ch'u-t'u chung-yao wên-wu chan-lan t'u-lu*, Peking, 1958, pl. 107, fig. 2; *Kaogu*, 1964, no. 12, pl. 7, fig. 5.

118
Lady Wên-chi's Return to China
Northern Sung period, ca. A.D. 1100
Remains of a hand scroll now mounted as album leaves, ink and colors on silk,
a: 24.7 x 49.8, b: 25 x 46.6, c: 24.8 x 67.2,
d: 25 x 55.8 cm.
Museum of Fine Arts, Boston, Denman Waldo Ross Collection. 28.62-28.65

The romantic story of Lady Wên-chi's captivity in Mongolia and her return to China twelve years later, after she was ransomed and had to leave her Hsiung-nu (Hun) husband and their two children, is a typical northern frontier saga of the Han period. Poets and painters have often used the story in their work. The four album leaves were originally part of a series of eighteen paintings, a number derived from that of the poems attributed to Lady Wên-chi. It is possible that they were originally mounted in the same manner as the hand scroll by Ma Ho-chih, in which poems and their illustrations alternate (see cat. no. 120). Of the paintings of this scroll only these four remain; none of the calligraphed poems has been preserved.

The four leaves represent four sections of a scroll; these deal with Wên-chi's departure from Mongolia and her return to Ch'ang-an, the Chinese capital. The silk is of the same fine, tightly woven type as that of cat. nos. 115 and 120. The leaves have sustained damage in several places and under ultraviolet light a large number of retouchings appear. The differences in size between the leaves suggest that the original height was cropped in the process of remounting. Several later colophons have been added to the leaves. A label that is mounted to the right of the first leaf erroneously states that the paintings represent "Auspicious omens foretelling the accession to the throne of Emperor Sung Kao-tsung by Hsiao Chao." This label should not be taken seriously, as it not only misidentifies the theme of the leaves but also attributes them to an artist with whose work the pictures have no stylistic affinity. It must have become attached to the painting at a later date. A painting attributed to Hsiao Chao and representing the omens of Kao-tsung is now in the Tientsin Museum, China. The collector's seals of Liang Ch'ing-piao on the mounting of the Boston leaves indicate that they were once part of his famous collection.

In the first three leaves the action is laid in the northern steppes. The first leaf shows a large *yurt* in a sparsely wooded, undulating landscape. The *yurt* is protected from the wind by four leather-colored screens. The chief personages, Wên-chi and her husband, are seated in front of the *yurt* at an oblong table on which dishes, Chinese chopsticks, and spoons have been laid out. The tableware seems to be of gold and silver. Short-legged, saddled ponies are waiting outside the screened area.

In the second leaf the painter represents the same tent, but from another perspective, giving a frontal view. He vividly depicts life in a nomad camp at a watering place, revealing many interesting details of the life style of the north that are not documented in other paintings. The green grass grows on both sides of the winding stream. Wên-chi is seated in a subdued mood, facing her husband, who seems to be arguing with her. In the lower left corner two servants are preparing the lamb stew. The fire and smoke under the cauldrons are clearly visible. Flags and drums are tied together and placed in front of the tent. In the background are oxen, horses, and chariots.

The third leaf breathes a spirit that is quite different from that of the previous two leaves. Here the *yurt* is empty, and the focus has shifted away to the crowd outside. The center of the composition is occupied by a chariot drawn by camels. Along the path, upper left corner, between the hills the mounted escorts are waiting. The differences between their headgear and banners suggests that those on the left are Chinese, those on the right the northerners. On the right side of the leaf we see how the nomadic prince takes leave of his wife, Wên-chi. All bystanders are crying; and the prince, who is drawn in a typical Chinese manner of showing sorrow, has covered his face with his hands to hide his tears.

118

fig. 125

fig. 126

222

118

118

A Chinese maid tries to console him. To distinguish the chieftain from the other personages he is represented considerably larger than they are. To his right, Wên-chi is trying to tear herself away from her two young sons, one of whom is seen clinging to his mother's dress. The protracted drama of parting seems to have bored one of the camel drivers, who is standing behind his chariot yawning impatiently. A servant in typical Sung servant's dress has joined the waiting drivers.

The fourth leaf represents the arrival in Wên-chi's hometown, Ch'ang-an. On the right is a walled compound, in the open hall of which Wên-chi is being welcomed by friends and relatives of all ages. Several servants busy themselves taking her luggage to another part of the house. The front gate is crowded with men and women bringing welcoming gifts. Farther down the street we see the chariot, but the camels of the steppes have been replaced by Chinese oxen. The Chinese drivers regale themselves with delicacies after the long voyage home.

Published: Kojiro Tomita, "Wên-chi's Captivity in Mongolia and Her Return to China," Museum of Fine Arts, Boston, *Bulletin,* vol. 26, no. 155 (1928), pp. 40-45.

In an article treating the considerable number of paintings dealing with the Wên-chi story, Liu Ling-ts'ang reached the conclusion that the version in the Boston Museum is surpassed in quality by the scroll in the Palace Museum, Taipei. Although this conclusion seems to be open to debate, the Palace Museum version has the advantage that it is complete, illustrating all eighteen episodes.

In his article Liu Ling-ts'ang leaves undecided the question of which ethnic group is represented in the paintings, but archaeological evidence clearly indicates that the artist was familiar with the customs of both the Chinese and the Khitans. Long ago other scholars, including Torii Ryūzō, had already tried to compare the Boston album leaves with several stone reliefs found in a tomb of the Liao period in today's Liaoning Province (northeast China). Perhaps the most striking parallel is that between a relief representing a camel-drawn chariot (fig. 125) and the chariot shown in the paintings. After 1949 many additional stone reliefs and tomb wall paintings were excavated, confirming Torii's theory that the Hsiung-nu (Huns) in the Wên-chi album are in reality portrayed contemporary Khitans. Chariots drawn by camels seem to be a typical feature of Liao culture. In addition to Torii's example, this vehicle appears several times in wall paintings in excavated tombs. In 1962 Chinese archaeologists excavated four Liao tombs in the vicinity of Ta-t'ung, Shansi Province. On the west wall of tombs no. 6 and no. 5 the same type of chariot is depicted (fig. 126). The wall painting in tomb no. 6 is of special interest, as the tomb is datable to A.D. 1093. The famous wall paintings in the Ch'ing-ling mausoleum of the Liao emperors provide additional proof of the Liao background of the Wên-chi album.

Among the many utensils represented in the four paintings are vases of typical Liao shape. On the extreme right of the third leaf several wine jars are shown; they are decorated with grooved bands, a common feature of Liao wares, and are covered by cups (fig. 127). The rather formal and symmetrical table setting points to a mixture of Chinese and nomadic taste. The branded horses are known from several paintings attributed to artists from the north active during the tenth to eleventh century. The stirrups are all of late Liao style.

The album leaves also vividly depict the difference in mood and atmosphere between life in the steppes and life in the capital. The change in brushwork which occurs from the third to the fourth leaf, where the scene shifts from the steppes to the capital, is particularly striking. The figures in the fourth leaf can be compared with those in the scroll *The Night Revels of Han Hsi-tsai,* attributed to the tenth century artist Ku Hung-chung (Palace Museum, Peking), *The Return of Duke Wên of Chin,* a hand scroll newly acquired by the Metropolitan Museum, New York, and the hand scroll in the Tientsin Museum attributed to Hsiao Chao (see above). The last two works are fine narrative figure paintings of the early Southern Sung dynasty. A comparison with the fourth of the Wên-chi leaves suggests that this last painting may be slightly earlier than the other two and later than the *Night Revels.*

It is an interesting phenomenon that during the later part of the Northern Sung dynasty, when Khitans and Chinese were peacefully living as neighbors, the Chinese artists became interested in the way of life of the northern frontier regions. They represented this life in their paintings, borrowing the contemporary life style of the Khitans for historical subjects dealing with other unrelated northern tribes.

fig. 127

References: Torii Ryūzō, *Sculptured Stone Tombs of the Liao Dynasty,* Peking: Harvard-Yenching Institute, 1942, pp. 121-123, pls. 37-38; Liu Ling-ts'ang "Representations of the Eighteen Songs in Chinese paintings" (text in Chinese), *Wen Wu,* 1959, no. 5, pp. 3-5; Shên Ts'ung-wên, "Notes on paintings of the Lady Wen-chi's return to China" (text in Chinese), *Wen Wu,* 1959, no. 6, pp. 32-35; Yen Yu, "The Liao and Chin tombs with stone engravings at Ta-wo-p'u, Chin-hsi County, Liaoning" (text in Chinese), *Kaogu,* 1960, no. 2, p. 30, fig. 2 and pl. 4, fig. 1; Wang Tsêng-hsin, "A Liao dynasty tomb with stone engravings excavated at Chin-ch'ang, Liaoyang County, Liaoning" (text in Chinese), *Kaogu,* 1960, no. 2, pp. 25-28; *T'ien-ching shih i-shu po-wu-kuan ts'ang-hua hsü-chi,* Peking, 1963, vol. 2, pls. 1-6; *Chinese Art Treasures,* Geneva: Skira, 1961, pl. 132; Tamura Jitsuzō and Kobayashi Yukio, *Ch'ing-ling,* Tokyo: Zauhō Press, 1952, vol. 2, pls. 26-44; Ta-t'ung City Museum, "Four painted tombs of the Liao dynasty excavated at Wo-hu-wan, Ta-t'ung, Shansi Province" (text in Chinese), *Kaogu,* 1963, no. 8, pl. 6, fig. 6 and pl. 7, fig. 5; Liaoning Provincial Museum, *Liao tz'u t'u-lu,* Peking, 1961, pl. 65; National Palace Museum, *Masterpieces of Chinese Album Painting in the National Palace Museum,* Tokyo: Gakken Press, 1971, pp. 3-4; Kirin Provinical Museum et al., excavation of the Liao dynasty tomb no. 1 at Kulun Banner, Jerim League (text in Chinese), *Wen Wu,* 1973, no. 8, pp. 2-13, 30-35, pls. 1-2.

119
Ladies Preparing Newly Woven Silk
Emperor Hui-tsung (1082-1135), Northern Sung period
Hand scroll, ink, colors and gold on silk, h. 37 cm., l. 145.3 cm.
Museum of Fine Arts, Boston, Chinese and Japanese Special Fund. 12.886

This masterpiece of Chinese figure painting by the Sung emperor Hui-tsung is the result of a combination of two of the emperor's hobbies, painting and collecting. Although unsigned, the painting carries an inscription by Emperor Chang-tsang of the Chin dynasty (reigned 1188-1208), who attributes the painting to Hui-tsung and calls it a copy after a painting by the T'ang artist Chang Hsüan (first half of eighth century), which was, according to the catalogue *Hsüan-ho hua-p'u,* in Hui-tsung's collection. The painting and the brocade section preceding it are still the original of Chang-tsung's time, as is indicated by his seven seals, traditionally impressed only on the most important works in his collection. Chang-tsung's label is written in a style that closely resembles Hui-tsung's handwriting.

Throughout the painting the lines are light and sensitive and are drawn in slightly varying thickness, which is a characteristic of the brushwork of this painting. The composition consists of three groups of figures. The first and the last group are made up of four persons diagonally arranged, with only the small child acting as an interloper and providing a lively contrast with the quiet, dignified pose of the older ladies. Only the two ladies in the central section are seated, making elegant gestures with their hands as they go about their various tasks. The white line of the spun silk has become almost invisible.

The young maid is squatting next to a charcoal brazier. She fans the fire with a round fan that is decorated with a delicate winter scene of a pair of ducks among reeds. The maid turns her head to the left, thus creating the visual connection between the central and left groups of figures in the

painting. The compositional theme here is surprisingly close to the scroll "Scholars of the Northern Ch'i Dynasty Collating the Classics" (cat. no. 117).

Published: Kojiro Tomita, *Portfolio of Chinese Paintings in the Museum (Han to Sung Periods),* Boston, 1933, pls. 52-55. *Li-tai Jên-wu-hua hsüan-chi,* Shanghai: People's Art Press, 1959, pl. 21; Yashiro Yukio, "Emperor Hui-tsung's copy of the scroll *Ladies Preparing Newly Woven Silk* by Chang Hsüan," *Bijutsu Kenkyu,* no. 41, 1935, pp. 1-8, pls. 2-4.

In 1971 the hand scroll was the subject of a detailed study by Miss Mitsuko Gomi, in which she raised several interesting points. Noticing differences in the hairdo and in the textile designs on the dresses of the ladies on the first and second half of the scroll, she concluded that the last part of the scroll must have been painted by a different hand. Also, in her opinion, the style of the figures conforms more closely with that of the painter Chou Fang than with that of Chang Hsüan, whom he followed. Some of the suggestions made by Miss Gomi are based on archaeological evidence, especially tomb figurines. However, although her arguments are of great interest, not all of them appear to be conclusive. Moreover, there are many additional archaeological data that can throw light on the questions she has raised. It would seem, therefore, that it is possible to pursue the arguments further.

The difference in hairdo between the women of the first and the last groups in the hand scroll is real, but it is not necessary to assume that this implies either a difference in time or that another artist finished the painting. For instance, the excellent study on the Northern Sung tombs at Pai-sha, Honan Province (one datable to A.D. 1099) by Professor Su Pai demonstrates that both hair styles occur in the wall paintings of Sung tombs that are most likely to date from about the same period (fig. 128). The hairdo with a prominent widow's peak, referred to in Sung literature as Yün-chien ch'iao-ngo, i.e., "cloud tip over the forehead," occurs together with the parted hairstyle, exactly

119

in the same way as the two appear together in the *Ladies Preparing Newly Woven Silk*. The parted hair style is a familiar T'ang fashion, whereas the hairdo with the widow's peak was not known during that dynasty. In addition to the wall paintings at Pai-sha, there is an even earlier datable example of it in the tomb of Chao Tê-chün (datable A.D. 937-958), which was discovered near Peking in 1959. The wall paintings in this tomb show two ladies with the same type of "cloud tip over the forehead." It has long been a common practice in China for painters to draw one section of a scroll and later—from

a few days to long over a year—to come back to work out the rest of the composition. In this way, the later part could very possibly be executed differently, especially in such details as the hair style and designs on the textiles. Most likely the ladies in the Boston Museum, whether by Hui-tsung or not, entered our scroll at separate times rather than descending from the brush tip all at once.

In tomb no. 6 excavated at Shih-chuang, Hopei Province, in 1960, a wall painting was found that illustrates the process of preparing silk (fig. 129). The wall painting is about 240 cm. in width and about 90 cm. in height. Four

activities connected with the preparation of silk are represented. On the right a young man enters the painting carrying water. Next to him three women are ironing silk. To their left a woman is putting the ironed silk away in a large trunk while a cat is watching her work, crouched on top of the trunk. On the left a woman is beating the silk. Bolts of silk are draped over a bar above her head.

The scene of the three women ironing silk is of special interest as it is a typical Sung version of the scene representing the same activity in the *Ladies Preparing Newly Woven Silk*. Although the process of beating the silk

119

is quite different in these two pictorial illustrations, Boston's is obviously the imperial method. As is the case with the *Clear Weather in the Valley* (cat. no. 121), there can, of course, be no doubt that the Boston version is artistically far superior to the wall painting in the tomb. The close similarity in composition of the two groups of ironing women make it rather doubtful that the two are as far apart in date of origin as the time of Chang Hsüan's activity (first half of the eighth century) and the early twelfth century, the date the tomb has been assigned by Chinese archaeologists.

As Miss Gomi has pointed out, however, the Boston hand scroll reveals many typical T'ang details. Unless we assume that the process of ironing silk remained completely unchanged through almost four centuries, it would seem that the distinguished ladies of the T'ang court are performing somewhat anachronistic duties. The answer probably is that the artist of the *Ladies Preparing Newly Woven Silk* represented the process of preparing silk as he knew it from his own time, but that he adopted T'ang models for his composition, as was common practice during the Northern Sung period.

Perhaps the most interesting point raised by Miss Gomi is the suggestion that the prototype of the painting should be associated with the painter Chou Fang rather than with Chang Hsüan. She is probably correct in doubting the early eighth century origin of the style of the painting, for neither tomb figurines nor wall paintings of that period, both of which are now abundantly available for comparison, reveal similar stylistic characteristics. However, there is no close affinity either between the Boston hand scroll and the paintings attributed to Chou Fang or to tomb figurines of the middle of the eighth century.

227

119

The Boston figures, therefore, are most likely to be Northern Sung recreations based upon T'ang models.

References: The Archaeological Team of the Provincial Bureau of Culture, Hopei, "Report on the excavation of tombs of Sung period at Shih-chuang, Ching-hsing County, Hopei," (text in Chinese), *Kaogu Xuebao,* 1962, no. 2, pp. 31-73, pls. 14-16; Su Pai, *Pai-sha Sung-mu,* Peking, 1957, p. 79. fig. 75; Archaeological Team of Peking, "Report on the excavation of the tomb of Chao Tê-chün and his wife of the Liao period at southern suburb of Peking" (text in Chinese), *Kaogu,* 1962, no. 5, pp. 246-253, pl. 9; Liu Lin-ts'ang, "Underground painting gallery of twelve hundred years ago" (text in Japanese), *People's China,* 1973, no. 6 (supplement), p. 26; Liu Lin-ts'ang, *T'ang-tai jên-wu-hua,* Peking, 1958, pp. 26-33; Ma Tê-chih and others, "Tomb of Hsien-yü T'ing-hui," in "Report of the excavation of three tombs of T'ang period at the suburb of Sian City" (text in Chinese), *Kaogu,* 158, no. 1, pp. 47-52, pl. 5; Gomi Mitsuko, "Genetic problems of the scroll *Ladies Preparing Newly Woven Silk*" (text in Japanese), *Bijutsu-shi,* no. 81, 1971, pp. 1-16.

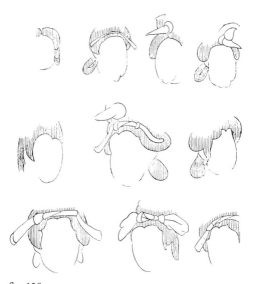

fig. 128

fig. 129

120

Six Illustrations from the Book of Odes
Hand scroll, ink and colors on silk,
27 x 383.8 cm.
Painting by Ma Ho-chih (12th century),
calligraphy by the Sung emperor Kao-tsung
(1107-1187)
Museum of Fine Arts, Boston, Marshall H.
Gould Fund. 51.698

The material used is a fine silk of smooth texture, of a type similar to that used for Emperor Kao-tsung's album leaf (see cat. no. 115). The entire scroll consists of sections of painting alternating with sections of calligraphy, the format of which can be traced back to the fourth century A.D. The calligraphed text is that of six odes from the *Hsiao-ya* section of the *Book of Odes,* the famous Chinese classic; the paintings illustrate these odes. The calligraphy is a typical example of the emperor's early style, developed during the Shao-hsing era (1131-1162), quite distinct from his later style, which is exemplified in the fan-shaped album leaf (cat. no. 115).

The paintings are characteristic examples of the style of Ma Ho-chih. All motifs, whether human figures, trees, rocks, or water, are executed in softly flowing, undulating brush strokes. This unique manner of painting differs greatly from that of later followers of his style, as is demonstrated, for example, in an album by Hsiao Yün-tsung (1596-1673) in the National Palace Museum, Taipei. Of the six illustrations the first and the last are river scenes, the second a mountain landscape, whereas the other three show personages performing ceremonies at court.

This hand scroll, one of the finest extant works by the master, formerly belonged to the Manchu palace collection. Both the outer label and the first section are inscribed by Emperor Ch'ien-lung (reigned 1736-1796), whose seals are impressed on all sections of the painting. Other collector's seals include those of the famous seventeenth century collector Liang Ch'ing-piao. Attached to the pictorial section are two colophons, the first by

the Ming painter Wên Chêng-ming, written in 1547, and the other by Ch'ien-lung, written in 1770. Wên Chêng-ming's colophon calls this hand scroll the best work by Ma Ho-chih that he had ever seen.

After the revolution of 1911 the painting left the imperial collection. When it came to the Boston Museum, its condition had much deteriorated. It was remounted by Yasuhiro Iguchi in 1970.

Published: Kojiro Tomita and A. Kaiming Chiu, "Scroll of Six Odes from Mao Shih," Museum of Fine Arts, Boston, *Bulletin* 50, no. 281 (1951), 41-49.

The origins of Ma Ho-chih's personal style of figure painting has for a long time been a matter of discussion among scholars. In the Chinese tradition his style has always been associated with that of Wu Tao-tzu, the great eighth century painter, but this explanation is not entirely satisfactory, especially as it fails to be supported by archaeological evidence. In recent years a large number of wall paintings have been discovered in tombs of members of the imperial clan who died around the turn of the eighth century. In none of these superb wall paintings, which date from the years of Wu's activity, do we see any affinity with the later works of Ma Ho-chih.

One of the peculiar features of Ma's treatment of his figures is what has been called *chien-shang fei-wên*, i.e., "flying lines over the shoulder." The three principal figures in the court scenes of the *Six Illustrations from the Book of Odes* all display this feature, although with varying degrees of emphasis: on both sides of the shoulders the folds are indicated by two or three additional strokes that extend beyond the outline of the shoulders.

The figures in a painting, which is generally accepted as a Sung copy of the *Lives of Famous Women* by the fourth century figure painter Ku K'ai-chih (Palace Museum, Peking), interestingly enough display this same mannerism. Although it is difficult to establish how faithfully this copy was executed,

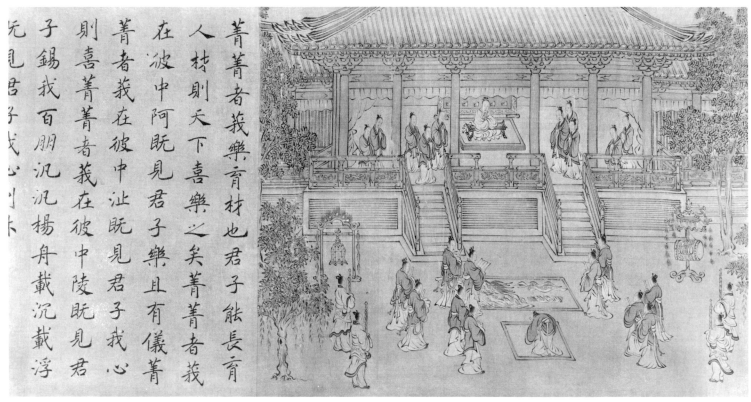

120

the fact that this same feature may be seen in this picture constitutes an argument in favor of an early date for the "flying lines over the shoulder." A famous set of fifteen engraved stone slabs in the Confucius Temple at Hangchow, Chekiang Province, illustrates seventy-three personages, consisting of Confucius and his disciples (fig. 130). Each figure is accompanied by an inscription supplying the identification; they are written by Emperor Kao-tsung. The original upon which these engraved pictures are based has traditionally been attributed to the Northern Sung master Li Kung-lin. The almost mechanical repetition of the "flying lines" is one of the typical stylistic traits of the set. If these illustrations were indeed after a design by Li Kung-lin, one might suppose that Ma Ho-chih was inspired by them, and took them as an ex-

ample. From literary sources we learn that Li Kung-lin followed both Ku K'ai-chih and Wu Tao-tzu. However, judging from some of Li's most representative works, such as *The Five Horses* and the *Illustrations for the Classic of Filial Piety* (collection Wen Fong, Princeton University), one gets the impression that the influence of Wu Tao-tzu completely dominated what little influence of Ku K'ai-chih there may have been in Li's oeuvre.

In 1972, when the archaeological journal *Wen Wu* resumed publication, the first, third, and eighth issues all discussed a set of five lacquered wooden panels, excavated from the tomb of the high official of the Northern Wei dynasty Ssu-ma Chin-lung, who died in A.D. 484, in the vicinity of Ta-t'ung, Shansi Province. The five panels are decorated with figure scenes in four superimposed registers.

Although they do not occur as consistently as they did on the Hangchow slabs, the "flying lines over the shoulder" are also in evidence here. It stands to reason, therefore, that this feature dates from at least the fifth century (see fig. 121).

In 1957 the Academy of Sciences of the People's Republic of Korea excavated several large tombs of the Koguryo period in the Anak area. Tomb no. 3 was identified as the tomb of King Micheon, datable by an inscription in Chinese characters to A.D. 357. On a wall painting in this tomb King Micheon is flanked by two officials (fig. 131). Even from the poor reproductions at our disposal it is quite evident that the costumes of these two officials show exactly the same treatment of the folds around the shoulders as the above-mentioned Chinese works.

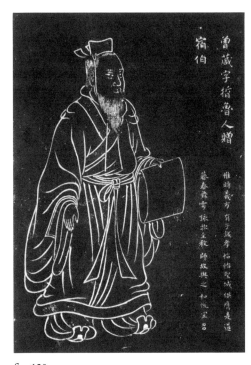

fig. 130

fig. 131

All this tends to show that the "flying lines over the shoulder" could well have been a common feature in Chinese figure paintings since the fourth century, and that in this respect the *Lives of Famous Women* reflects faithfully this feature of the original.

The attribution of the stone slabs at Hangchow to Li Kung-lin should perhaps be re-examined in the light of this new evidence. There is no concrete indication, neither stylistic nor documentary, that the slabs should be attributed to the famous Northern Sung artist. Emperor Kao-tsung, a great admirer of the master, does not even refer to Li's name in his imperial inscription accompanying the slabs. The possibility that they should be attributed to Ma Ho-chih can no longer be excluded now that new evidence has revealed a stylistic feature so closely connected with his name.

References: Shansi Provincial Museum, Ta-t'ung City, "The tomb of Ssu-ma Chin-ling of the Northern Wei dynasty at Shih-chia-chai, Ta-t'ung, Shansi Province" (text in Chinese), *Wen Wu,* 1972, no. 3, pp. 20-33; Institute of Archaeology and Anthropology, *Anak Che 3-ho Pun Palgul Pogo* [Report on the excavation of tomb no. 3 at Anak], P'yongyang, 1958, pls. 30-32; National Palace Museum, *Ku-kung Shu-hua-lu,* Taichung, 1956, ch. 6, pp. 141-142; *Shih-chü pao-chi* [catalogue of painting and calligraphy in the collection of Emperor Ch'ien-lung], part 1, ch. 36/7a-8b, Han-fên-lou ed., Shanghai, 1918 reprint; Huang Yung-ch'uan, *Li Kung-lin Shêng-hsien-t'u Shih-k'o,* Peking, 1963; Ma Ts'ai, *Ku K'ai-chih yen-chiu,* Shanghai, 1958, pl. 6; Richard Barnhart, "Survivals, revivals and the classical tradition of Chinese figure painting," *Proceedings of the International Symposium on Chinese Painting,* Taipei, 1972, fig. 7 & 8.

121

Clear Weather in the Valley
Traditionally attributed to Tung Yüan
(907-960), but probably early 13th century
Hand scroll, ink and light colors on paper,
h. 37.5 cm., l. 150.8 cm.
Museum of Fine Arts, Boston, Chinese and
Japanese Special Fund. 12.903

This masterpiece of landscape painting shows a country house at the foot of a mountain range, surrounded by trees. To the right is a mountain stream coming out of a valley in the background. Continuing toward the left the foreground is taken up by the country house flanked by trees. The house is opened to the spectator, revealing details of its interior. A gentleman and his servant are approaching the main gate. The backdrop of this scene is formed by an imposing range of cypress-clad mountains. In a valley between two tops the roofs of two temple buildings are visible above the mists. Further to the left, passing the woods, the landscape suddenly opens up with a wide and distant view of clouded hills on the other side of a misty river, into which extends a wooded peninsula. Here and there travelers on foot or riding donkeys are seen. A ferry plies across the water toward the shore of the peninsula. At the far left of the composition, is a view of a shop with a "wine flag," shaded by large trees in the foreground.

The hand scroll has been cropped on the left side. In the middle of the edge three characters and two seals have been cut off almost completely. The inscription most likely reads: *Ts'ung-yün-shêng* in chancery script *(li-shu);* these three characters, together forming a man's *hao* or sobriquet, have not yet been successfully identified. They have not prevented a traditional attribution to Tung Yüan, the great tenth century southern landscape painter, from becoming attached to this painting.

Numerous collector's seals are impressed on both edges of the hand scroll, and mounted with the painting is a long section of colophons, the first of which is signed by

231

121

121

Tung Ch'i-ch'ang (1555-1636) and dated in accordance with 1633. It is followed immediately by a colophon written by Wang Shih-min, one of Tung's students, and done in the same year. One of the last connoisseurs to inscribe a colophon is the viceroy Tuan Fang, who added his contribution in 1911, shortly before he was assasinated by the soldiers of his regiment.

The painting obtained its present title from a label written by an as yet unidentified connoisseur. In the colophons, however, the title *Mountain Dwelling* is used. It has long been realized that the attribution of this hand scroll to Tung Yüan is unlikely to be correct and that the painting may have been painted as much as two centuries after the death of the great landscapist.

Published: Kojiro Tomita, *Portfolio of Chinese Paintings in the Museum (Han to Sung)* Boston, 1933, pls. 33-36.

An artistically most remarkable wall painting found in the tomb of the Taoist Fêng Tao-chên (1189-1265) was discovered in 1958 in the city of Ta-t'ung, Shansi Province (fig. 132). The painting measures 270 cm. in length and 91 cm. in height and is inscribed in the right upper corner as *Su-lin wan-chao,* i.e., "Sunset over scattered forests." According to the excavation report the landscape bears a striking resemblance to the actual scenery of Mount Ch'i-fêng outside Ta-t'ung City, the area in which, according to the mortuary inscription, the deceased resided most of his life.

Since the first publication of this exciting find several scholars in the West have tried to reconsider other paintings in the light of this new, exactly datable evidence. In 1965 Susan Bush tried to establish the style of the Chin period from the evidence produced by this tomb painting as well as two other works. However, the hand scroll *Clear Weather in the Valley* has not yet been studied from this point of view, although enough striking parallels have been found between it and the recently discovered tomb painting to warrant a close comparison.

fig. 132

These parallels are first of all to be found in the overall composition as well as in several details. Both paintings are dominated by a group of impressive, high-rising peaks, and in both the foreground is taken up by forests through which travelers make their way. Both paintings open up to a wide expanse on one side of the composition, where the peaks are replaced by distant mountains, rivers and boats, wrapped up in banks of mist. In both the contours of the mountains have been drawn in powerful brush strokes, accentuated by dots, and a variety of textural strokes enlivens the surface of the mountains. The trees in the foreground stand out against the lower slopes of the mountains because of intervening banks of mist. Both artists reveal an interest in the treatment of atmospheric perspective. But in spite of these numerous points of similarity the artistic quality of the hand scroll is undoubtedly far superior to that of the tomb painting. In the context of the style of the Chin period, as studied by Susan Bush, the Boston hand scroll stands out as a more subtle, refined and more mature masterpiece. It would seem most likely, however, that the two paintings are not far apart in date. The artists in northern China, under the Chin dynasty, cut off from the mainstream of artistic developments in the Southern Sung Empire, continued to emulate the example of the Northern Sung masters. The Boston hand scroll is a typical example of this trend.

References: Susan Bush, "Clearing after Snow in the Min Mountains and Chin Landscape Painting," *Oriental Art* 11 (1965), 163-172; Ta-t'ung City Museum, "Brief report of the excavation of the Yüan dynasty tombs of Fêng Tao-chên and Wang Ch'ing at Ta-t'ung, Shansi Province" (text in Chinese), *Wen Wu,* 162, no. 10, pp. 34-46 (esp. pl. 1); Wang Shih-ming, *Wang Fêng-ch'ang Shu-hua T'i-pa* (Ou-po-lo-shih ed.), n.p., 1909 reprint, ch. 2/9b-10a.

122

Doves and Pear Blossoms after Rain
By Ch'ien Hsüan (*chin-shih* in 1262, died
after 1322)
Hand scroll, ink and colors on paper,
30.5 x 97.8 cm.
Cincinnati Art Museum

Two doves are perched on a blossoming pear
tree, the branches of which stretch from the
lower left edge to the middle of the right edge
of the hand scroll. The birds occupy the center of the composition. The painting is executed in delicately drawn outlines, accentuated by washes and textural strokes in
various colors. The roughness of the bark
contrasts with the delicate drawing of the
blossoms and leaves, just as the somewhat
stylized shape of the birds provides a contrast with the naturalistic precision with
which the blossoms have been drawn.

This well-known painting has been generally admired and accepted by many scholars, in spite of the fact that very little is
known about the personal characteristics of
the artist's style. His way of rendering three-
dimensional forms has a simple, almost art-
less awkwardness, which has made others
question its attribution to Ch'ien Hsüan. In
discussing "The Problem of Ch'ien Hsüan"
Wen Fong expressed his doubts as to the reliability of the attribution on the argument
that the conservative and amateur quality of
the work is hardly in keeping with the oeuvre
of a great artist such as Ch'ien Hsüan. However, already in 1953 Richard Edwards had
pointed to the uniqueness of that same awkwardness as it is found in a hand scroll representing flowers and insects entitled *Early
Autumn* in the Detroit Museum.

The painting is signed: "The Old Man of
Cha River, Ch'ien Hsüan Shun-chü." It
carries seals and colophons of numerous
later collectors, beginning with Ch'ien
Hsüan's close personal friend Mou Yen and
the famous bamboo painter K'o Chiu-ssu
(1290-1343), and including collectors living
between the fourteenth and nineteenth
centuries.

The dates of Ch'ien Hsüan are uncertain,
but the gazetteer *Hu-chou fu chih* by Hu
Ch'êng-mou (author's preface dated A.D.
1739) lists Ch'ien Hsüan as a man who
passed the chin-shih (doctoral) examinations
at Wa-ch'êng County in A.D. 1262. He
probably lived beyond A.D. 1322, the year
his good friend Chao Mêng-fu died. The
Dove and Pear Blossoms probably dates from
the end of the thirteenth century.

Published: Sherman E. Lee and Wai-kam Ho,
Chinese Art under the Mongols, Cleveland,
Cleveland Museum of Art, 1968, no. 181; Wen
Fong, "The Problem of Ch'ien Hsüan," *Art Bulletin* 42 (September 1960), 173-189. Chêng Chên-
to, *Yün-hui-chai ts'ang T'ang Sung i-lai ming-
hua-chi,* Shanghai, 1947, pls. 7-9; Sherman E.
Lee, *A History of Far Eastern Art,* New York,
1964, p. 403, fig. 532; Wang Chi-ch'ien, *An Exhibition of Authenticated Chinese Paintings,*
New York, 1948, cat. no. 4.

In 1970 a highly unusual discovery was
made in the tomb of Chu T'an, the tenth son
of T'ai Tsu, the first emperor of the Ming
dynasty at Chou-hsien,Shantung Province.
Together with three other paintings and
pieces of calligraphy was found a remarkably
well-preserved hand scroll representing lotus
flowers by Ch'ien Hsüan (fig. 133). The
painting measures 42 x 90.3 cm., with the attached colophon section measuring 35 x 109
cm. The painting is executed in ink and light
colors on paper. There are three lotus leaves
and three flowers in full bloom or just beginning to blossom, arranged in a rather
orderly composition that is kept within the
limits of an invisible, almost rectangular
frame, the edge of which cuts right through
the leaves and stems at the bottom.

The composition is executed in strong yet
highly sensitive lines; the flowers are represented in almost three-dimensional shapes
with the petals either tightly closed or un-
folding in a regular pattern, suggestive of the
successive stages of continuous growth. The
most striking feature of the painting are the
dots on the stems of the leaves and flowers,
which were arranged, with obvious intent,
into a repetitive geometric pattern resembling the wedge-shaped Chinese character

jên (man). No other lotus painting showing
this stylized feature is known. The clear but
firm lines have a spontaneity that follows the
tradition of the ancient *pai-miao* technique
of line drawing of the Northern Sung period,
but the dots on the stems are an innovation
that is apparently without precedent. The
solid, evenly colored areas stand out against
the thin lines of the drawing and the empty
background. The artist's method of creating
contrasting opposites of new and old, fine
and coarse, solid and empty, may be characteristic of his time, for the same tendency
may be observed in *Sheep and Goat,* a
famous painting by Ch'ien Hsüan's friend
Chao Mêng-fu (1254-1322) in the Freer
Gallery of Art, Washington, D.C.

On the left side of the painting a seven
character *chüeh-chü* ("truncated verse") and
an inscription by the artist are written in five
lines of running script. Signed by the artist
himself, the inscription reads: "I changed my
nom de plume *(hao)* to Cha-hsi-wêng (Old
Man of Cha River) because more and more
forgeries of my work have appeared. I therefore had this new idea in order to put to
shame the fakers. Ch'ien Hsüan Shun-chü."
The inscription is followed by two square
seals of the artist. The information contained
in this inscription comes as a total surprise,
as none of the Chinese biographical records
have ever given this explanation for Ch'ien
Hsüan's well-known nom de plume, which
he also uses on the *Doves and Pear Blossoms
after Rain.*

This excavated painting by Ch'ien Hsüan
bears no collector's seals besides the official
"Szu-yin" half seal of the early Ming period,
at the lower right edge. The painting was
obviously part of the large and outstanding
collection of painting and calligraphy of the
Grand Princess of Lu (Lu-kuo Ta-chang
Kung-chu). Not only does her seal Huang-
tzu t'u-shu appear on two of the four paintings in the tomb, the colophons written on
these paintings were also executed by the
same artists in an identical style. The Ch'ien
Hsüan lotus painting, which bears an anonymous outer label reading "White lotuses by

122

fig. 133

Ch'ien Shun-chü" has colophons by Fêng Tzu-chên (1257-after 1327) and Chao Yen; both colophons are undated. Fêng's colophon ends with the phrase: "Ch'ien Hsüan has passed away; his work can no longer be obtained; treasure and protect it forever." The seal of Chao Yen, which the Chinese failed to identify, actually reads "Lu-chan," Chao's *tzu* name.

An album leaf found in the same tomb is impressed with the official half seal of the Hung-wu era (1368-1399). This indicates that the collection of the Grand Princess of Lu must have become the property of the first ruler of the newly founded Ming dynasty. Occasionally paintings were bestowed upon members of the imperial family or other meritorious courtiers. That Chu T'an inherited some of these paintings provides additional evidence of this recorded imperial custom.

The tradition of depositing paintings in tombs, though practised only rarely, can be traced back to late Chou times, as is evident from a painting found in a Ch'ang-sha tomb. Not until T'ang times, however, is there a record of art work that had been appreciated by the deceased and which, for that reason, were deposited with him in his tomb (cat. no. 114). Actual archaeological evidence of this custom exists only from the Sung period. In the Nelson Gallery of Art, Kansas City, is a painting attributed to Ching Hao that is thought to have been excavated from a tomb. From a Sung tomb, dated in accordance with A.D. 1094 and excavated in Huai-an County, Kiangsu Province, in 1959 the wooden roller of a painting was excavated. Unfortunately, the painting itself had completely disintegrated. Although there is, therefore, ample archaeological evidence of this custom the significant discovery of the paintings in Chu T'an's tomb is without any precedent.

References: Shantung Provincial Museum, "Report on the excavation of the tomb on Chu T'an" (text in Chinese), *Wen Wu,* 1972, no. 5, pp. 25-36, pls. 2-4; Liu Chiu-an, "Problems regarding the paintings found in the tomb of Chu T'an" (text in Chinese), *Wen Wu,* 1972, no. 5, pp. 64-65; Richard Edwards, "Ch'ien Hsüan and the Early Autumn," *Archives of the Chinese Art Society of America* 7 (1953), 71-83; James Cahill, "Ch'ien Hsüan and his figure paintings," *Archives of the Chinese Art Society of America* 12 (1958), 11-29; National Palace Museum, *Ku-kung Shu-hua-lu,* Taichung, 1956, ch. 4/74-77; Nanking Museum, "Report on the excavation of a painted tomb of Sung period at Huai-an, Kiangsu Province," *Wen Wu,* 1960, nos. 8-9, p. 46, fig. 3 (inside back cover). John Pope and Thomas Lawton, *The Freer Gallery of Art: China,* Tokyo: Kodansha, n. d., pl. 47; Hu Ch'êng-mou, *Hu-chou Fu Chih* (author's preface in 1739), n.p., n.d., ch. 31/22b.

Selected Bibliography

Books and articles in English containing information on recent archaeological discoveries in China.

Akiyama, Terukazu, et al. *Arts of China: Neolithic Cultures to the T'ang Dynasty: Recent Discoveries.* Tokyo and Palo Alto: Kodansha International, 1968.

Akiyama, Terukazu, et al. *Arts of China: Buddhist Cave Temples: New Researches.* Tokyo and Palo Alto: Kodansha International, 1969.

Barnard, Noel, ed. *Early Chinese Art and Its Possible Influence in the Pacific Basin.* Vol. 1, *Ch'u and the Silk Manuscript.* New York: Intercultural Arts Press, 1972.

Bulling, A. Gutkind. "Archaeological Excavations in China, 1949-1966." *Expedition* 14, no. 4 (summer 1972), 2-12.

—. "China: Archaeological Excavations 1966-1971." *Expedition* 14, no. 5 (fall 1972), 22-39.

—. "Studies and Excavations Made in China in Recent Years." *Oriental Art,* n.s. 11, no. 4 (winter 1965), 235-242.

Chaves, Jonathan. "A Han painted tomb at Loyang." *Artibus Asiae* 30 (1968), 5-27.

Chêng Tê-k'un. *Archaeology in China.* Vol. 1, *Prehistoric China,* Cambridge: Heffner, 1959; vol. 2, *Shang China,* 1960; vol. 3, *Chou China,* 1963; supplement to vol. 1, *New Light on Prehistoric China,* 1966.

Fêng Hsien-ming. "Important finds of ancient Chinese ceramics since 1949." *Wen Wu,* 1965, no. 9, pp. 25-26. Translated by Hin-cheung Lovell. London: Oriental Ceramic Society, 1966.

Forman, Werner and Bedřich. *Ancient Relics of China.* Peking: The People's Publishing House, 1962.

Goodrich, L. Carrington. "Archaeology in China: The First Decades." *Journal of Asiatic Studies* 17, no. 1 (1957), 5-15.

Haskins, John F. "Recent Excavations in China." *Archives of the Chinese Art Society* 10 (1966), 42-58.

Hsia Nai. "Arts and Crafts of 2300 Years Ago." *China Pictorial,* January-February 1954, pp. 31-35.

—. "New Archaeological Discoveries." *China Reconstructs,* July-August 1952, pp. 13-18.

—. "Opening an Imperial Tomb." *China Reconstructs* 7, no. 3 (March 1959), 16-21.

—; Ku Yen-wu; et al. *New Archaeological Finds in China.* Peking: Foreign Languages Press, 1972.

Hulsewé, A. F. P. "Texts in Tombs." *Asiatische Studien* 18-19 (1965), 78-89.

Juliano, Annette L. "Three Large Ch'u Graves Recently Excavated in the Chiangling District of Hupei Province." *Artibus Asiae* 34 (1972), 5-17.

Karlgren, Bernard. "Some pre-Han mirrors." Museum of Far Eastern Antiquities, Stockholm, *Bulletin,* no. 35, 1963, pp. 161-169.

Loehr, Max. *Ritual Vessels of Bronze Age China.* New York: Asia Society, 1968.

Loewe, Michael. "The Wooden and Bamboo Strips Found at Mou-chü-tzu." *Journal of the Royal Asiatic Society,* 1965, pp. 13-26.

Mino Yutaka. *Ceramics in the Liao Dynasty North and South of the Great Wall.* New York: China Institute in America, 1973.

—and Wilson, Patricia. *An Index to Chinese Ceramic Kiln Sites from the Six Dynasties to the Present.* Toronto: Royal Ontario Museum, 1973.

Revue bibliografique de sinologie. Paris and The Hague: Mouton, vol. 7, 1957; vol. 9, 1971. (The archaeological section of this journal contains numerous English and French abstracts of Chinese archaeological publications that appeared between 1955 and 1963.)

Rudolph, Richard C. "A Decade of Discovery: China (1947-1957)." *Archaeology* 10, no. 4 (1957), 236-237.

—. "Revelation and Revolution in Chinese Archaeology." *Archaeology* 25, no. 2 (1972), 146-148.

—. "The Revolution in Archaeology: 'Make the Past Serve the Present'." *Understanding China Newsletter* 8, no. 5 (September-October 1972), p. 1, cont. on p. 7.

—. "Two Recently Discovered Han Tombs." *Archaeology* 26, no. 2 (1973), 106-115.

Singer, Paul. "The 'Unique' Object in Chinese Art." *Oriental Art,* n.s. 7, no. 1 (1961), 32-34.

Soper, Alexander C. "Early, Middle, and Late Shang: A Note." *Artibus Asiae* 28 (1966), 5-36.

—. "The tomb of the Marquis of Ts'ai." *Oriental Art,* n.s. 10, no. 3 (autumn 1964), 152-157.

Tregear, Mary. "Early Chinese Green Wares in the Collection of the Ashmolean Museum, Oxford." *Oriental Art,* n.s. 13, no. 1 (spring 1967), 29-35.

Tseng, Hsien-ch'i, and Dart, Robert Paul. *The Charles B. Hoyt Collection in the Museum of Fine Arts, Boston.* Vol. 2, *Liao, Sung and Yüan Dynasties.* Boston: Museum of Fine Arts, 1972.

Wang Yu-Chuan. "Relics of the State of Ch'u." *China Pictorial,* August 1953, pp. 31-32.

Watson, William. *Ancient Chinese Bronzes.* Rutland, Vt.: Tuttle, 1962.

—. *Archaeology in China.* London: Parrish, 1961.

Weber, Charles D. "Ritual Vessels of Bronze Age China," parts 1-3. *Artibus Asiae* 28 (1966), 107-140, 271-302; 29 (1967), 115-174.

Wirgin, Jan. "Sung Ceramic Designs." Museum of Far Eastern Antiquities, Stockholm, *Bulletin,* no. 42, 1970.

Young, Jean. *Art Styles of Ancient Shang.* New York: China Institute in America, 1967.

Lenders
to the Exhibition

ANONYMOUS	no. 43
THE ART INSTITUTE OF CHICAGO	no. 13
ASHMOLEAN MUSEUM, OXFORD	nos. 44, 65, 66
MR. AND MRS. EUGENE BERNAT	no. 25
BRITISH MUSEUM, LONDON	no. 102
THE BROOKLYN MUSEUM	no. 79
BUFFALO MUSEUM OF SCIENCE	no. 81
CENTER FOR ASIAN ART AND CULTURE SAN FRANCISCO	nos. 93, 94
CINCINNATI ART MUSEUM	no. 122
COLLECTIONS BAUR, GENEVA	no. 108
MR. AND MRS. MYRON S. FALK, JR.	nos. 26, 34, 109, 110
FIELD MUSEUM OF NATURAL HISTORY CHICAGO	no. 22
FOGG ART MUSEUM HARVARD UNIVERSITY	nos. 111, 112
MUSEUM FÜR OSTASIATISCHE KUNST COLOGNE	no. 16
MUSEUM VAN AZIATISCHE KUNST RIJKSMUSEUM, AMSTERDAM	nos. 11, 12, 68
PRINCETON UNIVERSITY MUSEUM	no. 114
ROYAL ONTARIO MUSEUM, TORONTO	nos. 2, 7, 36, 47, 77, 103
THE SACKLER COLLECTIONS	nos. 3, 14, 15, 38, 55, 57
SEATTLE ART MUSEUM	nos. 20, 24
MR. LAURENCE SICKMAN	no. 69
DR. PAUL SINGER	nos. 1, 5, 17, 29, 33, 35, 37, 39, 41, 50, 60, 62, 67a-d, 92, 98, 100
STAATLICHE MUSEEN PREUSSISCHER KULTURBESITZ, MUSEUM FÜR OSTASIATISCHE KUNST, BERLIN-DAHLEM	no. 10
THE UNIVERSITY MUSEUM PHILADELPHIA	no. 101
VICTORIA AND ALBERT MUSEUM LONDON	no. 9
WANGO H. C. WENG	no. 113
WILLIAM ROCKHILL NELSON GALLERY OF ART, KANSAS CITY, MISSOURI	nos. 18, 19, 19a, 45, 46, 48, 49, 70, 90, 91, 104, 105, 106
YALE UNIVERSITY ART GALLERY	nos. 27, 56, 78, 80, 82